THE
BEACH BOOK

Also by Nancy Bruning
The Cold Weather Catalog (with Robert Levine)
Swimming for Total Fitness (with Jane Katz)
Hardcore Crafts
Lady Luck's Companion

THE BEACH BOOK

by Nancy Bruning

Designed by Ann Perrini

Houghton Mifflin Company   Boston   1981

Library of Congress Cataloging in Publication Data

Bruning, Nancy.
  The beach book.

  1. Outdoor recreation — Miscellanea. 2. Beaches
— Recreational use — Miscellanea. I. Title.
GV191.6.B78   796.5'3   80-28390
ISBN 0-395-30523-3 (pbk.)

Printed in the United States of America
AL 10 9 8 7 6 5 4 3 2 1

Author's Note: Before you send away for any books or products listed in *The Beach Book*, be sure to check with the supplier for the current price and availability. Prices go up and models change or are discontinued faster than books get published!

Typesetting: Ettlinger, Chase & Lobel, Inc. (Louise Lippin)

ACKNOWLEDGMENTS

The Beach Book has provided me with the perfect excuse for sunning, swimming, diving, sailing, traveling...and for discovering, visiting, and dreaming about some of the best beaches in the world. (All in the name of research!) Better yet, it has given me the opportunity to meet and work with a whole slew of talented fellow beachniks. Of them special thanks goes to:

• Ann Perrini, to whom *The Beach Book* owes it superb design.

• Marianne Dickinson, Michael Gross, and David Seidman, who helped with the writing and research.

• Illustrators Todd Ballantine, Don Brown, Phillip Jones, and Dean Williams.

• Kitty Mackey of *Travel & Leisure* magazine, Art Santucci and Tony Tedeschi of Communication Brokers International, and Catherine Wood of the American Express Travel Service, among other members of the travel industry, and Richard Raymond, coastal consultant and director of the Subcommittee on Ports and Terminals, New York State Assembly, and Jane Katz, all of whom generously shared their time and knowledge.

• Anita McClellan, my editor and fellow beach nut, who managed to throw very little sand in my typewriter; and Susan Protter, my agent, who supplied piña coladas and tuna salad sandwiches.

• The J.C. Archives, which generously allowed me to reproduce postcards from their collection.

• Sheila Smith and the Picture Collection of the Cooper-Hewitt Museum Library, Smithsonian Institution, New York, and the Kubler Collection, from which I reproduced several pieces.

• My special friends for whom the phrase "beach, beach, beach" has a special meaning.

• My parents, who introduced me to the pleasures of the beach before I could say the word.

As for the rest of you: *You know who you are!*

(Anne Bruning)

Portrait of the author as a young beachnik.

FOREWORD

Are you...

> bored with the same old beach you've been going to for years?

> tired of the same old bologna sandwiches and tepid iced tea?

> sick of using 4286 matches to light one measly cigarette?

> a little nervous about surrendering your tender, precious body to the pounding surf?

> dying to go au naturel, but "oh so shy"?

Have you been (sun)burned once too often?

Are you under the impression that melanin is something that grows on vines and makes an interesting little frozen daiquiri?

Do you think just because you're 1500 miles from the ocean there's no place for you to surf?

Do you want to know something about all those shells, plants, and other creatures that you meet where the land meets the sea?

Do you approach the surfside object of your desire with lines even sillier than "Hi. Drown here often?"

Do you suspect there's more to going to the beach than getting hot, sweaty, sticky, sandy, chilled, hungry as a horse, thirsty as a sponge, bored to tears — but don't know where to look for the solution?

Greetings, Beach Lover — your search has ended! THE BEACH BOOK is here, especially created to banish those Beach Blanket Blues forever. It's a guide book, a source book, a how-to book, and a picture book that mixes fact and fun to capture the excitement and serenity, the beauty and the mystery, the good times and the nostalgia inherent in your favorite escape.

CONTENTS...

CONTENTS...

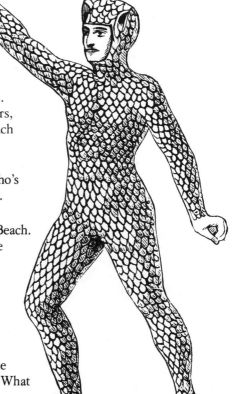

BEST BEACHES...

Do you love the beach, but hate figuring out which one to go to? Are you tired of your usual stomping grounds, but wary of trying some place new? Do you know which beaches are best for sightseeing, nature watching, skinny-dipping, island hopping? Or which supply the most adventure, the greatest luxury, the liveliest sports? Where you should take your family, where you can meet the most (or the fewest) people? Where the nearest water is if you're a thousand miles from the sea or a million light years from home? Is the beach you have in mind pastoral, peaceful, dramatic, deserted, crowded, honky-tonk, idyllic, elegant? Guess no more — just turn to the appropriate guide.

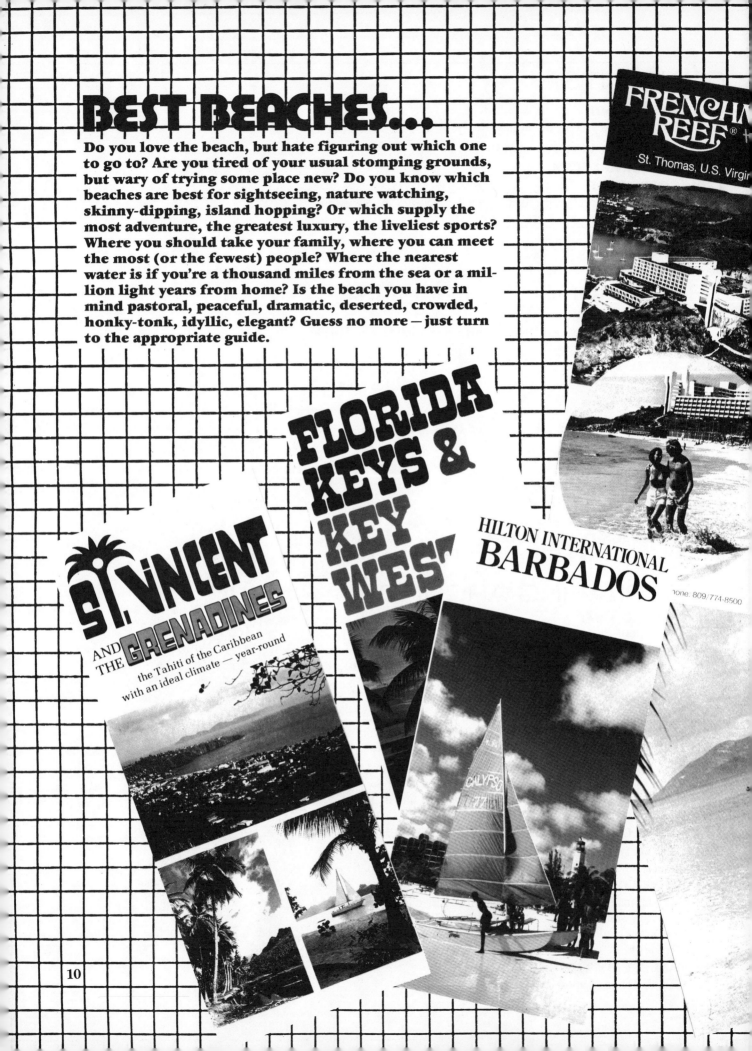

FRENCHMAN REEF®
St. Thomas, U.S. Virgin
Phone: 809/774-8500

FLORIDA KEYS & KEY WEST

ST. VINCENT AND THE GRENADINES
the Tahiti of the Caribbean
with an ideal climate — year-round

HILTON INTERNATIONAL BARBADOS

CALYPSO

10

11

AN ADVENTURER'S GUIDE

Off-the-beaten-path beaches for thrill seekers and risk takers.

A Walk on the Wild Side

Adventure travel means facing the unknown, meeting new challenges, walking on the wild side, taking risks. Luckily for beach-loving, self-reliant outdoorsy types, there are plenty of vacation adventures on or near the water. Luckily for everyone, these simple pleasures can be enjoyed on a shoestring.

This type of travel almost always entails camping of some sort — in other words, roughing it. But in case you haven't noticed, camping ain't what it used to be. There are thousands of campgrounds, and many are right at the water's edge. Some are privately owned, many are in national or state parks: As of this writing, there are 10 national seashores in this country. Camping today runs the gamut from the old pitching-a-simple-tent-where-you-please (and digging your own latrine, and running into town for containers of water) to the more comfortable, organized facilities, electrical hookups for RVs, even cabins with a variety of amenities. (But it's still always the maid's day off — and maybe the bugs' night out — so if you'd rather skip the sandy sleeping bags and if you prefer your adventures to include clean sheets, there are usually alternate lodgings nearby.)

Living under various degrees of such primitive conditions and dunking the old bod in the bay may be enough excitement for you. If not, all the campgrounds listed here also offer many other facilities and activities for stretching the mind, the body, and the soul: hiking or biking along wilderness trails; canoeing, rafting, or floating along "flat" or "white" water strictly for fun or as a means of transportation. And since you'll be in wilderness areas, bird and wildlife watching is often superb. (See *A Nature Lover's Guide* and *A Sightseer's Guide* for more ideas.) To supplement this information, see the list of books and outfitters in ADVICE TO ADVENTURERS at the end of this mini-guide.

13

Great Places to Pitch a Tent

Gulf Islands

United States

• *Gulf Islands National Seashore, Florida and Mississippi.* Unreserved campsites, electrical hookups. Sparkling white sandy beaches; swimming, boating, scuba diving, hiking, picnicking, tours, bicycling, playground, ball field, and ball court on the mainland (Mississippi) and idyllic islands (Florida).

• *Cumberland Island National Seashore, Georgia.* Majestic beaches and dunes, marshes, and freshwater lakes makes this, the largest of Georgia's Golden Isles, one of the finest natural campsites on the East Coast. Swimming, fishing, hiking, bird and wildlife watching, tours, and educational programs.

• *Cape Cod National Seashore, Massachusetts.* Beautiful ocean beaches, dunes, wooded areas, ponds, and marshes, plus historic Cape Cod homes. Camping in nearby private campgrounds (reservations recommended), or the state-run one in Brewster (no reservations). Swimming, surfing, biking, horseback riding, picnicking, hiking, shellfishing.

• *Fire Island National Seashore, New York.* Watch Hill Campground, reservations required. Swimming, fishing, clamming, boating along the Atlantic Ocean or the bay. Bike riding, picnicking, guided nature walks, wildlife watching. To get there, drive or take the train to Sayville or Patchogue, then take the ferry.

• *Cape Hatteras National Seashore, North Carolina.* (See *A Sports Lover's Guide.*)

• *Cape Lookout National Seashore, North Carolina.* Beautiful sandy barrier islands add up to 58 miles of ocean beaches. Fishing, swimming, boating, shell collecting, birdwatching. Camping is primitive thus far. Beware of biting insects!

• *Hawaii Volcanoes National Park, Hawaii.* Lush, rare vegetation, active volcanoes, and access to the sea. (See also in *A Sightseer's Guide.*)

• *Haleakala National Park, Maui, Hawaii.* Terrific scenery in this park, which encompasses the side of Mt. Haleakala and a piece of the Kipahulu coast: overlooks, rain forests, black sand lava beaches, cliffs, scenic pools; has rare and endangered species of wildlife, picnicking, walking, hiking and swimming for the experienced and adventurous. Primitive campsites and a few cabins, reservations required.

TOO MUCH TOGETHERNESS

Campers should be aware that the unaccustomed closeness that comes from spending time together in tents, campers, or boats can do relationships more harm than good. Normal physical and psychological releases are disrupted, as well as division of labor and routine habits. Space is at a premium and there's no way to have a room of one's own. The result? Smoldering distrust and irritability, anger, hostility, depression, and boredom. George R. Bach, a California psychologist, has said, "Isolation can be dangerous; 72 hours seems to be the maximum that people can remain exclusively together without an intermission." The solution? Plan short trips, include interesting activities, consider traveling with other couples or in a group.

Cinnamon Bay, St. John (Rockresorts)

The Caribbean

Most of these tropical paradises don't have organized campgrounds and you can pitch your pup just about anywhere. There are more comfortable campsites, though, that throw in all the camping gear you need:

Jamaica

Strawberry Fields, on the north shore between Ocho Rios and Port Antonio. Choose screened tents on platforms or fully equipped seaside cottages; you can even go for the Modified American Plan (MAP), which includes breakfast and dinner. Reservations are a must, especially around Christmas. Campers can swim, snorkel and dive; other activities away from the campgrounds include surfing (best at Boston Bay, on the north coast, east of Port Antonio), boating (rent yachts or small boats), river rafting (on the Rio Grande near Port Antonio), fishing, golfing, horseback riding, hiking (especially at Dunn's River Falls in Ocho Rios), riding mopeds. The action at night is at Ocho Rios (music, dancing, drinks).

St. John, U.S. Virgin Islands

The Virgin Islands National Park has two great campgrounds:

Cinnamon Bay Campground will rent you everything you need to be comfortable in their cottages and platform tents. These campgrounds are near the famous and lovely Caneel Bay.

Maho Bay Campground is a private operation that supplies platform tents (no cabins) with beds and lights. These are in thickly wooded areas with a view of the beach. The meals prepared there emphasize natural and fresh local foods. (For more information about St. John and the U.S. Virgin Islands, see *A Nature Lover's Guide.*)

Tortola, British Virgin Islands

Brewers Bay has a campsite, where you can rent tents and the whole shebang, right on the beach.

Puerto Rico

This pleasure island has the most campsites of any island in the Caribbean: over a dozen, and more are being added all the time. Their offerings vary from bare sites to trailer hookups. Some of the best are: Lago Mar Trailer Camp, near Isabela; Villa Pilaza, near Boqueron; and the government-operated one at Playa El Combate.

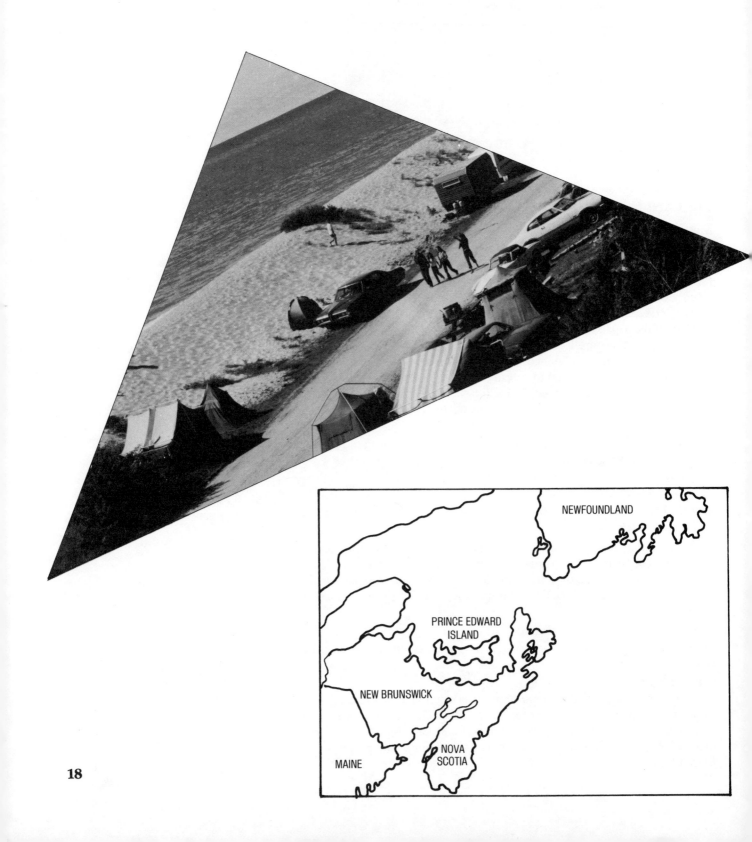

(Prince Edward Island Tourism)

Canada

Canada, too, beckons campers and adventurers with its delicious wilderness areas. Many campgrounds are privately run, but the excellent national and provincial parks also have campsites within them or nearby. In many parts of Canada, the water's too brisk for all but the brave, even in summer. The scenery, sports, and warmer inland lakes make up for that. Or you can visit areas where the water is warmer, such as those listed here.

Prince Edward Island is in the south of the Gulf of St. Lawrence, where the waters are comparatively shallow and warmed by the summer sun. There are 70 campgrounds — in green fields and close to the swimming action. If you want, you can rent a trailer and have it towed to the campsite. (For more information about P.E.I., see ATLANTIC CANADA in *A Family Guide.*)

Fundy National Park, New Brunswick. Famed for its tides, which are the highest in the world, the Bay of Fundy's shoreline is rugged and full of cliffs, coves, abundant tidal life, and fish that bite. Hiking trails, a heated saltwater pool, golf, tennis, boating, nature programs, and crafts courses complete the picture.

Kouchibouguac National Park, New Brunswick. The vast sweep of uncrowded sandy beach on warm Northumberland Strait is the park's main feature. You'll also be able to enjoy canoeing, bicycling, clamming, fishing, guided nature walks, forest marshes, tidal lagoons, and meandering rivers.

Mexico

In Mexico, it's easy to camp "in the wild," right on the beach. Camping is also allowed in some national parks, but that's just as primitive. Privately run campgrounds, with trailer hookups, showers, rest rooms, lounge buildings, laundries, and stores are cropping up all over. Some of them are in or near these beach towns: Acapulco, Bahía Kino, Tijuana, Ensenada, Manzanillo, Mazatlán, Puerto Vallarta, Veracruz.

19

Advice to Adventurers

Raw nature can be nice, but naughty. Always know what you're getting into. Hikers should stick to marked trails or take a guided tour the first time around. The same goes for water adventurers: canoers, rafters, kayakers, and divers should turn their lives over to a good guide or outfitter-guide if they're inexperienced or unfamiliar with the territory to be explored. If you do venture into the wild, don't go alone, and make sure you tell someone where you're going and when you expect to return.

As for camping, Carl Franz advises in his *The People's Guide to Mexico:*

> Everyone wants both a beautiful and a comfortable campsite. Unfortunately the most comfortable places are not always the most aesthetically pleasing. You may find yourself — and your group — torn between camping in a grove of trees, with lots of shade and places to hang hammocks, or on the beach with beautiful sunsets and the sound of the surf. I advise you to choose in favor of the most *comfortable* location. You'll find that you will be able to enjoy everything much more: sleeping, the weather, the food and the view. If you have to stake your sleeping bag down to keep from sliding over a cliff, the fabulous sunrises and sunsets will soon begin to pale in comparison to a good night's sleep.
>
> Camping on the beach means camping in sand. Sand can drive you crazy. It will soon be in your hair, food, clothes, crotch, books and toothbrush. In addition to the sand, there's the salt mist from the spray and from the wind blowing over the sea. This mist soon has everything either damp or feeling slightly greasy and salty. Avoid this by camping back from the beach if possible. You'll be amazed at how much easier and more enjoyable your camp life will be.
>
> Camping away from the beach often means, however, that you lose cooling breezes that keep the temperature more reasonable and act as a barrier against mosquitoes. We've found that some beaches were made unlivable by mosquitoes unless we camped right on the edge of the water. What little wind there was kept the bugs from harassing us.

Franz also reminds his readers to camp near food and fresh water, and warns against camping in direct sun: Either build a sun shade or locate an overhanging cliff of the noncrumbling variety or a large tree. (Watch out for coconut palms, though, which have the nasty habit of dropping their fruit without the slightest thought about where it will land.)

More information about camping in Mexico will be found in Franz's *The People's Guide to Camping in Mexico* (John Muir Publications, rev. ed. 1980; paper). It does more than tell you where to camp and what to expect when you get there. It also features inexpensive adventures such as kayaking and backpacking along the Sea of Cortez, boating, bicycling, diving, fishing; and lists survival skills, including "how to pack a kitchen in a suitcase" — all in entertaining anecdotal form.

MOVING RIGHT ALONG

You can canoe and hike in most of the national seashores and parks listed earlier. Two popular seaside trips are:

A Canoe Trip

The Russian River, near the Pacific Ocean in California, lets you get whiffs of the salt air every now and then. The trip, which takes you through forests, vineyards, and redwoods, is safe almost all year round, no matter how much (or little) experience you have.

The United States Canoe Association also suggests these lakes and rivers: the Great Lakes; Allegheny River, Pennsylvania; Ausable River, Mississippi; Brazoa River, Texas; St. Joseph River, Indiana; Susquehanna River, New York; Wabash River, Indiana — and the rivers in the towns of St. Charles, Illinois; Muscoda, Wisconsin; and Milford, Ohio.

A Hike

The Bruce Trail in southeastern Ontario is 430 miles long, but you can begin almost at any point and enjoy a shorter trek — from one day to, say, a week. There are campsites and water sources all along the trail and commercial lodgings in nearby towns. The best part of the trail is on the Bruce Peninsula that juts out into Georgian Bay. Here's where you'll find limestone cliffs, caves, 39 varieties of orchids, birds, bays and inlets, rocky beaches, and giant offshore boulders. Georgian Bay Islands National Park, which includes Flowerpot Island, is at the tip. The water-sculpted rocks and caves are a big attraction in this section, known as Thousand Islands. (For more information, contact Bruce Trail Association, P.O. Box 857, Hamilton, Ontario L8N 3N9, Canada.)

OUTFITTERS

For groups that outfit adventure trips (that is, provide most of your supplies and act as organizers and guides), see the two adventure travel guides listed in The Adventuresome Reader, below.

The Sierra Club

The Sierra Club advises potential adventure seekers to choose their trips carefully according to their abilities and interests, and Sierra Club outings make it easy even for beginners to take part in wilderness adventures. Once you've chosen the trip you're interested in from their outings catalog (available free), write for the trip supplement which gives more details. Never-to-be-forgotten trips of the past include: sailing and whale watching in Baja, Mexico, and Alaska; special family trips; camping, hiking, bicycling, and backpacking trips along waterways in many places, such as Hawaii, Cape Cod, Chesapeake Bay, the California coastline, Canada, and Greece; water trips (kayak, raft, canoe, boat) in the Grand Canyon, Oregon, Alaska, Utah, and more. (For more information, write to the *Sierra Club,* 530 Bush St., San Francisco, CA 94108.)

American Youth Hostels, Inc.

Inexpensive adventure outings for adults and youth groups. They sponsor bicycling and camping trips along the coasts of Virginia, North and South Carolina; Puget Sound and San Juan Islands in Washington and British Columbia; the Hawaiian Islands; the Atlantic Coast from Boston to Bangor; the Delaware Bay area in Delaware, Maryland, and Virginia; California coast; Prince Edward Island and Nova Scotia. They also have trips to Polynesia, Ireland, and Great Britain. (For more information, write to *American Youth Hostels, Inc.,* National Office, Delaplane, VA 22025.)

THE ADVENTURESOME READER

For more information about camping and adventure travel, refer to the following publications.

• *The Worldwide Adventure Travel Guide,* published by the American Adventurers Association (Suite 301, 444 NE Ravenna Blvd., Seattle, WA 98115), is revised every year. In it you'll find over 3000 adventure trips including land adventures, air adventures, water adventures, and underwater adventures.

• *Adventure Travel* by Pat Dickerman (available from Adventure Guides, Inc., 36 E. 57th St., New York, NY 10022) gives helpful hints for various types of adventures and a state-by-state guide to adventure specialists and their services in hiking, sailing schools, scuba diving, and so on. It's for families, individuals, and couples who want to explore the wilderness, but who don't know where to go or how to arrange for a guide or outfitter.

• *Outdoor Life* is a magazine geared toward fishing, canoeing, kayaking, boating, camping, and hunting. (For subscription information, write to Outdoor Life, P.O. Box 2854, Boulder, CO 80322.)

• These government publications are available from the Consumer Information Center, Pueblo, CO 81009 (most cost only a few dollars):

Guide and Map to the National Parks. Publication No. 149H. Seasonal and year-round activities of nearly 300 parks; includes highway maps.

Index to the National Park System and Related Areas. Publication No. 207H. State-by-state listing of all areas managed by the National Park Service (parks, monuments, seashores, etc.) with a brief description of each; also includes information on the Wild and Scenic Rivers System and the National Trail System.

Camping in the National Parks. Publication No. 179H. Lists 100 parks with camping areas; includes maps and information on fees, camping season, number of sites, and other facilities.

Camping on the Public Lands. Publication No. 670H. Lists 180 camping sites on government-owned lands (excluding the national parks) in the western states and Alaska, including many wilderness and primitive areas; gives directions and describes the facilities available at the different sites.

• For detailed brochures about specific national parks, write to: National Park Service, Office of Public Information, Washington, DC 20240.

• Rand McNally publishes five editions of their *Campground and Trailer Park Guide.* All are updated annually and the complete edition lists nearly 19,000 campgrounds in the U.S., Canada, and Mexico, along with their facilities, amenities, cost, seasons, and so on. They also publish these related books: *National Park Guide, Vacation & Travel Guide,* and *Backpacking & Outdoor Guide.*

• *The Bantam Great Outdoors Guide to the United States and Canada* by Val Landi (Bantam, 1978; paper) contains information on accommodations, wilderness trails, canoeing waters, recreation and scenic highways, fishing, hunting, guide services, and outfitters. Bantam also publishes a three-volume guide for specific areas (Canada, the eastern U.S., and the western U.S. and Alaska).

• *Women in the Wilderness* by China Galland (Harper & Row, 1980; paper) describes women who have tested themselves in the wilderness and includes information on how to start to explore on your own, such as a directory of programs run by and for women.

• *Canoe Trails Directory* by James C. Makens (Doubleday/Dolphin, 1979; paper) describes 1000 waterways in the United States. It gives directions to streams, decribes access points, portages, mileage, fishing potential, what to expect, and special areas of scenic beauty.

Lynn Beach (Barry Pakoff)

A DAY TRIPPER'S GUIDE

You're visiting a big city to see Aunt Tillie, visit an old college buddy, attend a business meeting, play tourist. Inject a little fresh air and watery R&R into your stay by visiting a beach that's a mere pail-and-shovel's throw away.

(Cape Cod Chamber of Commerce)

Boston, Massachusetts

Located right on the Atlantic Ocean in Massachusetts Bay, Boston has a wealth of nearby public beaches. For something special:

• *Cape Cod* can be a rather long day trip. (Although it's only about sixty miles from Boston to where Cape Cod takes off from the mainland, the Cape itself is sixty-five miles long; so the length of the trip depends on your final destination.) But its natural beauty is worth the trip no matter how far away you are. The Cape Cod National Seashore area has lovely scenic ocean beaches, dunes on the march, woodlands, and freshwater ponds and marshes. You can watch wildlife, listen to nature talks, swim and surf (but watch out for rip tides), drive beach buggies, ride horseback, fish, picnic, hike, beachcomb, and bike ride. Accommodations and food are available nearby, but not right on the National Seashore. Other good beaches on the Cape include Hyannis, Brewster, Chatham, Eastham, Provincetown, Sandwich. Drive or take a ferry to the Cape; if you have time, visit nearby Nantucket and Martha's Vineyard (see *An Island Lover's Guide*).

• *Cape Ann,* about 27 miles northeast of Boston, is accessible by car or train. Gloucester harbor is the place to see fishermen and lobstermen at work, or charter a boat and catch your own. Eastern Point (no cars allowed) is a dune-edged road perfect for biking and hiking, climbing and picnicking. Rockport and its environs have both rocky beaches (and a view "to Ireland") with pounding surf and hard-packed sandy stretches suitable for swimming and surfing. There's a wildlife preserve at Halibut Point on the northernmost tip for a bit of quiet contemplation and picnicking. Reservations are a must if you stay the weekend or longer during the warmer months.

• *Crane Beach,* just north of Cape Ann in Ipswich, has been called the nicest beach in Massachusetts and one of the best in the country. It's a seven-mile stretch of white sandy beach with beautiful dunes.

• *Plum Island,* farther north, near Newburyport, is a state park with a wildlife refuge and a nine-mile strip of pristine sand in the Atlantic.

• Even closer are Boston's harbor islands. *Georges, Gallups, and Lovell* islands are accessible by ferry. On Grape and Bumpkin islands in Hingham Bay you can swim, picnic, fish, or take in a bit of history.

CAPE COD IN WORDS AND PICTURES

When you go, don't forget to bring a copy of the classic *Cape Cod* by Henry David Thoreau (College & University Press, 1951; paperback).

Over Cape Cod and the Islands: An Aerial View by Stephen Proehl (Houghton Mifflin, 1979; paper) is a stunning portfolio of the Cape's shoreline, interiors, and outlying islands.

Santa Monica (Budd Symes)

158—Edgewater Beach Hotel and Apartments, Chicago

Chicago, Illinois

Chicago is fortunate in that it's right on Lake Michigan, so its waterfront is characterized by green parks, cool sandy white beaches, and deep blue waters. The miles of sandy beaches are fully patrolled by lifeguards, and you can swim, scuba and skin dive, fish, and rent boats.

• *Lincoln Park Beach,* on the Gold Coast, is the most fashionable one to go to; the farther north you go, the less popular (and crowded) the beaches are.

• *Highland Park* is a popular marina.

Houston, Texas

Galveston Island, a leading Gulf Coast resort area, is only about 50 miles south of Houston. Stewart Beach is the most popular public beach, and you can swim, surf, sail, water-ski and deep-sea fish all over the island, all year round. The island's 32-mile white sandy beach faces the Gulf of Mexico, with Galveston Bay out back. You can reach the island by ferry or causeway, and feast in seafood restaurants and marvel at the restored turn-of-the-century homes and lush oleander blossoms. For overnight trips, a variety of accommodations are available, including camping in Galveston Island State Park.

Los Angeles, California

The beaches here have much in common with those near San Diego as far as conditions and activities go. However, they're even more heavily used and therefore some are less idyllic in terms of cleanliness and elbow room.

• *Long Beach,* a seven-mile-long strip of sand with calm water, is very popular.

• *Cabrillo Beach* is the sight of a marine museum, tide pools, and good swimming and surfing.

• The *Channel Islands* are the site of a national park and home to many species of wildlife. Picturesque Santa Catalina, immortalized in song, is reachable by sea (there are excursion boats) or air (regular or sea plane).

• South Bay Beaches (*Torrance, Redondo, Hermosa, Manhattan*) are clean, sandy, and good for swimming, surfing, and other sports, but the parking problem can be acute.

• *Marina Del Rey* is for the sailing set, and has a small beach for swimming. *Venice* has a good beach, and is worth a trip for the parade of humanity along the boardwalk — most of it on roller skates. *Santa Monica* has an old-timey carnival-like pier and a long stretch of state-owned beach that is very popular with locals.

• *Malibu,* one of the most beautiful stretches of seashore, has many public beaches. The best may be Leo Carillo State Beach, but unfortunately you need a car to get there.

Coney Island (New York Convention and Visitors Bureau)

Breakers at Hammels.   Coney Island, N. Y.

New York, New York

The farther you get from the teeming masses, the better the beaches get. From the ridiculous to the sublime:

• The public beaches nearest the city are reachable by mass transit and reflect the density and ethnic diversity of its population. Without fail, hot weather spawns sunbathers that resemble so many sardines packed in oil — most playing loud radios, some playing bongos, a few being obnoxious but not necessarily dangerous. You'll find boardwalks, playgrounds, sports facilities, rest rooms, fast-food concessions, and peripatetic snack vendors. Water pollution is a definite deterrent to some, but if you absolutely must get a whiff of salt air and feel the sand and surf between your toes, these are the beaches you can get to for the price of a token (or two).

In Brooklyn, there's *Coney Island* (rides, games, aquarium, and the world-famous Nathan's for clams, corn on the cob, softshell crab); a bit quieter are *Brighton Beach* (popular with the very young and the very old, who've been coming all their lives) and *Manhattan Beach* (near Sheepshead Bay, a seafood and fishing spot).

In Queens, there's *Jacob Riis Park* (huge pool, some nude sunbathing, and a large gay clientele); the *Rockaways* (10-mile-long beach, amusement park).

In the Bronx, you have *Orchard Beach* (on Long Island Sound, near City Island, a historic fishing and boating town).

• *Jones Beach* is a state park on Long Island. It's the best public beach, not too crowded, and still a reasonable distance from Manhattan. This beautiful wide sandy beach is five miles long and accessible by car or public transportation (bus or a combination of train and bus). It's relatively clean, has two miles of boardwalk, a bay side, saltwater pool, bath houses, fishing, cafes, restaurant, snack bar, picnic area, game fields, and archery range. Dancing and theater at night.

(Chuck DeLaney)

• *Robert Moses State Park,* on Fire Island, is a long haul, but worth it — less crowded, cleaner, and quieter than any of the other beaches; if you're willing to walk a bit, you may find yourself a deserted stretch of beach. Snacks and rest rooms. Drive over the causeway that connects the island to Long Island, or take a bus from Manhattan or a train to Babylon to connect with a bus.

Golden Gate National Recreation Area

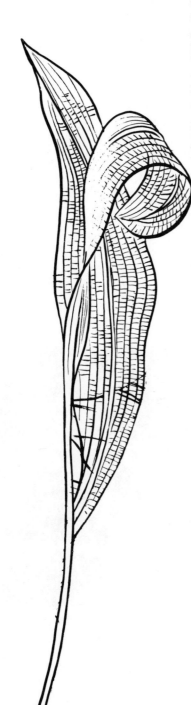

Philadelphia, Pennsylvania

Philadelphians are within about 100 miles of most of the great beaches on the Jersey Shore. *Atlantic City* is closest, with its gambling casinos and high-rolling nightlife. *Ocean City* is the most family-oriented beach. *Wildwood* is known for its youth-attracting rambunctiousness, amusements, and nightlife. (For more information about Jersey Shore beaches, see *A Family Guide.*)

San Diego, California

As you might suspect, any soul near San Diego is automatically in beach country. The wide, sandy shoreline near here is relieved by cliffs edging right up to the sea. Even in summer, the Pacific is "refreshing" (about 65° F), but rip tides and strong currents often make for unsafe swimming, surfing, and diving. (This varies from beach to beach and day to day — signs are posted and lifeguards will tell you where the water's safe.) There are plenty of other activities on and near the beaches: sailing, nature watching, clamming, fishing, horseback riding, jogging, volleyball; roller skates and bicycles are common on boardwalks. The sunsets can be pinky-pretty. Most beaches have rest rooms, showers, fire rings, and picnic areas. Beaches are usually crowded: the traffic congested and parking a problem unless you arrive early. Luckily, plenty of buses go past the beaches.

• *Mission Bay,* San Diego's Coney Island, is especially crammed.

• *Windandsea,* great for surfing, is less crowded and popular with the young set.

• *La Jolla Point* is romantic and cozy, with little coves, lava flows, seals, sea lions (and whales in winter).

• *Tory Pines State Reserve* is known for its scenery, nature hikes, and hang gliding.

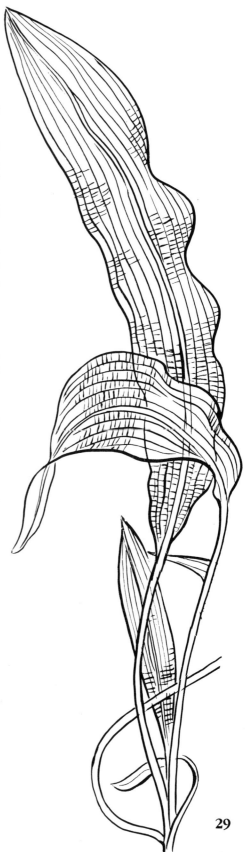

San Francisco, California

San Franciscans are fortunate — a cosmopolitan city and good beaches that are accessible by car or public transportation:

• In Marin County, the 37,000-acre *Golden Gate National Recreation Area* follows the city's northern and western shorelines. You can picnic, swim, fish, hike, and camp at Muir Beach, Stinson Beach, and Rodeo Beach amidst beautiful scenery.

• *Santa Cruz* has been the seaside respite for San Franciscans since the turn of the century.

• *Point Reyes National Seashore* is about one hour from the city (by car only). It has long beaches and towering cliffs, with lagoons and wildlife colonies. You can swim, surf, fish, hike, bike, horseback ride, picnic, and watch the birds. (There are campgrounds if you'd like to stay.)

Washington, D.C.

You can rent rowboats, canoes, and paddle boats in the Tidal Basin right in Washington, but if you need more beachiness than that, you have two options: nearby Chesapeake Bay beaches and faraway Atlantic Ocean beaches.

• *Chesapeake Bay* is 185 miles long, most of it in Maryland, and a fishier, crabbier, clammier place is hard to find. It's America's largest estuary — 46 rivers and streams flow into it, fringing the land with ribbons of water. You can drive or walk to the ends of its myriad fingers by following any unpretentious road, which inevitably leads to water. A better way to explore the inlets and bays is by boat. There are commercial ferry rides and sightseeing cruises, but you can charter a boat, too. Best yet may be if you can wangle a Chesapeake "waterman" into taking an impromptu trip across the bays and rivers. The area is thick with wildlife, especially in its numerous wildlife refuges. *Kent Island,* between western and eastern shores, has a subdued atmosphere and is where you can visit the Chesapeake Bay Study and Hydraulic Model Complex.

Also near Washington is Annapolis, the heart of Chesapeake's heavy boating action. There are several good beaches on the western shore from *Sandy Point* on south.

The towns themselves are picturesque and prerevolutionary; locals are friendly fisher folk, some of whom have retained Elizabethan English to this day. Seafood lovers will think they've died and gone to heaven. As James Mitchener has said, Chesapeake is a "sequestered paradise — one of the most remote corners of the nation."

• *Ocean City,* also in Maryland, is on the Delmarva Peninsula. This old seaside resort, with a bay on one side and the ocean on the other, is a beautiful long stretch of wide sandy beach. It's also a bit honky-tonk due to the boardwalk and amusement park and gets pretty crowded. Drive, fly, or take a train or bus to this seaside mecca and swim, surf, and deep-sea fish in true Atlantic Ocean style.

A FAMILY GUIDE

Where to take the kids — of all ages — when the beach isn't enough.

Atlantic Canada   (See map on page 18)

The provinces and waters of Atlantic Canada are guaranteed to elicit oohs, ahhs, and oh wows from all who see and hear them. The Bay of Fundy is the center of attraction, with the highest tides in the world. Twice a day, one hundred billion tons of salt water (25 to 50 feet high) head toward shore all at once, covering barnacle-encrusted legs of wooden wharves, reefs, sandbars, beaches, and mud flats. As it retreats, it leaves barnacles, sea anemones, and periwinkles behind. It also leaves herring in the special *weirs* (a sort of net) that fishermen set out before high tide, enabling them to simply walk out and harvest their catch when the tide is low. All through the provinces of Nova Scotia, New Brunswick, and Prince Edward Island there are rugged coastlines with caves and water-carved archways, quaint fishing villages, historical landmarks, and museums. The Cabot Trail on Cape Breton, Nova Scotia, is particularly breathtaking, but there are many other scenic and nature routes to walk, hike, bike, or drive.

Other Features: Swimming in "the warmest saltwater north of the Carolinas" (70°F in summer), at beaches along the Northumberland Strait, Chaleur Bay, and numerous little coves elsewhere where the water is shallow enough to warm up. There's plenty of more invigorating saltwater; lakes for freshwater enthusiasts; and a heated saltwater pool in Fundy National Park. Deep-sea and fresh-water fishing, clamming, sailing, water-skiing, scuba diving, canoeing in nearby lakes, golf, tennis, horseback riding, nature watching (seals, whales, porpoises, and seabirds — from sea gulls to puffins).

Appearance and Ambiance: Sandy uncrowded beaches along bodies of both salt- and freshwater, with an overwhelming sense of the timeless power and strength of the forces of nature. Beaches supervised by the National Parks System offer the most recreational facilities and lifeguard service. The atmosphere is relaxing and friendly.

Climate: Summer, when the temperature is in the 60s and 70s, is when most people visit; autumn is cooler, but with beautiful foliage.

Accommodations and Food: Modern resorts and hotels, historic inns, cabins, camping. Seafood galore: Nova Scotia salmon, Solomon gundy, smoked eel and mackerel, and all the lobster you can eat. Perfect picnic conditions — you can buy fresh fruit and vegetables (or pick your own at certain farms).

Nightlife: Plays, musicals, lounge music, dancing.

Getting There and Getting Around: Planes, trains, and buses to major cities and vacation spots. Ferries go to the numerous islands; many are part of the highway system and toll-free. Excellent scenic roads (Prince Edward Island has three all its own) to drive; rent a car or bike. English is spoken in this part of Canada; use Canadian currency; credit cards accepted widely.

CANADIAN CRUISES

• *Prince of Fundy Cruises* (Portland, ME 64101) has a variety of tours to Nova Scotia and the Bay of Fundy. They range from one-way specials to round trips from Portland that last 6 days and nights. You can take your car, camper, motorcycle, or bicycle to use when the boat docks in Nova Scotia.

• *The Bahama Cruise Line* (747 Third Ave., New York, NY 10017) offers seven-day cruises along the magnificent St. Lawrence River. The *Veracruz,* which leaves from New York or Montreal, shows you Prince Edward Island; the Gaspé Peninsula and its famous landmark, the Percé Rock; Bonaventure Island and its bird sanctuary with thousands of gannets, gulls, puffins, and kittiwakes; and the river's school of white whales.

The Grand Strand, South Carolina

There's always something going on along the sixty miles of public, sandy beaches and around the 400 swimming pools, including sports, arcades, amusement pavilions, parks, bingo parlors, and special events such as fishing tournaments, workshops, art and craft shows, bikini pageants, and jogging competitions.

Other Features: Excellent swimming, surfing, golf (34 championship courses), 125 tennis courts, surf, pier and deep-sea fishing, horseback riding, shell collecting; soak up some history (Charleston's a hop-skip-and-jump away); visit floral and sculpture gardens; take a historic river tour past old plantations. Visit nearby barrier islands such as Isle of Palms, Kiawah, Seabrook, Edisto (see *An Island Lover's Guide*).

Appearance and Ambiance: Clear blue surf caresses white, sandy beaches that are wonderfully flat and surprisingly wide (one eighth of a mile at North Myrtle Beach at low tide — the "widest beach in the world"). Some deserted, some lively and crowded. Highlights are Little River, Cherry Grove, Ocean Drive, North Myrtle Beach, Surfside, Garden City, Huntington State Park, Litchfield, Pawley's Island, Debidue.

Climate: Both water and air temperatures average mid 50s in winter; low 80s in summer.

Accommodations and Food: Luxury resorts, hotels, motels, efficiency apartments, cottages, 12,000 campsites. Food ranges from foot-long hot dogs to gourmet meals; don't miss local dishes and seafood, like hush puppies, crab soup, and fish stew.

Nightlife: Hotel nightclubs, discos, dancing, music of all kinds, intimate lounges, and piano bars; theaters, concerts, movies, midnight cruises, amusement parks.

Getting There and Getting Around: Fly direct from many major cities; car rental at Myrtle Beach Jetport and downtown; taxis and limos, too. Bus and train service; drivers can use several interstate highways to get to U.S. 17, which winds along the coast. The Intracoastal Waterway provides access by boat. Bike riding.

(Harvey Stein)

The Jersey Shore

There's always something to do for every member of the family, regardless of age, along the string of beaches collectively known as "the Jersey Shore": from heart-stopping amusement park rides to beachside playgrounds, shuffleboard, and everything in between. Not only that — the 125 miles of wide, gently sloping sandy white ocean beaches have plenty of well-trained lifeguards. In fact, Wildwood, near Cape May, has been singled out as "the World's Finest and Safest Bathing Beach."

Other Features: Never a dull moment. Every game imaginable along the livelier boardwalks and piers; sightseeing boat cruises, boats to charter; surfing, water-skiing, scuba diving; surf, pier, and deep-sea fishing; rafting, canoeing, and fishing along lakes and rivers; tennis, golf, shell collecting, bicycling, hiking, birdwatching; historic walks and tours, especially in Ocean City and Cape May; visit the Twin Lighthouses on Atlantic Highlands, the highest point on the East Coast between Maine and Florida.

Appearance and Ambiance: Wide, white, sandy beaches, sheltered dunes, marsh grass. Ocean temperature reaches about 70°F in July, but the many inlets and the tidal bay are warmer. Quiet resort towns burst into various degrees of healthy honky-tonk along the boardwalks, particularly in Wildwood and Atlantic City. Dress is casual; semicasual even at Atlantic City casinos.

Climate: The beach season is from late May to September; the average temperature hovers around 80°F between June and August, and is about 10° cooler at night. Expect cloudy or partly cloudy days at least two thirds of the time in summer.

Accommodations and Food: Grand old resorts, luxury hotels, reasonably priced seaside cottages and apartments, camping — you name it. Permits are issued for beach fires and cookouts; picnicking; snacks along the boardwalk; some "gourmet" restaurants; excellent French restaurants near the Cape.

Nightlife: Jumpin', especially at Wildwood and Atlantic City. Dancing, concerts, theater, floor shows, boardwalk games and many nearby amusement parks, horseracing.

Getting There and Getting Around: Air service to Newark, Atlantic City, Cape May; bus and rail service to and between many cities and beaches; ferry from Lewes, Delaware, to Cape May. Highways are many and modern; the islands are connected by Ocean Drive. Inland and ocean boats to charter; many marinas. Bikes to rent.

There is something about growing up by the sea which gives one a sense of the mystery in the universe, some unaccountable force which acts in ways which are not meant for us to understand. And there is also the feeling of adventure and freedom associated with the vast waters which roll on to other continents carrying homeless flotsam in its currents...always was one of my ears tuned to the relentless shuffling of waves on beach, on a kind of harmonious whispering of natural phenomena which guided all my real or imagined pursuits. I was the son of some lost sea god, and I could do no wrong. The sea, I felt, was my real home, and if I ever had a goal in life it was to recall the art of breathing underwater. I'd still like that. I'd still like to crawl to the shoreline, porpoise through the gullies, pass over the silent sandbars and go all the way out there and live on the bottom for a while.
— from *Atlantic City Proof* by Christopher Cook Gilmore (Simon & Schuster, 1978)

Clearwater Beach

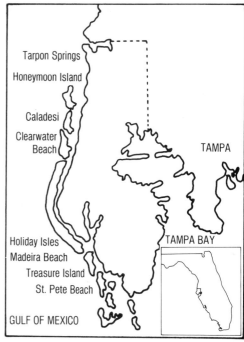

The Pinellas Suncoast, Florida

Twenty-eight miles of calm, warm-watered beaches that meander through eight very different communities with tons of things to do and see.

Other Features: Great swimming, fishing, beachcombing. Sail, water-ski; bet on the horses, the hounds, and jai alai; play golf, tennis, volleyball; watch nature (there's a seabird sanctuary in the Holiday Isles); snorkel, parasail, jet-ski, windsurf, ride your bike. Visit many nearby attractions and amusement parks, such as Disney World (see NOT FOR KIDS ONLY).

Appearance and Ambiance: Soft, white, wide, sandy beaches on islands and inlets with the warm turquoise waters of the Gulf of Mexico on the west; bays and the intracoastal waterway on the right. Uncluttered beaches with sea oats, sand dunes, seabirds. Dress is casual, but you won't be out of place if you dress up for evening.

Climate: So good that St. Petersburg guarantees 361 days a year of sunshine. The newspapers are free on sunless days and fewer than 300 have been given away since 1910. Average temperature is 74°F.

Accommodations and Food: Very varied — from campgrounds and cozy beach cottages to luxurious resorts. Food ranges from elegant to barefoot dining; many seafood and ethnic (Chinese, Polynesian, Italian, Greek) restaurants; picnicking, snack bars, and alcohol bars on the beaches.

Nightlife: First, watch the sun set over the Gulf; then whoop it up at nightclubs that feature all kinds of music from bluegrass and rock to classical — opera and theater, too. Discos, piano bars.

Getting There and Getting Around: Twenty minutes from Tampa Airport, from which buses and limousines service all eight communities. By car, take U.S. 19 or I-275. Auto-Train leaves from Lorton, Virginia, and Louisville, Kentucky, and goes to Sanford, which is near Orlando and Disney World. (For more information about Auto-Train, call toll-free 800-424-1111.) The modern system of causeways makes getting to the beaches easy; Caladesi Island is accessible only by boat. Bus tours available.

Florida's compact Pinellas Coast combines calm water and soft sand with attractions and activities that are just a hop-skip-and-jump away.

Not For Kids Only

Sometimes more than a beach is required to keep everyone amused; that's where theme parks come in. There's nothing like an amusement park to set the child in all of us free, if only for a day. Adults may rationalize going on knuckle-whitening rides because the kids need supervision, but those who are honest with themselves know better. Fortunately for the beach lover, many such parks are near or on bodies of water, in vacation meccas such as Florida, New Jersey, and California. But, as you'll see from this selection, there are some surprises in store. Many have gentle, relaxing, scenic rides and exhibits, so kids from 6 to 60 will find something of interest. Some combine entertainment with education, especially the aquarium-and-water-show centers (the old "spoonful of sugar" trick), which can add an interesting fillip to kids' responses to "What did you do on your summer vacation?" "I petted a dolphin, rode the largest roller coaster, saw a shark."

Write ahead for more information, such as maps, seasons, hours, admission fees, recommended nearby accommodations. Don't forget to bring a camera and your sense of fun.

KIDS AND CARS

"Are we there yet?"
"I'm hungry."
"I have to go to the bathroom."
"I'm going to be sick."
"I can't see anything."
"I'm bored."
"But we played that already."
"I'm cold."
"I'm hot."

38

California
Sea World
1720 South Shores Rd., Mission Bay, San Diego, CA 92109. Near Southern California beaches. Unusual marine exhibits, entertaining animal shows, lush botanical settings. SRI International (formerly the Stanford Research Institute) has called Sea World "a marvelous collection of shows, playgrounds, aquariums, birds, tide pools, and education."

Six Flags Magic Mountain
Magic Mountain Parkway, Valencia, CA 91355. Nestled in rolling hills in scenic north Los Angeles County — near two large lakes (Pyramid Lake in the Angeles National Forest and Castaic Lake). Called "the roller coaster capital of the world" because its 35 rides include 5 roller coasters, such as the world's largest steel roller coaster and the world's largest double-track wooden roller coaster. Water shows spotlight dolphins and Acapulco cliff divers. Lifelike puppets, rock 'n' roll slide show, country music show.

Marineland
Palos Verdes Dr. South, Rancho Palos Verdes, CA 90274. Set high on rugged coastal cliffs; world's largest oceanarium. Shows and exhibits of whales, dolphins, sharks, octopuses, etc. The Skytower ride rises 340-plus feet above sea level and offers a breathtaking view of the Pacific coastline. There's also a coastal cruise and a swim-through aquarium — the park supplies the necessary equipment.

Florida
Miami Seaquarium
On Virginia Key. 4400 Richenbacker Causeway, Miami, FL 33149. Near southern Florida's beautiful beaches, especially the Keys. Shows and exhibits of whales, dolphins, birds, turtles; underwater feedings.

Ocean World
One mile east of U.S. 1, on A1A. SE 17th St. Causeway, Ft. Lauderdale, FL 33316. One and a half miles west of Ft. Lauderdale Beach. Water shows of dolphins, sharks, sea lions, birds, fish, and alligators.

Sea World
At the intersection of I-4 and Bee Line Dr. 7007 Sea World Dr., Orlando, FL 32809. Near Central Florida beaches and Disney World. (See California's Sea World, above, for description.)

Walt Disney World
Lake Buena Vista, off intersection of I-4 and U.S. 192. P.O. Box 40, Lake Buena Vista, FL 32830. Dozens of major attractions in the Magic Kingdom. Vacation Kingdom, which surrounds the Magic Kingdom, is a total resort — choose from luxury hotels, motels, "treehouse" and Polynesian villas with kitchens, camping — with golf, tennis, horseback riding. Between the Vacation Kingdom and other areas in Disney World, there are plenty of places to swim, sail, water-ski, go boating — heated swimming pools, lagoons and lakes containing over 650 acres of water, 5 miles of beaches. River Country is a whole land devoted to swimming and water play where you can shoot the (manmade) rapids in an inner tube. (There are also plans in the works to devote part of Future World to the sea as a future environment for man.)

Other places in Florida to visit are *Shark Institute,* in Layton, on Long Key. *Silver Springs,* near Ocala on S.R. 40. *Marineland,* between St. Augustine and Daytona Beach on A1A. *Weeki Wachee,* near Orlando on U.S. 19 and S.R. 50. *Monkey Jungle, Parrot Jungle, Planet Ocean,* and *Miami Serpentarium,* all in Miami.

Hawaii
Sea Life Park
Makapuu Point, Waimanalo, Oahu, HA 96816. Manmade Hawaiian reef is home to hundreds of kinds of native sea life, seldom seen anywhere else in the world. Performing whales, dolphins, more; replica of whaling ship that inspired *Moby Dick.*

New Jersey
Great Adventure
Just off the New Jersey Turnpike on Rt. 537. Box 120, Jackson, NJ 08527. Near the Jersey Shore and its many safe beaches. More than 100 rides, shows, and attractions, including the world's largest drive-through safari.

New York
Playland
Exit 19 of I-95. Rye, NY 10580. Right on the boardwalk on Long Island Sound where you can swim, sunbathe, picnic, fish; playing fields, nature walks, too. One hundred rides and attractions; buildings in the art deco style.

Ohio
Oceana
At Cedar Point in Sandusky, OH 44870. Next to Cedar Point's amusement park and bathing beaches on Lake Erie. Aquarium and stadium for viewing dolphins and sea lions. The park has six roller coasters, four antique carousels, two water flume rides — a total of 57 rides in all.

Sea World
On Ohio Route 43, 1100 Sea World Dr., Aurora, OH 44202. Near Geauga Lake (see California's Sea World, above, for description).

Rhode Island
Rocky Point Park
Route 17, Warwick Neck, Rhode Island 02889. On Narragansett Bay, with 100 rides and games, including 1600 feet of waterways, Olympic-sized saltwater pool.

Texas
Sea-Arama
Seawall Blvd. at 91st St., Galveston, TX 77552. On Galveston Island's West Beach. Exotic fish, killer whales, dolphin show, reptiles, and more.

Utah
Lagoon Amusement Park, Utah
On I-15. P.O. Box 102009, 464 South Main St., Salt Lake City, UT 84110. Near Great Salt Lake, at base of Wasatch Mountain Range. Rides, including the Tidal Wave; rodeos, shows, pioneer village, million-gallon swimming pool; adjoining campground.

KIDS AND CARS, Con't.
On long trips, singing "100 Bottles of Beer on the Wall" and playing endless games of I Spy soon lose their charm. If car trips seem to bring out the little devils in your little angels, here are a few tips that will accomplish your two most important goals: keeping the kids from getting bored and keeping them from throwing up.

• Let them plan the trip along with you so they can't complain if they aren't having a good time.

• Plan to make frequent pit stops — for leg stretching, a fast game of Frisbee, snacks, meals and bathrooms.

• Sit older children up front so they can catch the sights out of the front window; bobbing up and down with no distractions but the dashboard or the back of the front seat adds to antsy-ness and car sickness, too. (Tiny ones should be provided with safety seats and stay in the back seat.)

• Keep windows partly open for ventilation.

• Cover sticky or scratchy upholstery with a smooth old sheet; bring a fluffy pillow for comfy naps.

• Dress children comfortably. Stay loose; consider pajamas, shorts, warm-up suits. Keep extra sweaters handy, not locked up in the trunk.

• Bring toys and games designed for automobile travel, such as magnetic checkers and Scrabble; toys with no loose parts to be misplaced (Etch-a-Sketch, etc.) are also recommended.

• Provide damp washcloths or foil-packed cleansing cloths for sticky snacks — fruit (prewashed), individual cans of juice, and nut-and-dried-fruit munchies.

• Rotate drivers and referees.

• Let older children help plan the trip and act as navigators — read maps, directional signs, watch for landmarks.

A HIDEAWAY GUIDE

Where to find serenity, seclusion, and a slower pace...the art of doing nothing with no one.

(Bahama News Bureau)

The Bahama Out Islands

Most of the 700 Bahamas are Out Islands — off the beaten path and a far cry from the sophistication and action found in the more popular Nassau and Freeport. They're low-key, quietly beautiful, and oriented toward the simple pleasures of sun and water.

Other Features: Swimming in the Atlantic, warmed by the Gulf Stream. Scuba and snorkeling in colorful coral reefs. Sailing along 2000 cays. Fishing for white marlin, bluefin tuna, sailfish, swordfish. (Twenty-five world-record game fish have been caught in the Bahamas.) Shell collecting — for pink-tinged beauties. Sightsee by air, taxi, or on foot. Some golf, tennis.

Appearance and Ambiance: Peace, tranquillity, a Robinson Crusoe no-one's-ever-been-here-before atmosphere prevails on these tropical, sun-drenched isles with uncrowded, white sandy beaches. Thousands of flamingos (the national bird of the Bahamas) mingle with colorful tropical flowers; some islands have green hills, soaring cliffs, or powder-pink sand. Relaxed, do-what-ever-you-want-to-do attitude. Dress is casual except at resorts, but don't wear your bathing suit to town.

Climate: Winter temperature averages 72°F; summertime 85°F, but it can get as hot as southern Florida (its neighbor), which is too hot for some. Rainfall varies, but most comes in the fall (hurricanes and possibility of storms in September). The best time is November through April.

Accommodations and Food: Some of the Out Islands are so "out" that they have no tourist accommodations. Those that do take care of visitors (Abaco, Bimini, the Berry Islands, Andros, Long Island, Exuma, San Salvador, Cat Island, Eleuthera, Spanish Wells, and Harbour Island) have small hotels and inns, some relatively unpretentious resorts, some cottages. Air conditioning is a rarity. Dining is low-key in mom-and-pop restaurants and usually depends on the day's catch. Hotels have dining rooms with limited menus. Bahamian bread makes a good breakfast; fruit is plentiful for snacking (pick your own bananas and mangos or buy at local fruit stands).

Nightlife: A drink during sunset, then dinner and quiet conversation, soft, gentle music, moonlight strolls.

Getting There and Getting Around: Fly directly from Ft. Lauderdale, Miami, Nassau, or Freeport. Boats may also be chartered or you can sail there on your own. On the islands, your best bet is private taxis, which can be hired for days and half days (and come with commentary at no extra charge). Also for rent are horses to explore empty beaches, small boats for poking around the many secluded coves, and bicycles to travel along the hard, sandy roads. Few cars are used, but golf carts are used off the courses.

**NASSAU AND FREEPORT —
WHERE THE ACTION IS**
Should you tire of doing nothing and get antsy for a little more "civilized" action during your stay in the Out Islands, you can always pop over to Nassau on the island of New Providence or Freeport on Grand Bahama for a fix. There you'll find shopping, yelling, and traffic jams by day and casinos, nightclubs, and dancing at night. Also, sightseeing, tropical gardens, nature watching.

Tortola (Dave Kendall)

The Baths, Virgin Gorda (Sally Cummings)

The British Virgin Islands

The British Virgin Islands personify the Caribbean the way it used to be: unspoiled beaches, sun, and sea. Many of the 50-odd off-the-beaten-path islands, cays, and rocks are uninhabited. Most visited are: Tortola, which houses the capital, Road Town; Virgin Gorda; and Anegada. Others include Peter Island, Norman Island, Jost Van Dyke, and Beef Island. Aside from sunning and swimming, the main activity is sailing for fun and fishing in the world's best sailing waters. Rental boats come with crews, or you can "bare-boat" it.

Other Features: Snorkeling and diving galore among the coves, caves, and cays that are rich in aquatic life and wrecks that date back to pirate days. There are hills to climb and horseback ride over, and some tennis.

Appearance and Ambiance: Some of the most beautiful, scenic beaches in the world with powdery white sand and low surf that's perfect for swimming. Best beaches are the Baths on Virgin Gorda, where you can crawl through openings between huge, mysterious rock formations to find shallow pools and grottoes; and Tortola's Cane Garden Bay. Atmosphere is warm and friendly; dress is casual, even at luxury resorts.

Climate: Perfect; trade winds keep temperature between 75 and 87°F all year round.

Accommodations and Food: Everything from luxury condominium-type resorts to moderately priced accommodations; some camping in the rough, campground at Brewer's Bay on Tortola. Hotel and local restaurants serve haute cuisine, roast beef, and Yorkshire pudding, but best of all is local fare, which includes seafood cooked to perfection — lobster, fresh fish, fish stews. Some picnicking.

Nightlife: Mostly snoozing; some boozing at local clubs where people play fungi (*fun-gee*) music and welcome visitors.

Getting There and Getting Around: Definitely half the fun. Fly to Tortola or Virgin Gorda from Antigua, St. Thomas, San Juan, or St. Croix; take a ferry from St. Thomas to Tortola; or charter a boat. Once there, the best way to see the islands is by boat: start on Tortola and island-hop, using your boat as a floating hotel. Land transportation includes vans, taxis, Land Rovers, bicycles, and mopeds. Currency is the U.S. dollar; language is lilting English.

**God loves an idle rainbow
No less than laboring seas.
— Ralph Hodgson**

Na Pali, Kauai (Aloha Airlines)

Far From the Madding Crowd

Bear these general principles in mind when the world seems too much and you
need a get-away-from-it-all vacation full of peace and quiet.

• If you're a stickler for creature comforts, expect to pay handsomely for your
privacy by patronizing exclusive beach resorts (see *A Luxury Lover's Guide*),
which have private beaches, villas, even individual swimming pools!

• Try traveling off-season, which will give you more elbow room anywhere —
at lower prices.

• Another approach, which costs little or nothing, is to pitch a tent on remote
stretches of sand (see *An Adventurer's Guide*).

• Your biggest hassle and a large part of your expenses will probably be transportation. After all, hideaways are by nature relatively remote and inaccessible.
Islands and peninsulas are a natural choice (see *An Island Lover's Guide*),
especially the barrier islands. The Caribbean, too, has so many tropical playgrounds that many of them have yet to succumb to the tourist trade.

• When you're in the Florida Keys, many of which are nicely devoid of the
thronging masses, don't stop at Key West — keep going, toward the Marquesas
Keys, which are home to ospreys, bald eagles, herons, migratory birds, and sea
life.

• Head up north for cool, salt-tinged solitude. Prime choices include Grand
Manan, Campobello, and Deer islands in New Brunswick, Canada; Maine's
Vinalhaven and Monhegan islands; and the Pacific wilderness of Olympia
National Park in Washington.

*Note: Remember that "no man (or woman) is an island" — if you wander off
by yourself, you also wander away from help in case of accident or emergency.
A solitary tourist may be prey to any number of mishaps from a variety of
sources.*

AN ISLAND LOVER'S GUIDE

Where to fulfill one of society's most beguiling fantasies: escape to a sea island.

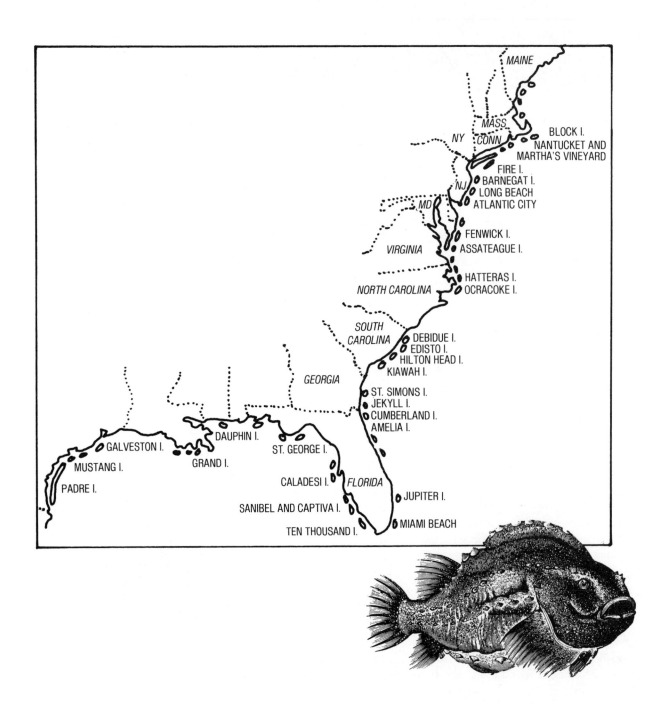

Jekyll Island

The Barrier Islands

Beginning in Maine and extending all the way down the Atlantic Coast, around the tip of Florida, and into the Gulf of Mexico to Texas, there exists a slender chain of islands. As far as nature is concerned, they are mere narrow, fragile landforms of ever-shifting sand that function as living buffers between the sometimes angry ocean and the mainland. To the beachgoer they also happen to be some of the most beautifully perfect beaches on which you could hope to leave your footprints.

There are 295 islands off the shores of 18 states, and each has a character all its own. For example, South Carolina's Seabrook, Edisto, Fripp, and Hilton Head; Georgia's St. Simons; and Florida's Amelia and Miami are all known for their sumptuous resorts and golf and tennis facilities. Diverse and distinct communities on New York's Fire Island cater to various special-interest groups such as campers, families, gays, the well-to-do, artists, and the swinging singles crowd. In Massachusetts, Martha's Vineyard, Nantucket, and Cape Cod have long been refuges for artists and writers as well as being whaling and fishing centers.

Many islands haven't been sullied by developers' shovels. You must take along your own food and shelter, or seek room and board on the mainland and daytrip to the unspoiled strand of your choice. Some have been designated national seashores and are protected from possible runaway development; these include Cape Cod (see BOSTON, *A Day Tripper's Guide*), Fire Island, Assateague (see *A Nature Lover's Guide*), Cape Hatteras (see *A Sports Lover's Guide*), Cumberland Island, Canaveral, the Gulf Islands, and Padre Island.

Barrier islands teem with wildlife: Nantucket, Block Island, Chincoteague, Pea Island, Pelican Island, and others have national wildlife refuges. Depending upon the location, you'll find woods, marshes, beach plums, rose hips, rabbits, ospreys, deer, crabs, beach grass, swans, geese, palmetto, mangroves, oak, pines, shells, and a huge variety and abundance of sea life.

No matter which island you choose, expect offshore sandbars, crashing surf, and a superb sand beach on the ocean side, then fragile dunes, interior lowlands, followed by a peaceful bay with wetlands.

VISIT THE VINEYARD

On the Vineyard, *edited and with photographs by Peter Simon (Doubleday/Anchor, 1980; paper), is a collection of reminiscences, commentaries, and photographs by some of Martha's Vineyard's illustrious residents including Art Buchwald, John Updike, Robert Crichton, Ruth Gordon, Garson Kanin, and Carly and Peter Simon.*

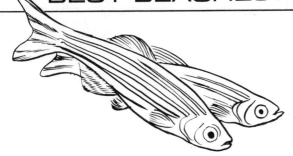

The Caribbean in a Nutshell

The Caribbean has something for everyone. Some individual islands and island groups are described in other mini-guides in this book, but here's a quick run-down of the outstanding features of the most popular pleasure islands.

Cuba. **Beautiful scenery, friendly people, superb food.**

Cayman Islands. **Terrific beaches, water sports; diving and snorkeling heaven.**

Jamaica. **Best beach is at Negril;** *ganga* **("grass"), reggae music (and unfortunately, some hostility) fill the air.**

Haiti. **Great food; unspoiled, primitive, hard-to-get-to beaches; for the adventurous.**

Dominican Republic. **Good values; Spanish traditions.**

Puerto Rico. **Jumping nightlife; good beaches, especially Luquillo Beach.**

British Virgin Islands. **Get-away-from-it-all atmosphere; extraordinary sailing waters.**

U.S. Virgin Islands. **Fairly serene; lots of sports; National Geographic called Magen's Bay on St. Thomas "one of the ten best beaches in the world."**

St. Maarten/St. Martin. **Part Dutch, part French; pretty, spectacular beaches; higher-priced accommodations.**

Anguilla and St. Barthélemy (St. Barts). **Quiet, get-away-from-it-all atmosphere.**

St. Kitts and Nevis. **Quiet, few visitors; do-it-yourself entertainment.**

Antigua. **British tranquillity.**

Guadeloupe. **French Creole customs; nude beaches.**

Martinique. **The "Riviera in the Caribbean"; very French, and with a (dormant) volcano yet.**

St. Lucia. **Good beaches and lots of sailing.**

Grenadines. **Over 100 islands and cays with some of the best cruising in the world.**

Barbados. **Tea and cricket and the British way of life on pink and white sand beaches, all of which are public.**

Trinidad and Tobago. **Steel bands and carnivals on Trinidad; better beaches and snorkeling at Buccoo Reef on Tobago.**

Dutch ABCs. **Aruba is known for its luxury and gambling; Bonaire for its flocks of flamingos and diving; Curaçao has beaches that are nothing to write home about, but shopping that is.**

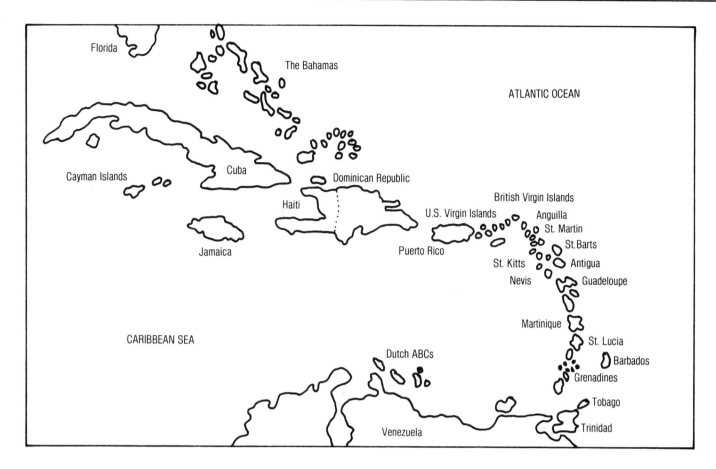

The Caribbean Islands

Flamboyant trees, brilliant shrubs, warm turquoise water, soft golden beaches, rainbows of tropical fish, piña coladas, soothing sun, balmy breezes, an easy-does-it pace, a "rainy season" that brings the mere possibility of a brief shower. The Caribbean Islands have all this in common; but they're also incredibly diverse. That's what makes them interesting and keeps visitors coming back for more. No wonder they're called "the Paradise Islands."

Some are romantic, some dramatic, relaxing...or exciting. Many have terrific sports facilities, nightlife, a party scene; others supply you with peace and quiet. You can battle the Atlantic surf on the windward (northeastern) side of the islands or laze in the calmer Caribbean leeward (southwestern) side. Sleep under the stars in campgrounds or luxuriate in plush hotels. Slurp a sloppy picnic mango or dine in utmost elegance. Live in your bathing suit or bring your most expensive designer glad rags. Bring the kids and let a family-oriented resort watch 'em or go alone and rediscover each other and the Caribbean together. Shop for luxury items from around the world or take home locally crafted souvenirs.

Though English will usually be understood, be prepared to hear a variety of other languages: Spanish, French, Creole, Dutch, Papiamento, and an English that is often given a local twist by incorporating other languages and dialects. Though American currency (cash, traveler's checks, credit cards) is widely accepted, converting to the local currency is recommended. The number of cruises and package tours are mind-boggling, and getting there by plane or boat is simple. The same is true of interisland transportation.

SO YOU WANT TO BUY AN ISLAND?

"When you sell an island, you are helping someone fulfill a dream. It's such an emotional thing, there's no logic to it at all." So says a broker who's been selling them for 10 years. He also observes:

• There are two types of people: Those who want islands and those who think it's the most frivolous thing in the world.

• Island buyers are apt to be lawyers or doctors with artistic bents.

• Island buyers are rarely cigarette smokers and are never Republicans.

• Island buyers should look for: good anchorage, interesting rock formations on the shoreline, a small sand beach, enough height to stay visible at high tide, trees and wildlife, open areas of good soil for planting, fresh water, unlikelihood of natural disasters such as hurricanes.

Florida Keys

Special Islands

LONG ISLAND, NEW YORK

New York's oceanfront is 250 miles of coastline with enough variety to please everyone. The sandy south shore, facing the Atlantic Ocean, has vast, smooth beaches and good surf. Jones Beach (see NEW YORK, *A Day Tripper's Guide*) is here and Captree State (fishing, swimming, picnicking), South Hampton (elegant resorts, estates, yachts, motels, hotels, inns), Westhampton (big with the artist crowd; hotels and inns), Easthampton (lively, young, "in" bars, boutiques, hotels, motels, and inns). At the tip is Montauk, with spectacular beaches and a wooded countryside, high cliffs, dunes, tranquillity, great fishing, sailing, and swimming; a variety of accommodations. The north shore, which faces Long Island Sound, is peppered with bays, harbors, and pebbly beaches. Nearby is *Shelter Island* in Gardiners Bay, a tranquil unspoiled idyll with beautiful beaches, calm water, and land and water sports.

THE FLORIDA KEYS

Stretching out from Miami into two seas, the Florida Keys are 150 miles of 45 islands that encompass amazingly different worlds. On one side you have the Atlantic and freighters; on the other, the Gulf of Mexico and quiet wading birds and mangroves. The only living coral reef in the U.S. is on Key Largo, and the fabled "last resort" is on Key West. Prefab and fast food mingle with nineteenth-century buildings and developing artists. Drive from island to island via the Overseas Highway, which ends on Key West; continue the trip via chartered boat or sail along the entire chain. Along the way, swim, fish, dive, watch the wildlife, beachcomb; at night, camp or stay at resorts. Applaud the sunset (a tradition), or bar hop and story swap (another tradition).

For more specific needs, see also the islands described in these mini-guides:

• *An Adventurer's Guide:* Includes Great Places to Pitch a Tent, for island aficionados.

• *A Day Tripper's Guide:* Islands near the major cities of Boston, Houston, Los Angeles, New York, and Washington, D.C.

• *A Family Guide:* Atlantic Canada's Prince Edward Island and Bonaventure Island.

• *A Hideaway Guide:* The Bahama Out Islands, the British Virgin Islands, and other solitary islands that are far from the madding crowd.

• *A Luxury Lover's Guide:* Aruba, Bermuda, and other islands where the livin' is easy.

• *A Nature Lover's Guide:* Assateague, the U.S. Virgin Islands, and more island nature to sample.

• *A Sightseer's Guide:* Islands off the coast of Maine, the San Juan Islands off the coast of Washington, and the three Caribbean islands off Mexico's Yucatán Peninsula.

• *A Single Traveler's Guide:* The Hampton beaches on New York's Long Island, New York's Fire Island, and St. Barts in the Caribbean.

• *A Sports Lover's Guide:* Cape Hatteras' Outer Banks, and additional islands on which to be a good sport.

ISLAND DREAMERS

For many travelers, the South Sea Islands are the ultimate in romantic adventure. In *A Dream of Islands, Voyages of Self-Discovery in the South Seas* by Gavan Daws (Norton, 1980), discover how five "misfits" lived out their dreams during the Victorian era. Writers Herman Melville and Robert Louis Stevenson, painter Paul Gauguin, a missionary, and a political adventurer are the five in question, and their search for answers led them to both success and disaster.

A LANDLOCKED GUIDE

Inland waters for stranded beach lovers who can't make it to the continent's edge.

**WHERE TO GET WET:
WATER WATER EVERYWHERE**

Did you know there are more miles of inland shores than ocean beaches in this country? Of course, except for the Great Salt Lake and the Salton Sea, the salt air is missing; but that's about all that is. The thousands of lakes, ponds, rivers, springs, and pools scattered all over the continent supply all the scenic beauty, sandy (or rocky or pebbly) beaches, water sports, and beachside activities you could ask for — and usually much closer to home.

The state tourist offices listed in FOR YOUR INFORMATION will be a tremendous help in ferreting out the bodies of water nearest you. In this mini-guide, you'll find a sampling of the most outstanding to help get you going.

(Arizona Office of Tourism)

BEACH STONES
The Great Lakes are a plentiful source of gemstones such as agate, chert, jasper, granite, quartz, and basalt. Lake Superior yields the greatest finds, but all the lakes' shorelines are rich enough to fatten up any beachcomber's rock collection.

Surprising Lakes

Finger Lakes region, New York, has spectacular waterfalls; fast-running streams; 600-foot gorges; green, grapevine-covered slopes; and eleven lakes with 600 miles of shoreline. Swimming, fishing, boating, and hiking are big.

Glacier National Park, Montana's one million magnificent acres, is the site of six large, cool, crystal clear lakes, each at least five miles long, plus hundreds of smaller lakes, ponds, waterfalls, and streams. You can swim, picnic, go boating, hiking, camp, and understand why the Blackfoot Indians considered this beautiful area sacred. Visit nearby Flathead Lake — maybe you'll catch a glimpse of the fabled lake monster!

Grand Lake, Colorado, in Rocky Mountain National Park, is a sparkling alpine lake nearly two miles above sea level. Boating, water-skiing, hiking, and brisk swimming are yours, along with snow-capped mountains in the middle of summer.

The Great Lakes don't get their name from their size alone, although standing on their sandy beaches it's hard to believe you're not facing across thousands of miles of ocean. Michigan, known as the Great Lakes State, is two peninsulas bounded by Lakes Erie, Huron, Michigan, and Superior. The 3000-mile shoreline is longer than the Atlantic coast from Maine to Florida; that's not even counting the 36,000 inland lakes, streams, and rivers.

Great Salt Lake, Utah. The 20-percent-plus salinity means you bob like cork on the surface of this huge (30-by-70-mile) lake in the middle of the desert. Make sure you don't get your face wet (oh, the sting!) and be thankful for the open-air freshwater showers. (Utah has many fine, spacious state parks with fresh, blue-water, manmade reservoirs.)

Lake George, New York, has sandy beaches and a mixture of commercial amusements and untouched rustic splendor. There's more than ample room for the 100 islands in this 32-mile-long lake with water that's clear enough in parts to drink.

Lake Mead, Nevada. A trip to this desert playground is the perfect way to cool down after a hot night at the blackjack tables in nearby Las Vegas. It's a manmade lake (formed by Hoover Dam) with 550 miles of shoreline and great boating, water-skiing, fishing, and diving. The swimming is brisk, but countless swimming pools surrounding the lake are more comfortable. If you lose your shirt while gambling, you can forgo the expensive motels and hotels and camp along the lake shores.

Lake Tahoe, California, is the largest mountain lake on the continent and the second highest in the world. Much of the lake has water so clean and clear you can drink it! Most visitors, though, would rather swim in it, boat on it. take fish out of it and camp, hike, or play golf or tennis near it. Of course, there's always gambling and big-time entertainment, too.

Salton Sea, near Palm Springs, California, is a beach in the desert. Go swimming, boating, fishing, and water-skiing in this 38-mile-long sea that used to be a part of the Gulf of California. Visit nearby bubbling mud pots or miniature volcanoes that are believed to be directly over the San Andreas Fault.

NATIONAL PARKS

The following offer nature at its wildest and most beautiful. You'll usually find facilities for swimming, boating, hiking, fishing, wildlife watching, canoeing, and picnicking; and sometimes diving, water-skiing, bike riding, and horseback riding. Facilities for camping range from primitive to modern.

• *Indiana Dunes National Lakeshore* on Lake Michigan contains 200-foot-high sand dunes.

• *Chickasaw National Recreation Area,* Oklahoma, has a manmade lake, cold mineral and freshwater springs, and bromide waters in a woody, green setting.

• *Isle Royale National Park,* Michigan, is a wilderness island in Lake Superior that is reachable by boat or plane. The boat tours are recommended.

• *Ozark Scenic Riverway,* Missouri, is real canoe country, especially the Current and Jacks Fork rivers.

• *Sleeping Bear Dunes National Lakeshore,* Michigan, has famous immense beaches and sand dunes, forests, and islands.

STATE RESORT PARKS

Twenty-one states run resort parks; the finest are in Kentucky, Alabama, Georgia, Oklahoma, Tennessee, and West Virginia. Others are in Arkansas, Illinois, Indiana, Minnesota, Mississippi, Missouri, Nebraska, New York, Ohio, South Carolina, South Dakota, Texas, and Virginia. These are resorts with a variety of accommodations and rates and all the trimmings: championship golf courses, tennis courts, trap ranges, swimming pools, sandy lake beaches, marinas for houseboats, pleasure boats and fishing boats for hire, game rooms, horseback riding, lounges, and ballrooms.

• To find out more about national and state parks, see the sources listed in *An Adventurer's Guide.*

McCredie Hot Springs, Oregon (Jayson Loam)

Olympic Hot Springs, Washington (Jayson Loam)

Hot Stuff

Hot Springs National Park, Arkansas, is the state's most popular thermal resort. It not only has 47 mineral springs nestled in five thousand acres of Ouachita Mountains, but nearby De Gray Lake and a national forest for swimming, fishing, boating, and hiking.

Eureka Springs, Arkansas, has 63 springs and is near 28,000-acre Beaver Lake.

Saratoga Springs, New York, gives Easterners a chance to drink (and bathe) to their health. A long-time favorite of the well-heeled wet set, historic Saratoga still boasts dozens of natural springs, many of which are enclosed by pillared Victorian structures. For a therapeutic dunking, the bathhouses have super-evanescent waters that tingle and relax. Try the mud baths too. For a beachier ambiance, zip over to one of the nearby lakes.

Warm Springs Desert Oasis, Nevada. Glorious natural pools in the middle of the desert, the largest of which is 40 by 65 yards, 6 feet deep, and 85°F all year round.

To learn about more hot spots to soak in, get Jayson Loam's *Hot Springs and Pools of the Northwest* (Colorado, Oregon, Washington, Idaho, Utah, Montana, and Wyoming) and *Hot Springs and Pools of the Southwest* (California, Nevada, Arizona, New Mexico). These illustrated guides will tell you all about large and small mineral springs resorts (many of which have natural hot soaking pools and cooler swimming pools), vapor caves, RV parks with therapy pools, primitive springs, health spas, and more — all set in the raw rugged scenery characteristic of their states. (Capra Press, 1979; or available from the author, P.O. Box 841, Van Nuys, CA 91408.)

QUARRIES

Spring-fed excavations are natural splashing grounds for old swimming hole aficionados of all ages. Some — such as *the Quarry* in Hamburg, New Jersey — have facilities for swimming, boating, even scuba diving. At the Quarry, the water's so clear (with visibility up to 30 feet) that you can see perch, bass, catfish, sunfish, and underwater rock formations. At Huntington, Indiana, a great spring-fed quarry and manmade beach is the site of an annual open-water competitive swim. (For information on ocean rough-water swims, see LA JOLLA COVE in *A Sports Lover's Guide.*)

55

(Budd Symes)

Extraordinary Pools

Barton Springs, Austin, Texas, is a naturally fed swimming pool that's 960 feet long. (A mere 176 lengths equals the English Channel!) It's a favorite with serious swimmers (who complete their workouts by 7 a.m.) and recreation swimmers alike. The water is clear, crisp, and unchlorinated — visibility is up to 25 feet with goggles — with a temperature of 68°F all year round. The environs include a park with facilities for picnicking and canoeing plus a rose garden.

Big Surf near Tempe, Arizona, is touted as a manmade ocean — a wave-making machine creates 3- to 5-foot waves. Hundreds of miles from the ocean you can actually surf (on rented boards), swim, body surf, go rafting, or thrill it up as you swoosh down the three-hundred-foot-long twisting surf slide. Kids have their own shallow water area.

Glenwood Springs in Colorado is the place to go if you want the unique experience of taking the plunge in the world's largest open-air hot springs swimming pool. Wintertime brings clouds of fog to eerily envelope swimmers — a favorite way to spend New Year's Eve.

The Grand Hotel Swimming Pool on Michigan's Mackinac Island makes it easy to imagine you're smack in the middle of an Esther Williams movie — after all, it was used for one of her water ballet extravaganzas in the 1940s. The pool, which is open to the public, is definitely the stuff of which daydreams are made: 150 feet long, it winds its serpentine way through giant begonias, geraniums, and lilacs on unspoiled, no-cars-allowed Mackinac Island in Lake Michigan.

The International Swimming Hall of Fame, Fort Lauderdale, Florida, includes a 50-meter Olympic-sized pool and diving complex. Though its proximity to the ocean means it isn't strictly in the landlocked league, it is one of the best environments for swimming. The Hall of Fame also boasts exhibits of swimming memorabilia and superstars plus an auditorium and souvenir bookshop.

Tip: You'd be surprised at the number of excellent pools open to the public. Many are at universities; ask around. Depending upon the geographic location, they may be outdoors and surrounded by other recreational facilities for you to enjoy. The state and national parks that dot the countryside are another likely place to douse your body in the essence of chlorine.

POOL POINTERS

If you're lucky enough to own your own pool, get a *solar pool blanket* like the one pictured here, made by the Sealed Air Corporation, Park 80 Plaza East, Saddle Brook, NJ 07662. It performs a multitude of handy functions:

- Raises pool water temperature 10° in season.
- Cuts heating costs 70 percent or more.
- Reduces water evaporation 90 percent or more.
- Extends your swimming season.
- Helps keep the pool clean.

The *Sun Dome* by Fabrico, 4242 South Pulaski Rd., Chicago, IL 60632, is available in 12-, 15-, and 18-foot diameters. Placed over your pool, it extends the swimming season, protects swimmers, and keeps out dirt, leaves, and insects.

"The hottest safety device since the life preserver" is a two-piece, *pool-to-house alarm system* marketed by Pool Patrol, Inc., 371 Greenwich Ave., Greenwich, CT 06830. The float, which resembles a UFO, uses wireless radio signals to transmit its warning up to 200 feet away if a child, adult, or pet enters an un-supervised pool.

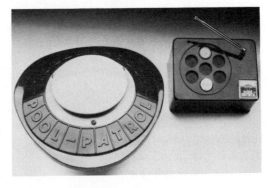

It's just one of those days. The blue sky beckons, but alas, Nancy is stranded in the big city with no money, no time, no energy, no wheels, and plenty of suntan lotion. With a firm commitment to the credo "'Tis better to catch one UV ray than to curse the darkness," she gathers her paraphernalia, emerges from her tiny apartment, and begins to climb. And there, at the top, in all its glory is — the roof! Resplendent in tar paper, tastefully decorated with a few dead leaves and TV antennae, shimmering in the heat waves — her very own...

TAR BEACH!

(Marianne Dickinson — suit by Danskin)

TAR BEACH COMFORT TIPS

To make your stay on Tar Beach more pleasant, take all the equipment and refreshments you'd normally tote to the beach, plus a few more to stave off inevitable boredom. Since you don't have far to go, even a portable TV doesn't seem quite so silly. Most important of all, you need something to take the place of a cooling body of water: a plant mister or a wet washcloth usually do the trick.

59

A LUXURY LOVER'S GUIDE

You prefer your beaches private, magnificent, and at your doorstep...your hotel swimming pools large and multiple... your food exceptional...the service unobtrusively first class... the atmosphere cushy and hushed enough to hear an ice cube clink...the golf and tennis facilities immaculate and uncrowded ...and plenty of room to park your yacht. If your idea of roughing it is whirly-birding to the remote Na Pali coast of Kauai for a charming little picnic — have we got a beach for you!

(Aruba Beach Club)

(Aruba Beach Club)

Aruba

An up-and-coming Caribbean island with many sleek, modern, luxury hotels on extraordinary beaches.

Other Features: Excellent pool and ocean swimming, snorkeling and scuba diving (visibility is 90 feet, with coral, sea fans, tropical fish); water-skiing; Sunfish, pedal boats, sea "jeeps," and larger craft to be rented; deep-sea fishing; tennis, golf, horseback riding, and "dune sliding" (an Aruba specialty); shop for jewelry, china, crystal, and other luxury items that are nearly duty-free, though not all are bargains; visit Oranjestad, the capital, with its Dutch-gabled houses.

Appearance and Ambiance: Pure white sandy beaches with warm, clear water along its "Turquoise Coast"; dramatic, pounding surf and jagged rocks along its west coast. Inland, you'll find more cacti and divi-divi trees than palms on this dry island, as well as mysterious stone monoliths. A blend of laid-back sophistication with relaxed, friendly atmosphere and islanders. Dress is casual for daytime; dress-up for evenings is common, especially at the casinos.

Climate: One of the most stable in the Caribbean — average temperature is 75° to 85°F. Trade winds keep humidity low, but they are especially strong in February and March: One visitor suggests you watch children carefully — they might be blown into the pools, which have whitecaps!

Accommodations and Food: Primarily first-class luxury high-rise hotels, with some moderately priced low-rises cropping up. Native cuisine includes lamb or goat stew, and fish chowder made with coconut milk; much Indonesian food; also American and Continental. You can picnic on Dutch cheese and fresh fruit at Manchebo Beach or Eagle Beach.

Nightlife: And how! Hotels have casino gambling, dancing, floor shows.

Getting There and Getting Around: Flights from New York, Miami, San Juan; docking facilities for cruise ships and private boats; ferries and commuter planes for interisland travel. Taxis, buses, rental cars, bikes, and sea excursions get you around the island. Official currency is Netherlands Antilles florin or guilder, but U.S. dollars and credit cards are accepted everywhere. English, Dutch, and Spanish are widely spoken.

CARIBBEAN CASINOS
Aruba isn't the only island paradise in the Caribbean that gives you the chance to leave with more money than you arrived with. In fact, junkets — packages that include air fare, hotel, even meals and entertainment all paid for by the casino — exist to woo the would-be high rollers. Islands where you can "roll them bones" legally include (asterisks indicate most popular spots):

Antigua
Aruba*
The Bahamas*
Bonaire
Curaçao
Dominican Republic
Guadeloupe
Haiti
Martinique
Puerto Rico*
St. Kitts*
St. Maarten/St. Martin*

61

(Bermuda News Bureau)

Bermuda

Understated, casual elegance is the byword on this utterly civilized, veddy British subtropical island in the Atlantic. It's the ultimate tourist island (tourism is their only industry), without being touristy. Bermuda is synonymous with "the good life"— old world charm and first-rate, genuinely friendly service with a smile— and you don't have to spend a fortune to enjoy it. (Unless of course you want to.) No wonder visitors keep coming back.

Other Features: Many water sports: swimming; diving in crystal clear waters around reefs and wrecks, or don a Jules Verne-type helmet and stroll along the sea floor; boating (crewed or bare-boat; sloops to Sunfish); water-skiiing. On land play golf or tennis on uncrowded courses and courts; ride horseback (English saddle, of course); take a low-key hike; watch rugby, cricket, soccer games, a boat race, a motorcycle scramble. Shop for high-quality bargains; visit St. George, founded in 1612 and recently restored. Try to catch the colorfully costumed goombay dancers at Christmastime.

Appearance and Ambiance: The south shore has the best beaches — picture-postcard-pretty expanses and little coves of soft, pink-tinged sand and turquoise sea — most of which are open to the public and never crowded. Elsewhere you'll find lush green hills, pastel-colored cottages, blazes of flowers. Evening dress is dignified (jackets and ties, fancy gowns prevail at dinnertime); daytime's more casual, but revealing outfits and bare feet are frowned upon anywhere but at the beach or poolside. Cooler nights dictate a jacket or other coverup.

Climate: Mild the year round: summer, when most swimming is done, averages 80°F. Winter temperature hovers around 65°F — perfect for the sporting life. The sun shines 340 days of the year, but the weather is changeable with frequent brief showers.

Nightlife: Big hotel shows including big name acts, steel bands, limbo, calypso. Dancing, discos, more intimate music and casual pubs, too.

Accommodations and Food: Formal, luxury resort hotels with all the first-class opulence you could want; smaller hotels; cottage "colonies"; economical apartments; casual guesthouses. Dinner ranges from burgers and french fries to elegant. Local fare includes fish, mussels, lobster, onion pie, black-eyed peas with rice. Buy picnic and cooking provisions at local supermarkets.

Getting There and Getting Around: Fly direct from many eastern cities; take a cruise ship. Taxis meet every flight and ship. No rental cars, but good public transportation and tours: buses, taxi tours, ferries, sea excursions, bus tours. Rented bicycles or mopeds are the best mode of transportation along the narrow, wall-lined streets, and be sure to stay to your left when riding. Entry requirements are a valid or expired passport, birth certificate, or voter registration card. Currency is the Bermuda dollar, but U.S. currency is accepted almost everywhere. Credit cards are accepted in only a few places.

Where the Livin' is Easy

These additional deluxe resort areas will also satisfy your yen for the posh life. They, too, have something very, very special (if it's good enough for Princess Margaret...) and represent the crème *de la crème*. They're expensive ($100 a day and up for a double in most cases), but just about anyone can be a Beautiful Person during the off-season, when prices take a nose dive.

UNITED STATES

California's La Costa in Carlsbad is a resort and hotel spa just two miles from the Pacific. It has an international reputation for attracting millionaires, movie stars, and other souls who want a deluxe diet-and-exercise plan. Palm Springs is an oasis at the edge of the Colorado Desert, with beautiful mountains for a backdrop. The hot, dry desert day gives way to star-studded skies and nightclub acts. Hobnob with Hollywood personalities like Joey Bishop at Newport Beach, which is just a clam's throw away from romantic Catalina Island.

Florida has long been a mecca for the monied class. Boca Raton is on the gorgeous Gold Coast; Palm Beach is where the diamonds outshine the sun and the jet setters settle; Amelia Island has wilderness and sunken forests, plus a panorama of the Atlantic; Key Biscayne is the spitting image of the South Pacific (and former vacation home for President Nixon); Miami, the former "Queen of the Gold Coast," has had a face-lift, but has retained huge oceanfront hotels and an array of nightlife; Sanibel-Captiva Islands' South Seas Plantations offer low-key elegance.

Georgia's Golden Isles include Jekyll Island with its "Millionaire's Village" where the Rockefellers, Goulds, Morgans, and Pulitzers used to live; and Sea Island with its lush atmosphere and semitropical foliage.

Hawaii's four major islands all have their share of luxury accommodations, such as the Mauna Kea Hotel on the Big Island.

Massachusetts boasts Hyannis, which will forever be associated with the Kennedy family, those champions of elegance and taste, and two pockets of understated luxury, Nantucket and Martha's Vineyard, where James Taylor, Carly and Peter Simon, Art Buchwald, Lillian Hellman, Vance Packard, William Styron, and John Updike — to name a few — rejuvenate.

New York's "the Hamptons" not only have Long Island's fine sandy beaches, they have famous writers and artists, too.

Oregon has posh resorts perched on high Pacific cliffs; especially spectacular are those around Lincoln City, Otter Rock, and Seaside.

Rhode Island and Newport are synonymous with yachting and those who can afford them. After attending the America's Cup, the Newport to Bermuda Race, or the Annapolis to Newport Race, visit the museum/mansions. Or stroll along Cliff Walk and its oceanfront mansions. Then take Newport Bridge to Conanicut Island or go south to Narragansett Pier, "one of the finest beaches in the world."

South Carolina's islands are a haven for those for whom the good life must include resort sports (and pros like Rod Laver and Evonne Goolagong) in an unspoiled, natural setting. Best are Hilton Head, Fripp, Kiawah.

Captiva

Sea Pines Plantation, Hilton Head Island

THE CARIBBEAN

• *St. Martin's* French side has La Samana, where movie and video stars soak up the sun and Casablanca atmosphere.

• *The Virgin Islands* have their share of deluxe resorts, especially Peter Island, which bills itself as "remote, beautiful, expensive, and exclusive." St. John's Caneel Bay is rimmed with seven beaches, and Trunk Bay Beach has been rated one of the world's top 10 beaches. The cognoscenti leave Little Dicks' main beach on Virgin Gorda behind, and sail to Spring Bay and the Baths for a picnic lunch.

• *Haiti* is rich in resorts. Habitation Le Clerc is one of the best.

• *Jamaica.* Port Antonio's Trident Villas and Montego Bay's Round Hill are luxury attractions.

• *The Grenadines* is where Princess Margaret has her vacation home, on Mustique. The nearby Cotton House is furnished with antiques, which is all right with frequent guests such as the Rolling Stones.

• *Grenada's* plush resort hotels are a new breed — luxurious space, oodles of comfort, relaxed style, and spectacular views.

• *Guadeloupe* caters to its preponderance of European guests by giving them first-class service in the Continental manner; the Hamak Beach Club is classy, informal, and a bit sui generis — President Carter has been a guest there.

Guadeloupe (Clement-Petrocik Co.)

MEXICO

Its west coast is called the "Riviera," and Manzanillo Bay has its superstars. The Las Hadas complex, the most glittering of all, resembles Morocco, and has eight lagoon-like pools, walled gardens, and private verandas.

*MEXICO FOR
ARMCHAIR TRAVELERS*
If you'd like the real personal approach — knee-slapping anecdotes, real-life experiences, facts and tips about Mexico and the Mexicans — from someone who's been there many times, you'll love The People's Guide to Mexico, *5th ed., by Carl Franz (John Muir Publications, 1979; paper).*

(Holland America Cruises)

RESORTS THAT FLOAT

Resorts That Float

You step on board, the gangplank is lifted, and the languor and luxury of life on board a cruise ship begins. Snoozing, feasting, sunning, playing on a veritable floating resort — there's always someone on hand to indulge your every whim — and living like royalty as you sail from port to port. What can compare to such enchantment and pleasure? Today, you can have it all for prices that compare with the familiar transportation/land accommodations packages.

Yes, times have changed for the cruising set; most ships have retained their aura of elegance, but are designed for moderate-income people. The Holland America Line, for instance, has a free limousine service to whisk you away to the pier and back home again at trip's end. Many have air/sea options, and offer reduced air fare to your point of departure (for popular Caribbean cruises, that means New York, San Juan, or Florida). Some have special rates and facilities for children, including baby-sitting services.

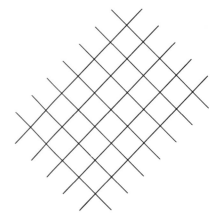

Choose your cruise according to how much time you have, where you want to go, and the environment that makes you most comfortable. Caribbean cruises generally range from between 6 and 16 days, with up to thirteen ports of call. Write the cruise lines listed on the opposite page for brochures, or ask a travel agent. Be ready to plan way ahead; 6 to 9 months is not unusual. The "Love Boat" type cruises, such as the Princess Cruises trip to the Mexican Riviera, sell out very fast.

Perusing the Cruises

American Canadian Line, Inc., P.O. Box 368, Warren, RI 02885; toll-free number: 800-556-7450. Mini-cruise ship (70 passengers), sails the Bahama Out Islands.

Princess Cruises, 2029 Century Park East, Los Angeles, CA 90067. Down the Mexican coast, through the canal to the Caribbean; South Pacific; Alaska.

Costa Line, Inc., P.O. Box 941, Woodside, NY 11377. Bahamas, Caribbean, South America, Mediterranean, all over the world.

American Hawaii Cruises, 1345 Avenue of the Americas, New York, NY 10019. Island-hops through Hawaii.

American Cruise Lines, Haddam, CT 06438; toll-free number: 800-243-6755. Intracoastal Waterway through wilderness areas and cities of the Old South: Hilton Head, Sea Island, Vero Beach, Lake Okeechobee, Fort Meyers, and more.

Holland America Cruises, Two Penn Plaza, New York, NY 10001. Caribbean, Alaska, Panama Canal, Pacific, Indonesia, and the world.

Cunard Line, 555 Fifth Ave., New York, NY 10017. Caribbean and South America — they own the QE II.

Sun Line Cruises, One Rockefeller Plaza, Suite 315, New York, NY 10020. Winter cruises to the Caribbean; summer cruises to the Aegean.

Royal Caribbean Cruise Line, 903 S. America Way, Miami, FL 33132. Caribbean.

Bahama Cruise Line, Inc., Ponce de Leon Blvd., Coral Gables, FL 33134; toll-free numbers: 800-522-5228 (NY State), 800-233-0908 (elsewhere). Caribbean, Mexico, Guatemala; their St. Lawrence River cruise stops at New York, Prince Edward Island, Gaspé, Quebec, Montreal, and the fjords of Saguenay River where whales are seen.

A NATURE LOVER'S GUIDE

Where the porpoises, fish, whales, seabirds, seals, and other water creatures play.

Assateague Island, Maryland and Virginia

This barrier island off the shores of Maryland and Virginia is a slender, thirty-seven-mile-long strip of wilderness. In fact, most of the Maryland section of the island is the Chincoteague National Wildlife Refuge. Take self-guided nature trails and hikes or attend interpretive programs in the summer; watch many kinds of waterfowl and other birds, as well as deer, foxes, raccoons, and the mysterious and unique Chincoteague ponies. These ponies may be the descendants of Spanish or English horses that were shipwrecked centuries ago. Their tiny size is due to their restricted diet.

Other Features: The island is a great place to go surf fishing, clamming, crabbing, canoeing, hiking, swimming, and shell collecting. There's a pony roundup and auction on the last Wednesday and Thursday in July.

Appearance and Ambiance: The sandy ocean beach slopes gently outward; there are lifeguards during the summer. The rest of the island is untouched salt marshes and pine forests.

Climate: Hot and humid in the summer, with hungry insects. Spring and autumn are best, with cooler temperatures and fewer visitors.

Accommodations and Food: As primitive as the island's beauty. Camping on the Maryland side (the national seashore) and picnicking. The most modern facilities are in the state park, which also serves meals in the summer. Otherwise, dine, shop for groceries, and stay in nearby Chincoteague, Virginia, or Berlin or Ocean City, Maryland.

Getting There and Getting Around: Drive from nearest large cities: Baltimore, Washington, Philadelphia, and Norfolk to Assateague State Park at the northern end or Chincoteague on the southern tip. In between the two ends is nothing but roadless island. To get from one end to the other, you need to drive back to the mainland or use a four-wheel-drive vehicle, for which you need a permit.

(San Diego Convention and Visitors Bureau)

(Tom Collins)

The Baja Peninsula, Mexico

About midway down the peninsula, near Guerrero Negro, are several warm, shallow lagoons that are breeding grounds for California gray whales. They leave the Bering Sea every year in October and make a 6000-mile swim to mate and calve here from November to April. It's an astounding sight, especially the trios: a mating male and female plus an assisting male (who helps the female assume the mating position), rolling slowly around. Meanwhile, other females are giving birth to sixteen-foot babies, which will be ready by April to leave this protected site for the long journey back to the Arctic.

Other Features: More wildlife to soak up, especially if you venture inland. Windswept cliffs, incredible flowering cactus and shrubs (two of which are found only in the Baja Desert) such as yucca, giant agave, gnarled, knobby elephant trees, whiplike cirio. Birdwatching (gulls, frigate birds, yellow orioles, ospreys, cormorants, egrets, pelicans). Rainbow-colored tropical fish for snorkelers and scuba divers. Fishing is superb. Swimming, clamming, horseback riding, and beachcombing; fishing villages to visit.

Appearance and Ambiance: The west (Pacific) coast has deep blue water that's slightly brisk up north; the east coast (Gulf of California/Sea of Cortez) is emerald green. Both offer virgin beaches and clean water. The best are: *Ensenada* (10 miles of sandy beaches); *Punta Banda* (on a bay, with 8 miles of coves and beaches); *Valle de San Quentin* (known for clams and horseback riding); *Malarrimo Beach* (a favorite with beachcombers); *Santa Rosalia; Loreto* (date palms on the beach); *La Paz* and *San Jose del Cabo* (great for swimming); and *Cabo San Lucas.* The interior is moutainous and desertlike, with a few green oases.

Climate: In the north, mild and dry during the summer; cool and somewhat wet in the winter. In the south, hot and humid during the summer; warm and dry in the winter.

Accommodations and Food: Resort lodges of various sizes on both coasts with many facilities including golf and tennis, swimming pools, camping. Some good restaurants and cafés; Mexican food and local seafood specialties. Shop at grocery stores and "traveling stores" for picnic fare, but fresh food and produce is sparse.

Nightlife: Best near large towns such as Tijuana, Ensenada, La Paz: dancing, music, bullfights, jai alai.

Getting There and Getting Around: Fly to Tijuana or La Paz from the mainland. Drive along the peninsula via the coast-hugging Transpeninsular Highway (new, but already succumbing to wear and tear, and dangerous at night). Buses run regularly up and down the highway and are comfy and cheap. You can also take a ferry from the mainland; small planes fly from town to town. Or take one of the travel packages that originate in southern California, including excursions that stop at unspoiled islands along the way. (Since the lagoons are a wildlife refuge, you need special permission to take a boat in; most people observe the whales from the shore, from excursion boats, or from hired planes.) Carrying cash, in pesos, is recommended if you stray away from major tourist areas, as is some knowledge of Spanish.

The U.S. Virgin Islands

St. Thomas, St. Croix, and St. John all offer extraordinary Caribbean diving opportunities for people of all levels of experience, whether you choose to join organized groups or go it alone. Lush, colorful tropical life is everywhere and so is rentable diving equipment.

St. John is the least developed island because the Virgin Islands State Park takes up two thirds of it. Take nature walks, guided tours, and slide lectures on land, or snorkel amidst schools of tropical fish and multitudes of coral (much of this park is underwater!). The marked underwater trail at Trunk Bay is ideal for beginners; so is the one at Buck Island on St. Croix, which also has coral canyons and drop-offs at Salt River and Davis Bay. On St. Thomas, beginners will be happy at Cow and Calf, St. James Island, and Stevens Cay. More advanced divers can go on unusual night dives, too.

You can also enjoy nature from glass-bottomed boats or the 14 feet-below-sea-level viewing tower at Coki Beach, St. Thomas.

Other Features: Other water sports abound — swimming, water-skiing, fishing, lots of sailing with yachts available fully crewed or as bare-boat (do-it-yourself) deals. Shopping for duty-free goods, tennis, golf, hiking in the state park on St. John.

Appearance and Ambiance: All beaches, which are white and sandy, are public. Magens Bay on St. Thomas has been called one of the world's ten most beautiful beaches many times. Trunk Bay on St. John is a huge sandy beach. St. Croix has the least impressive beaches, but Cane Bay and La Grange are pleasant. Dress is casual chic — T-shirts and cut-offs are okay at camp, but frowned upon elsewhere. Bathing suits are worn beachside only. A jacket or sweater comes in handy on cool winter evenings.

Climate: Average winter temperature is 77°F; in summer 82°F, with some days much hotter. A brief cooling shower is de rigueur after sunset.

Accommodations and Food: Luxury resorts, hotels, condominiums, cottages, nineteenth-century guesthouses; camping is great, especially at the state park. Dinner menus run the gamut from elegant Continental to Mexican, Chinese, steaks, and deli. Island cuisine tends toward seafood, fungi (cornmeal dumplings), and curries. You can pick up picnic fixings at delis and stalls that sell local fruits and vegetables, such as papayas, soursops, bananas, genips.

Nightlife: Low-key, mostly piano bars, bar bands, hotel music, some dancing; occasionally some great steel bands, jazz; outdoor barbeques and limbo shows; some discos on St. Thomas.

Getting There and Getting Around: Arrive on St. Thomas or St. Croix by air. Once there, island-hop via boat excursions, ferries, chartered boats, local air services. Taxis and a few buses; cars and scooters to rent.

OTHER GREAT DIVING SPOTS

• *The Caribbean* — Clear, warm waters protected by coral reefs, teeming with marine life and many shipwrecks that go back to pirate days. Highlights are *Bonaire, the British Virgin Islands, the Cayman Islands, Jamaica* (sponge forests), *Tobago* (Bucco Bay can be viewed while wearing sneakers and a mask).

• *The Bahamas* — Astoundingly clear waters.

• *Bermuda* — Dive among coral reefs or walk along the sea bottom near Flatts Inlet.

• *Mexico* — The islands of Cancun, Cozumel, and Isla Mujeres have coral reefs and technicolor fish

• *La Jolla Cove, California* — An underwater park with kelp, abalone, lobster, and an 11,000-foot drop-off.

• *Big Sur State Park, California* — Sea lions, many varieties of fish, whales, kelp beds.

• *Hawaii* — Abundant coral, lava formations, fish.

• *The Florida Keys* — Especially John Pennecamp's Reef in Key Largo.

• *Beliz* — This tiny colony in Central America has a 175-mile-long reef, which is referred to as the second largest in the world.

A Nature Sampler

More aquatic flora and fauna for your listening and glancing pleasure, all near or on wonderful beaches.

(Barry Pakoff)

Birds

Bird Boats: All along the East Coast there are weekend boat cruises for bird-watchers in spring and summer. The trips are not just for serious birders who are lured by the possibility of spotting relatively rare pelagic (ocean-going) birds that are otherwise seen only when storms blow them toward shore. Rank amateurs, too, get a rise out of the experience, and shark, whale, or porpoise sightings are also common. The Federation of New York State Bird Clubs in Sea Cliff, Long Island, sponsors trips that leave from lovely Montauk; the Maine Audubon Society in Falmouth, Maine, conducts trips out of Portsmouth, New Hampshire; there are also boats leaving from Ocean City, Maryland, and Hatteras, North Carolina.

Thousands of Flamingos live in Washington National Park on Bonaire in the Caribbean. See herons, terns, snipe, pelicans, parrots, too; and brilliantly colored fish in the surrounding reefs.

A Plethora of Pelicans have found refuge on Pelican Island near Sebastian, Florida. The rare brown pelicans practically cover the entire island in spring and summer.

Gobs of Gannets live on Bonaventure Island in the Gulf of St. Lawrence, Canada. These large white seabirds live in the world's largest gannetry and can be seen when you walk across the island's ocean cliffs, or by boat.

Recuperating Cormorants—along with other injured seabirds such as brown pelicans, white pelicans, herons, egrets, and ospreys—are cared for and then released at the Suncoast Seabird Sanctuary near Florida's Gulf of Mexico beaches around St. Petersburg.

Northeastern Whales

Many kinds of whales—finback, humpback, minke—and dolphins and porpoises, too, hang out in the Caribbean during the winter. But in the summer they migrate to feed off the coasts of New England and Canada, which makes those areas the best places to see them in the East.

Whale-watching boat trips leave from Provincetown, Cape Cod, and Portsmouth, New Hampshire. (For more information, write to Harvard University, Cambridge, MA 02138; and College of the Atlantic, Bar Harbor, ME 04609.) In Canada, whales are visible passing by the Gaspé Peninsula. The Zoological Society of Montreal (P.O. Box 80, Victoria Station, Montreal H2Z 2V4) conducts whale-watching weekends. ➡

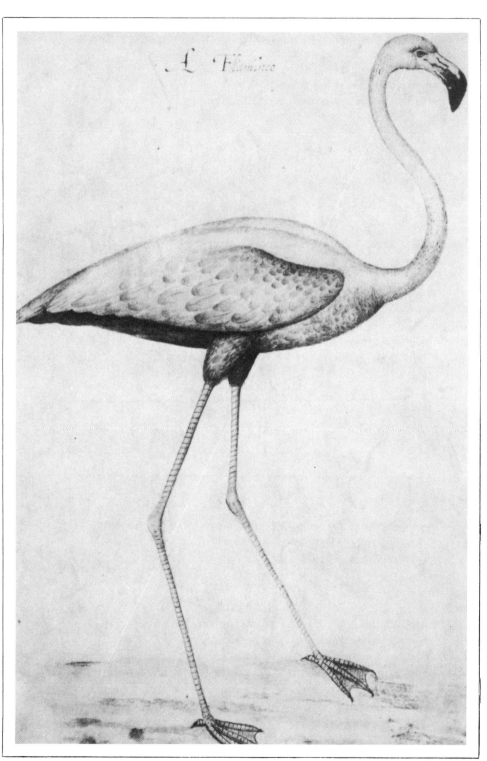

National Parks

These areas have been set aside by the federal government to preserve natural settings and curtail further development, allowing you to see the inhabitants, both plant and animal, in their natural environments. The on-site accommodations are generally limited to camping and, perhaps, a few cabins. Wildlife refuges and reserves are often a part of the park or are located nearby. Talks and guided tours are usually available. Some of the more nature-full seaside parks are:

Channel Islands National Monument, California: Sea lions, seabirds, unique plants and animals.

Point Reyes National Seashore, California: Long beaches, tall cliffs, lagoons, offshore bird and sea lion colonies.

Canaveral National Seashore, Florida: Birds, shells.

Biscayne National Monument, Florida: Coral reef.

Everglades National Park, Florida: The largest subtropical wilderness in the U.S.; abundant wildlife of all kinds.

Acadia National Park, Maine: See *The Coast of Maine* in A Sightseer's Guide.

Gateway National Recreation Area, New York and New Jersey: There are four units to this national park: the Jamaica Bay Unit in Brooklyn; the Breezy Point Unit in Queens; the Staten Island Unit on Raritan Bay; and the Sandy Hook Unit in New Jersey, which has the best beaches. Swimming, picnicking, sports, biking, fishing, birdwatching, crabbing, boating, and horseback riding can be enjoyed by the whole family.

Olympic National Park, Washington: Lush green rain forest, wild ocean shore, bird and wildlife watching.

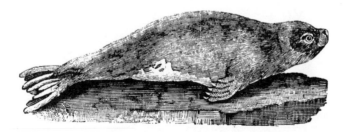

Expeditions

Society Expeditions (723 Broadway E., Seattle, WA 98102) runs unusual travel programs to remote corners of the world for those who want to see uncommon wildlife. Expeditions include: Patagonia, to see sea elephants, penguins, exceptional bird life, massive glaciers and icebergs in inland lakes; Galapagos, to see the rare and unusual, including giant tortoises, sea lions, boobies, frigate birds, penguins, cormorants, and marine iguanas.

The Barrier Islands

For wild, unspoiled nature, pick any of the barrier islands sprinkled along the Atlantic and Gulf coasts. Over the years, these sandy, fragile-but-tough strips and dots have been recognized as the national treasure they are. Many are protected from development and commercialization and have been designated part of the National Parks System. Selected barrier islands are described in *An Island Lover's Guide* and in *An Adventurer's Guide.*

Sanibel Island (Harvey Stein)

HOW TO READ A PALM

The royal palm *has a smooth gray trunk and grows to about 100 feet. Dark green feathery fronds grow out of the bright green leaf shaft.*

The cabbage palm *is easily identified by the "bootjacks" on the trunk left by old fronds, which are fan-shaped. This is Florida's state tree; the heart is edible, the berries have medicinal uses, brooms are made from the fiber, and the leaves are turned into rope.*

The Washington palm *has a slender trunk that reaches great heights. The leaves are fan-shaped with thorns on each side of the stalk; when old, the leaves form a gray "beard" around the trunk.*

The coconut palm *has a smooth, curving trunk that is quite swollen at the base. The feathery fronds grow up to eighteen feet long.*

The queen palm *looks like the royal palm, but with dried brown leaf shafts.*

The traveller's palm *looks like a huge flat fan.*

Shells, Shells, Shells

Sanibel and Captiva, islands off the southwest coast of Florida, are known for their shells. Strong winds and currents carry mountains of them from the Gulf of Mexico's bottom to the shore. Sanibel is the third-best shelling beach in the world (the first two are in Africa and the Southwest Pacific). If you go, watch out! You may develop the "Sanibel Stoop" from bending over so much. Expect to find scallops, cockles, coquinas, periwinkles, whelks, conches, and augers.

A SIGHTSEER'S GUIDE

The most beautiful beaches and scenic ocean vistas...sights that satisfy the eye and the soul.

(Hawaii Visitors Bureau)

The Big Island, Hawaii

(Hawaii Visitors Bureau)

Breathtaking in its diversity, the island of Hawaii ("the Big Island") in the Hawaiian Islands is so full of contrasts it seems to be several worlds at once—all of them unbelievably beautiful. While the azure surf is frothing at the black sand beaches at Kalapana, Punaluu, and Kaimu, the Mauna Loa volcano and Kilauea, one of its craters, are spitting and steaming in the Volcanoes National Park. As you walk through a mysterious "lava desert" moonscape in the Puna district, flower-filled gorges and cool green hills await nearby. Though the unpeaceful Pacific explodes against huge black boulders, sculptured pools beckon peacefully and waterfalls trickle daintily through lush rain forests or plummet dramatically down deep cliffs to the sea. One minute you're admiring the rainbow over Hilo Bay or frolicking among the rainbow-hued fish off the Kona Coast, the next you're snow-skiing down Mauna Kea's 13,000-foot-plus heights. All this—and beaches, too.

Other Features: Driving (in rented compacts or four-wheel-drive cars) along Hawaii's winding interior and coastal roads to catch the scenery is an adventure in itself. You can also enjoy scuba diving and snorkeling, surfing, deep-sea fishing (some of the best in the world is off the Kona Coast), horseback riding, hiking, golf, tennis, the orchid nurseries in Hilo, and many seasonal events and festivals.

Appearance and Ambiance: White sand, black sand, and rocky beaches —many are not for swimming because of the dangerous surf, strong currents, and lava formations. Good beaches exist, though, such as the ones at Mauna Kea and Hilo Bay; the Kona Coast (on the leeward side) is dry and has sandy beaches. Many rivers, lakes, lagoons, natural and manmade pools for luscious swimming.

Accommodations and Food: Hotels range from luxury resorts to a variety of lower-priced alternatives; a bungalow village à la South Pacific; inns; camping and cabins at seaside state and national parks. Fine hotel dining, Chinese and Japanese restaurants, fresh-caught fish.

Nightlife: Resort and hotel entertainment, bars, nightclubs, dancing.

Getting There and Getting Around: Fly from the mainland's west coast or take a plane, hydrofoil, or helicopter from another of the Hawaiian Islands. Public buses to go to major sights. There are also excursion buses and boats (including the glass-bottomed variety), rental cars.

HAWAII'S OTHER ISLANDS

Hawaii consists of eight major islands, six of which accept tourists (including "the Big Island") and offer spectacular scenery:

Maui—Kaanapali, the longest of Hawaii's beaches, has flat water and safe swimming. Don't miss the craters in Haleakala National Park, and the "Needle" in Iao State Park.

Lanai—The smallest island, owned mostly by Dole Pineapple Products. Good swimming and surfing beaches, shady picnic grounds. Beachcombing is excellent along the west (a.k.a. "shipwreck") coast.

Kauai—The Na Pali coast, accessible only by helicopter, is a virgin stretch of breathtaking beauty with 4000-foot cliffs and crashing surf.

Oahu—Home of Honolulu, Hawaii's teeming metropolis, and Waikiki, the famous oft-photographed beach with Diamond Head in the background. Plenty of other, nicer, wider, less-developed beaches, too, such as Makaha where the international surfing championships are held.

Molokai—Wild, quite undeveloped, called "the Forgotten Island." Untouched quiet beaches; the famous leper colony on Makanalua Peninsula is being phased out and its jagged cliffs turned into a park.

Monterey Cypress Tree

(Pismo Beach Chamber of Commerce)

The Central California Coast

All too often, dramatic geological features that set sightseers' hearts racing preclude other beach pleasures such as accessibility, safe swimming, and bearable water temperature. Not so this piece of Pacific coastline. California, from Pismo Beach to Monterey, lets you have your cake and eat it too. It's gorgeous to look at — with mountains meeting *la mer* in the usual dramatic fashion; it's also blessed with many stretches of long sandy coves and bays (those facing south are most protected) where the water is just warm and calm enough for taking the plunge.

Other Features: Beachcombing and fishing at unprotected beaches, surfing and diving for the experienced. Golf, horseback riding, tennis at some resorts, hang gliding, volleyball. Boating, water-skiing in nearby lakes and bays and rivers.

Atmosphere and Ambiance: Beaches vary from rocky and impassible to wide and sandy. Not quite as laid-back as Southern California; state parks and beaches are often crowded, but there are many isolated, secluded spots.

Climate: Summer days are often foggy, but it usually burns off by afternoon. Mild temperatures prevail year round: about 50-70°F in summer; 40-60°F in winter (the rainy season).

Accommodations and Food: Ranges from luxury seaside resorts to cozier quarters in small establishments, motels, cabins, and camping. Restaurants specialize in seafood (including abalone), may have any number of themes and decors, and serve from expensive gourmet meals and oriental specialties to family fare. Picnicker's delight.

Nightlife: Theater, roller skating, clubs, dancing.

Getting There and Getting Around: Fly to major cities, drive (rented or your own) along scenic coastal highway 1; buses, trains travel between cities and their routes hug the coastline. Some local public buses go to beaches. Rent bikes, mopeds.

Central California's coastline offers the combination of swimmable, accessible beaches and rugged beauty. For more of the former, dip down farther south to the Santa Barbara beaches, the Channel Islands, and beyond. If the latter is more to your liking, trek on up north where the coastline is even more rugged, dotted with ship-wrecks, and the site of two national parks, plus fantastic beachcombing and fishing. In between, enjoy Pismo Beach clamming and driving; Morrow Bay's state park; San Simeon Beach's nearby Hearst castle; Big Sur's rolling hills giving way to towering cliffs, sea otters, seals, sea lions, and whales at sea; Point Lobos' energetic surf and barking sea lions; the famous artist and writers colony at Carmel; the Seventeen-Mile-Drive on Monterey Peninsula, which reveals sweeping mountain and seashore vistas and wind-gnarled Monterey cypresses; the wide, sandy, tree-fringed state beach at Monterey Bay; and the amusement park at Santa Cruz.

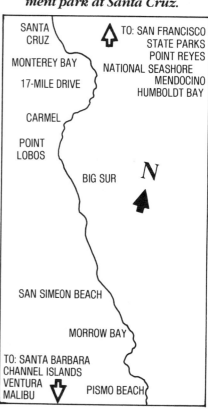

The Coast of Maine

This grandiose, rugged coast has many capes, beautiful deep harbors...hundreds of coves, points, bays, inlets, and islands. The thundering surf and majestic panoramas are a feast for the eyes and the ears. The best views and beaches are indicated on the map; everything comes to a crescendo on Mount Desert Island. Highlights on the island are Acadia National Park and Bar Harbor; Mount Cadillac, the highest point (1500 feet) on the East Coast, affords a breathtaking view of the surrounding ocean, islands, and countryside. Sights and sounds include "Thunder Hole" (named for the pounding surf), sheer cliffs, and "sandy" beaches made of minute shells. No wonder it's been called "the most beautiful island in the world," and that J.P. Morgan and Joseph Pulitzer built their 30-room "cottages" here.

Other Features: Boating, fishing, bike riding and hiking along seacoast and inland lakes, streams, rivers, and forests. Shipbuilding, museums, and small waterfront towns. Seals, porpoises, ospreys to glimpse.

Appearance and Ambiance: Countless rock-bound, pebbly beaches, with some sandy interludes; water is brisk (50°F in July). Authentic frontier, seafaring atmosphere steeped in history. Crashing, dramatic surf and quiet coves.

Climate: Pleasant summers (57-79°F); autumn has the most sunny days; winters are cold; spring comes late. Frequent fog. Bring foul weather gear just in case.

Accommodations and Food: Variety of accommodations and food up the entire coast, but both become sparse north of Mount Desert Island. Camping, hotels, cottages, motels, old resorts, rooming houses; great seafood...picnic and clambake country.

Nightlife: Hotel nightclub entertainment, bars, dancing.

Getting There and Getting Around: Planes and buses (no trains) go to coastal cities (Bangor, Portland, Bar Harbor, Rockland). By car, take the Maine Turnpike and U.S. 1 (cars may be rented at airports). All types of boats to charter; bridges and ferries (some car ferries) connect islands with each other and the mainland; romantic midnight cruises.

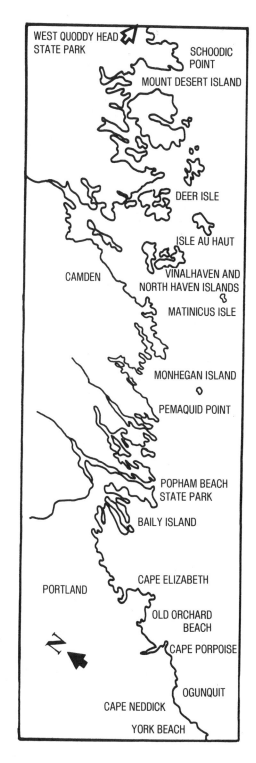

WEST QUODDY HEAD STATE PARK
SCHOODIC POINT
MOUNT DESERT ISLAND
DEER ISLE
ISLE AU HAUT
CAMDEN
VINALHAVEN AND NORTH HAVEN ISLANDS
MATINICUS ISLE
MONHEGAN ISLAND
PEMAQUID POINT
POPHAM BEACH STATE PARK
BAILY ISLAND
CAPE ELIZABETH
PORTLAND
OLD ORCHARD BEACH
CAPE PORPOISE
N
OGUNQUIT
CAPE NEDDICK
YORK BEACH

(Steven Mays)

COLUMBIA RIVER DETOUR
If Mount St. Helens behaves herself (remember the summer of 1980?), consider detouring along the Columbia River, the second largest river in the U.S. by volume, that slices right through a major mountain range and is bordered by playful waterfalls splashing over tall cliffs.

The Oregon-Washington Coast

This spectacular coast line is a sight you won't soon forget. The Oregon coast alone is 400 miles long — all of it dramatic, rugged boulder-strewn, surf-pummeled seascape interrupted by the odd pine-filled headland and hard, flat, sandy beaches. If you drive, you can park every few miles at oceanfront parks with picnic areas and camping facilities, each one with its own personality and access to the ocean.

Other Features: Stop at marine museums, picturesque fishing villages; observe sea otters, sea lions, schools of whales; visit aquariums, antique shops, lighthouses, amusement parks. The brave can swim, surf, and sail. Oregon's got strong outgoing tides, and danger signs are posted everywhere. There are few lifeguards, and the chilly waters (55-66°F in July) force many surfers and divers to wear wetsuits. There are some protected coves along the sea, where the water is calmer and warmer, but always swim during the incoming tide. Most swimming is done in the lakes that dot nearby camping parks. Beaches are for beachcombing (maybe you'll find glass Japanese floats), tide pooling, playing, driving, horseback riding, clamming, and crabbing.

Appearance and Ambiance: Secluded little coves and long stretches of hard flat sand that are always nearly deserted.

Climate: Temperate; high 50s to low 70s. Water temperature reaches 50°F in summer. Best beach weather is late summer and early fall, but the winter's dramatic storms attract a special coterie of storm watchers who prefer the coziness of sitting by the fireplace in a seaside resort. Bring warm clothes all year round, especially for cooler, wetter Washington.

Accommodations and Food: Quite diverse: award-winning luxury resorts, moderately priced hotels, rustic beach cabins, camping. The seafood is rivaled by none, and includes Dungeness crab, clams, octopus, Oregon shrimp, fish such as salmon and tuna, squid — for dinner or light meals and snacks. Also gourmet meals at elegant restaurants, moderately priced family fare, burger joints. Plenty of picnicking opportunities.

Nightlife: Not much. Large inns and hotels have nightclub entertainment and occasional "big names." Otherwise, linger over dinner, have a nightcap at the bar, or way up north, listen to the coyotes.

Getting There and Getting Around: Those who fly to the coast can rent a car or take buses to the parks. Commuter airlines and ferries go to San Juan Islands and other coastal highlights.

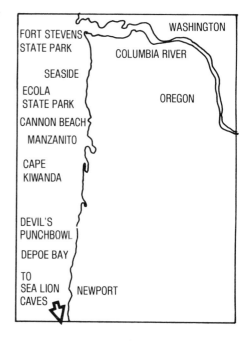

FORT STEVENS STATE PARK — WASHINGTON — COLUMBIA RIVER — SEASIDE — ECOLA STATE PARK — OREGON — CANNON BEACH — MANZANITO — CAPE KIWANDA — DEVIL'S PUNCHBOWL — DEPOE BAY — TO SEA LION CAVES — NEWPORT

The Oregon-Washington coastline has few parallels in the U.S. for sheer drama. Oregon's coastal highway stays close to the sea; highlights include: 12-foot Steller sea lions and puffins at the Sea Lion Caves; traditional resorts such as Newport and Seaside; sea-cut tunnels through which waves surge and "boil" up in a huge rock "cauldron" (at Devil's Punchbowl); 235-foot Haystack Rock at Cannon Beach. Farther north, in Washington, the road wanders inland occasionally; there you'll find Olympic National Park and the San Juan Islands.

(Chuck DeLaney)

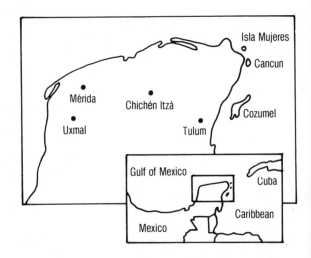

Soak up the sun along the Yucatán's beautiful white sand beaches; then soak up ancient history at the mysterious inland Mayan ruins.

The Yucatán Peninsula, Mexico

Mexico's Yucatán Peninsula and its lovely Caribbean islands are known as Mayan Mexico because of the proximity of the fifth-century A.D. ruins of that great civilization. The most impressive sites are at Chichén Itzá, Uxmal, and Tulum — steep but climbable pyramids, huge palaces, stages, astronomy observatories, and ball courts. The peninsula and islands themselves (Cozumel, Isla Mujeres, and Cancun) are a sight to behold too: soft, sparkling white sand beaches set off by brilliant turquoise waters, neon tropical fish, bright bougainvillea, and the occasional iguana and hummingbird.

Other Features: Excellent swimming, snorkeling, skin diving, and fishing; some golf and tennis. Isla Mujeres has sea turtles; Contoy Island, to which there are day excursions, is a bird sanctuary.

Appearance and Ambiance: Beaches are uncrowded, with bright white limestone sand, and warm, calm Caribbean waters. On the peninsula there are hot forest/jungles; Playa de Carmen has a lovely beach, Xelha's crystal clear lagoon is so full of fish you don't need a mask to see them. Of the islands, Cozumel is the largest and oldest tourist attraction; life is casual along the rough-water eastern shore and the calm, cove-studded western shore. Cancun, about 14 miles long and a quarter of a mile wide, has a lagoon between it and the nearby mainland; it's a bit more formal than Cozumel. Isla Mujeres, the latest to be "discovered," is only 5 miles long by half a mile wide and relatively undeveloped; there are few phones or paved roads.

Climate: Hot and humid most of the time: up to the 90s during May through November; the 80s otherwise. The rainy, windy season begins in June and lasts through September.

Accommodations and Food: Varies from island to island. Cancun has a posh newness with luxury hotels and family places. Cozumel is less posh with a range of old and new, expensive to inexpensive accommodations. Isla Mujeres has a handful of hotels, inexpensive rooms, and camping. Fresh pineapple or papaya for breakfast, seafood prepared in the local manner; plus turkey dishes (local specialties), steak-and-lobster houses.

Nightlife: Cancun's nightlife is lavish; otherwise, bars and small combos, a few nightclubs and discos.

Getting There and Getting Around: Fly to Cancun (the resort city) or Mérida on the peninsula. Getting around is much easier than it used to be. Take a bus tour, a plane, a taxi, or rented car to the ruins. Fly or ferry to and between islands; or drive along the causeway that connects Cancun to Cancun City on the mainland. Brush up on your Spanish, unless you plan to stay in the tourist areas. Use pesos or U.S. traveler's checks; U.S. dollars and credit cards are also accepted in many hotels, shops, and restaurants.

MEXICO'S PACIFIC AND GULF COASTS

Mexico has glorious beaches on its other coasts, too. They're all public — even those near resorts and hotels. (See *A Nature Lover's Guide* for beaches on the Baja Peninsula.)

The *Pacific Coast* beaches are the most popular, and no wonder: they're wide, white and sandy with warm water, world-famous sunsets, and a tropical climate that's sun-drenched the year round. *Mazatlán* is a very active resort peninsula. North Beach is a favorite with the locals; Las Gaviotas, Playas Sabalo, and Camaron are where the tourists go; the two nearby island beaches, *Venedos* and *Piedra*, are quieter. *San Blas* offers relaxation, lagoons, tropical fruit trees. *Puerto Vallarta* has beautiful, but very commercially developed, beaches for the most part; Palmas Beach, Conchas Chinas, and Las Estacas are exceptions. *Manzanillo* is full of luxury resorts, as is *Ixtapa*. Less popular (and less crowded) west coast beach areas are: *Mismaloya*, where *Night of the Iguana* was filmed, with tall cliffs, palms, and a lagoon; *Yelapa; Zihuatanejo; Puerto Escondido; Puerto Angel; La Ventosa*, near Salina Cruz; and the *Isthmus of Tehuantepec*. These beaches are remote, a bit harder to get to, with primitive accommodations, but definitely unspoiled.

On the *Gulf of Mexico* the beaches are relatively undeveloped. *Isla de Carmen* is the most frequented — especially by young folk — and is the most built up. It has white, palm-fringed beaches, dancing, bars, villas, and hotels. *Boca de Chachalacas* and *Veracruz* have dark, volcanic sand beaches. *Tecolutla* is a quiet one, with palms.

THOSE MYSTERIOUS MAYANS
To find out more about the mysterious Mayans and their ruins, pick up a copy of Incidents of Travel in Yucatán *by John L. Stephens (originally published in 1843, recently reissued in two volumes by Dover; paper). Amusing memoirs that combine archeology, adventure; illustrations.*

A SINGLE TRAVELER'S GUIDE

Where you won't be alone for long — unless you want to be.

(Morris Jaffe)

The Hamptons, Long Island, New York

Asparagus Beach in East Hampton used to be *the* beach to go to for "stalking" the opposite sex. Now, it's pretty much locals and tourists who are looking for the wild life but haven't heard the asparagus patch has wilted. Alfresco singles parties have moved to Gibson's Beach in East Hampton (nude bathing), Fowler's in South Hampton (largely gay), and Hot Dog Beach between West Hampton and Hampton Bays. Most accommodations are seasonal "shares" as on Fire Island; but hotels, motels, and inns are nearby, as are discos, clubs, bars, restaurants. Fly, drive, or take a bus or train to the Hamptons; wheels are needed to get around.

Fire Island, New York

Best known for its swinging single image, Fire Island is a series of communities that are often a mixture of singles of varying sensibilities, lifestyles, and families. During the summer, the population swells with weekend "shares" bought for the summer; but some communities have strict local ordinances and "grouper laws" that attempt to stem the tide of raucous singles. Unless you have accommodations on the island, a trip to Fire Island could prove uncomfortable — there are no public facilities except at Davis Park and Watch Hill. Nudity is okay at almost all the beaches, especially if you stray from the most heavily attended areas. A quick run-down: Kismet is a mix of families and "frenetic" singles. Ocean Beach seems uptight to some; there are more businesses and discos here than anywhere else on the island — and more people on the beach (on which there is no picnicking!). Ocean Bay Park has a loose, anything goes atmosphere. Cherry Grove is frequented by about 30 percent gay singles; the rest are families; all live together in a close-knit, yet loose community. The Pines is where the rich and the famous play; in about half of the *Architectural Digest*-type homes you'll find families, in the other half single gays.

CLUB MEDS

Though the management dislikes playing up the singles aspect, no section on beaches for singles would be complete without mentioning Club Med (see *A Sports Lover's Guide* for more information). Families and couples of all ages return again and again; but so do singles of all ages. Despite occasional charges of "forced frivolity" most visitors have a great time and thrive on the organized activities and "village" set-ups that make mingling easy and natural. Single travelers who book the package are given roommates, and when dinner is served, you're assured of company because you sit at tables for eight or more. And if you tire of the togetherness bit, the beaches are usually roomy enough for a solitary stroll. The Club recommends Club Med at Buccaneer's Creek on Martinique as the most singles oriented.

Daytona Beach, Florida

It calls itself "the world's most famous beach," perhaps that should be changed to "most gregarious." Bicycles, motor bikes, cars, lawn chairs, and sunbathers compete for space on this beach, the hard-packed sand of which is just made for "cruising." Make sure you look both ways before crossing the strand to the surf, which is as lively and challenging as the games that are part of the famous boardwalk. At night, bar hop, dance, listen to music. Speed's a part of the swinging scene, though the beach is no longer a racetrack; it's been replaced by the nearby Daytona International Speedway. World-caliber sports and stock car racing takes place during Speed Weeks in February, and other exciting racing events during the rest of the year. Daytona Beach may be reached by plane or car. Accommodations range from expensive resorts to moderate and inexpensive hotels, motels, efficiencies, camping.

(Club Med)

A SINGLE TRAVELER'S GUIDE

Fort Lauderdale, Florida

The atmosphere has been compared to that of Cannes, but that doesn't explain why thousands of college students flock to this Atlantic-splashed beach every Easter and summer vacation. It's popular with the just-out-of-college crowd, too. It certainly isn't the best beach Florida has to offer, though it is a long unbroken golden sweep because buildings have been kept to the west side of the oceanfront drive. Sidewalks extend right up to the sand, with boutiques, restaurants, and bars right across the street. The nightlife includes some surprisingly with-it live music. Fort Lauderdale is accessible by plane, train, bus, and car; accommodations include resorts, inns, hotels, motels, and camping.

(Solomon Martin Productions)

St. Barts, The Caribbean

And now for something completely different: a small (nine and a half square miles), intimate island, with a relaxed, no-pressure atmosphere and precious golden-sand beaches. The feeling is definitely French...beachside cafés for friendly lunchtime snacks and chats, where the wine and easy, good times flow freely. Swim, sun, windsurf, snorkel, sail, water-ski, fish, play tennis or golf, or ride horseback during the day. After dinner, stroll in the moonlight, gaze contentedly at the yachts bobbing in the harbor, go disco dancing, or boogie on down to one of the weekly parties for a little reggae or meringue. St. Barts' relaxed sociability is reinforced by the small hotels, chalets, and cottages. Go by small plane from St. Maarten, St. Thomas, or Guadeloupe; or ferry from St. Thomas.

Waikiki Beach, Oahu, Hawaiian Islands

Waikiki, the most visited of all of Hawaii's beaches, is a peninsula near Honolulu. Here you'll find all the excuses and inducements you could possibly want to help you meet people: romantic, tropical atmosphere and scenery, excellent dining, nightlife, willing instructors in surfing, outrigger canoeing, catamaran sailing, snorkeling and scuba diving, plus languorous swimming, zoos, outdoor theater, tennis courts, hibiscus garden, aquarium, native song and dance performances, fishing, and nearby yacht clubs. There are always special events, parades, and festivals that are also conducive to mixing and socializing. Fly (or sail) to Hawaii, then sightsee by bus or rented car. Take your pick of a large variety of accommodations.

GOING SOLO: TIPS FOR THE SINGLE TRAVELER

Neither the world nor the travel industry was designed with the single traveler in mind. Hotels quote double occupancy rates that they often charge whether there are two bodies in the room or one. Package deals are based on double occupancies. Eating out alone in a strange land can be a traumatic experience; being alone for a long time can be depressing. But there are advantages to "traveling light" and ways of circumventing the drawbacks.

• You're independent. You can leave when you want, stay as long as you want, and stay where you want.

• Your chances of meeting new people are greater. So is the possibility of having a surprising adventure, and of discovering new aspects of yourself. You can try out a new personality and enjoy new activities.

• When traveling alone, you'll probably need more comfortable accommodations than if you have a roommate to commiserate with.

• Go off-season if you want good service and a better crack at meeting the locals. Also, stay in out-of-the-way places or with a family. Read up on local customs and history so you'll be able to conduct an informed conversation.

• Daytime activities such as participating in sports, going on bus tours, and attending festivals are great ways to meet people for later, nighttime cavorting, and for the next day.

• Small, intimate beaches and hotels are most conducive to solitary adventurers: You're likely to get to know people because there are only a few places to spend time. Large resorts have more to do, and more people to meet, but they also have a frenetic, impersonal style that you might well have left home to avoid.

• Investigate travel agents and tour operators who specialize in matching up single travelers to share costs and rooms.

91

A SKINNY-DIPPER'S GUIDE

Bathing is a sport
Enjoyed by great and small
In suits of any sort
Though better none at all.

**THE UNSUITABLE WAY
TO HAVE FUN**
The answer to a shy dipper's prayers may be the Skinny Dip Clip. Simply remove your suit in deep water and attach this nifty little device. Your suit will stay safely afloat, freeing your mind and body for a carefree swim au naturel. Available for $5.98 from GDI Gifts, Box 1516W, 11 Ledgewood Rd., Manchester, MA 01944.

HOT CROSS BUNS?
Nothing can cool off your enthusiasm for free beaches faster than a pair of burned buns and/or breasts, a danger that many first-timers face. Make sure you use a highly protective sun screen on the parts of your body that rarely — if ever — see the light of day. (See BEAUTY AND THE BEACH, Before You Go for safe tanning tips; information on the new SPF rating system, which takes the guesswork out of how much protection you're actually getting; and tips on ways to soothe sun-ravaged breasts once it's too late and you've been overexposed.)

NEWS FOR NASCENT NUDIES

Are you just plain tired of sand gritting in your bathing suit; of tugging at straps; of drooping elastic; of hot, heavy fabric getting between you and the cool, caressing sea and fresh air; of the tan lines that conveniently let you see how you're coming along, but just may be the silliest-looking thing since hair spray? If so, you're ready for a nude beach — or, in today's parlance, a "free" or "clothes-optional" beach.

Unfortunately, going back to the simple life is not so simple. In Europe, toplessness is generally accepted even on public beaches, and except where strict religious tradition prevails, full nudity — if kept demure — is no big deal. Before you throw caution to the wind and your bathing suit to the ground, however, realize that much of the world, including the U.S., is a touch more uptight about this sensitive subject.

Though there's no federal law against public nudity in this country, state laws do exist, and it's a misdemeanor with the usual penalty of a $10 or $15 fine. But unless you're also engaged in "lewd conduct" or invade tried-and-true family or clothed beaches, regulations usually aren't enforced. More often a beach that's fine for free beachers one day becomes overrun with gawkers and irate citizens the next. In steps the law, purging the area of nude sunbathers, who simply move round the bend to the next beach where the whole scenario repeats itself in a never-ending cycle of legal and local tolerance giving way to prohibition.

Since nude beaches are in a constant state of flux, those who wish to enjoy the bluffs in the buff may find that looking for a receptive beach is a full-time job. You could limit yourself to the organized parks that exist, or pick up a copy of one of the guides on the subject (see Organized Nudity, right). If you want to go it on your own, avoid the possibility of exposing yourself to awkward situations, fines, or worse by keeping your eyes and ears open. The latest news on nude beaches spreads by word of mouth; since local ordinances and temperaments vary, check ahead with tourist offices and local authorities to see what's up. Use your common sense: If you arrive at what you've heard is a nude beach and no one is sans suit, leave yours on — at least until you've walked beyond the most populated strip.

Any deserted, secluded beach is suitable for going suitless. National seashores in particular are unspoiled, usually empty, and so ideal spots to grin and bare it. But think twice before you do so: Being naked and alone or with a small group of defenseless people puts you in a very vulnerable position — no hassles, but no protection against those who don't quite see things your way, either.

Some areas have a time-honored reputation: for example, the California coast, Riis Park and Fire Island in New York, parts of Cape Cod in Massachusetts, and Wreck Beach in Vancouver, Canada, which has the distinction of being "the most successful free beach in the western hemisphere."

In the Caribbean, you can frolic freely in the many islands and cays that have long remote stretches or cozy nooks and crannies suitable for skinny-dipping. In general, toplessness and often full nudity are accepted at even the more populated public beaches on the French Islands, with special mention going to Guadeloupe, Jamaica's Negril Beach, the British and U.S. Virgin Islands, Antigua, the Bahamas, Barbados, and Martinique.

In Mexico, private resorts can offer whatever they want to, but the public is usually hostile, so watch out and ask first at the local tourist office about regional attitudes at Mexico's many isolated beaches.

ORGANIZED NUDITY

The American Sunbathing Association is a family-oriented group based at 810 North Mills Ave., Orlando, FL 32803. Their nudist parks and recreation areas range from primitive campgrounds for tent-pitching to elaborate resort complexes. Potential members, who don't have to join with their families, are nevertheless screened. Once you join a club, you automatically receive a list of the other ASA clubs, have access to their facilities in the U.S., Canada, and around the world, and receive *The Bulletin* (motto: "If God had intended us to go around nude, He would have made us that way").

The *Skinny Dipper Guide to American Nudist Parks* (Hallwood Press, P.O. Box 10838, Dallas, TX 75207) gives information on membership and ground fees, regulations, and social climate and includes stories and articles on nudity.

To stay abreast of the free beach movement, join *The Naturists,* an "association of free beaches and other free spirits" (P.O. Box 132-S, Oshkosh, WI 54902). For a minimal membership fee you get a copy of the *Sun,* the yearly feature magazine of nude recreation that includes updates on new or changing conditions of clothes-optional beaches (also available to non-members). Members receive a 15-percent discount on other publications, including the *World Guide to Nude Beaches and Recreation,* which describes the best established and most beautiful places to go in over 60 countries — more than 1000 lake and ocean beaches, hot springs, resorts, nudist parks; plus tips for the beginner. (Stonehill Publishing Co., 1981. Available in bookstores, from the publisher, or from the Free Beachers Documentation Center, same address as The Naturists.)

A SPORTS LOVER'S GUIDE
For those who don't need to rest in order to relax.

Cape Hatteras, N.C. (Fishing)

Here, along the Outer Banks, is some of the best fishing (and deep-sea fishing) in the country. You can fish successfully and consistently 10 months out of the year. Though it's been estimated that about 20,000 anglers show up in April, there's plenty of room along the 175 miles of island beaches, and plenty of fish. At Gamefish Junction, for instance, where the warm Gulf Stream meets the cold northern currents, over 40 varieties of northern and southern fish await you. You'll find bluefish, tuna, marlin, mackerel, amberjack, dolphin, and bass; catch the Blue Marlin Tournaments in early June.

Other Features: Beautiful, untouched seascapes all along the Cape Hatteras National Seashore and the Cape Lookout National Seashore just to the south. (It's likely to stay that way, since commercial development surrendered to the ever-shifting beaches and came to a halt in 1974.) You can swim, stroll, hike, ride, sail, and view the protruding skeletons of shipwrecks. (Over 500 ships sank offshore, dubbing the area "the Graveyard of the Atlantic.") There are shorebirds and migratory birds galore, especially at Pea Island National Wildlife Refuge, where over half the world's snow geese spend the winter. The nation's highest sand dune (138 feet) is at Nag's Head, where sand-skiing and hang gliding are popular. The Cape Hatteras Lighthouse is the tallest in the country (208 feet).

Appearance and Ambiance: Wild, windblown, unspoiled sandy beaches— "motel row" north of Nag's Head is the only intrusion on the raw, salty beauty. Choose the "surf's up" Atlantic on the east or the calm Pamlico Sound on the west.

Climate: Crazy; frequent, but mild offshore storms; cloudy skies half the time; rainiest days in July, August, September. Temperature stays mild all year and rarely dips below 45°F in winter or climbs above 85°F in summer. Beach season begins in May.

Accommodations and Food: Wide range, from camping at seaside parks and funky atmospheric inns and lodges to a Holiday Inn; some oceanfront, many with pools. Unforgettable seafood, steak houses, continental restaurants, picnicking.

Nightlife: Low-key; some hotel nightclubs, a café or two.

Getting There and Getting Around: Fly to New Bern or Raleigh; Amtrak to Raleigh; drive to ferries, toll-free bridges, and causeways that link the barrier islands with the mainland and each other. Dune buggies and Jeeps to rent; boats to charter.

HERE, FISHY, FISHY

Salt Water Sportsman is a 40-odd-year-old magazine that gives the experienced saltwater angler the latest useful information and educates newcomers to the sport. Among other regular features, it provides expected fishing conditions in each coastal state. (For subscription information, write to *Salt Water Sportsman,* 10 High St., Boston, MA 02110.)

Field & Stream also supplies year-round fishing information for fresh- and saltwater. The February issue's annual round-up lists prime U.S. locations; June focuses on Canada; and January covers warm-water angling spots. (For subscription information, write to *Field & Stream,* 1515 Broadway, New York, NY 10036.)

Here's a sampling of some avid anglers' favorite saltwater spots: Cape Cod, Nantucket, and Martha's Vineyard in Massachusetts; Montauk, New York; the Jersey Shore; Bailey Island, Maine; the Rhode Island coast; Chesapeake Bay, Maryland; Florida's coasts; Galveston Bay and Aransas Pass, Texas; Channel Islands off California; Baja Peninsula, Mexico; and almost all of the Caribbean — especially for bonefishing.

Note: Write to local fish and game departments for information on licenses, permits, and the changing conditions and various peak seasons. Most books for the beach-loving angler are regional and boat oriented, but *All About Surf Fishing* by Jack Fallon (Winchester Press, 1975) covers all three coasts of the U.S. and is a good primer.

There's no substitution for local knowledge when it comes to surf fishing. Find yourself a reputable tackle shop and ask questions. They'll know what are biting, what they're eating, and what tide they'll be there on. Remember, the beach is always changing, the sand is shifting, and conditions are never quite the same.

— "Spider" Andreson,
Salt Water Sportsman

THE EXTREMES OF SWIMMING

Long and Challenging: For more information about rough-water swims (there are about 35 annually, most in southern California and Hawaii, including the two-and-a-half-mile swim at Waikiki that draws 800 participants), get the current issue of the *Rough Water Swimming Handbook.* It's inexpensive and is published by *Swim Swim Magazine,* P.O. Box 5901, Santa Monica, CA 90405. The editor, Penny Little, advises:

"Rough water" swimming doesn't mean aficionados always race in rough water. It *can* be rough, but the real challenge of this type of swimming lies in the distances covered and in the absence of lane lines and boundaries. Freedom, exhilaration and the challenge of the unknown combine to make open water competition a unique swimming experience.

Most adult rough water competitors are year-round lap swimmers who consider the summer events as frosting on the cake. Competition is generally relaxed and there is a carnival-like atmosphere at races despite the fact that swimming a mile or so in open water is really quite a feat! Entrants are enthusiastic and well trained endurance-type swimmers — much akin to marathon runners in their approach to their sport.

Warm and Languid: Even the most faint-hearted swimmers would find the 96.8° Persian Gulf a bit too warm for comfort. If you like your water bathtub-tepid, clear, and calm, the best alternative may be Magens Bay on St. Thomas in the U.S. Virgin Islands. This wide, palm-fringed, protected, white sand beach is considered by many to be the finest swimming beach in the Caribbean and one of the most beautiful in the world.

(Harald Johnson)

Brisk and Refreshing: In other words, freezing. A dip in any of the waters along Washington, Oregon, most of California, New England, and Canada would definitely be an eye-opener. But why not go all the way and get your goose pimples in Alaska? Kodiak Island and the Alaska Peninsula, in the southern part of the state, are where you'll find other hardy souls taking the plunge in the summer months, when the water temperature "soars" to about 50°F. Take a tip from the Polar Bear Club's president, though, and acclimate yourself to cold water gradually. The Polar Bears swim off Coney Island in New York all year round. They do it not only for the fun, sport, and camaraderie — they find it builds up their resistance to colds.

(Gail Seely)

La Jolla Cove, California (Rough-Water Swimming)

"How's the swimming?" is the first question in many a beach-lover's mind. For most of us, swimming — enjoyed in varying degrees — is central to the beach experience. Some like it hot (well, warm); some like it cold; some like it calm; some like it rough. *Serious* swimmers tend to like it competitive, and that's what La Jolla Cove has to offer. Every weekend after Labor Day for the last 50 years, it's been the site of the most popular rough-water swim in the country. At the start of this mile-long swim, about 1500 participants of both sexes and all ages appear at the water's edge to become, in the words of one competitor, "one boiling, frothing, arm-flailing mass." They follow a triangular, marked course as thousands of spectators cheer them on.

Other Features: If you don't swim, you can watch the natatorial masochists along with the usual 11,000 other onlookers. To see the satisfaction of having finished a mile in rough water on the swimmers' faces is to share their excitement and exhilaration. At other times, enjoy the sun, surf, and sand or visit nearby Scripps Institution of Oceanography, the Torrey Pines State Reserve and its fine beaches, and the famous clothing-optional Black's Beach.

Appearance and Ambiance: Typical southern California laid-back lifestyle. A rocky cove of a beach that's excellent for skin and scuba diving as well as swimming. Nearby La Jolla Point has lava flows and sea lions. La Jolla Shores is a good family beach that's wide and safe for swimming.

Climate: Mild year-round southern California weather.

Accommodations and Food: La Jolla is a good-sized city, with a variety of accommodations and eateries with a wide range of prices; camping at Torrey Pines State Park.

Nightlife: Almost everything — music, dancing, and so on — you'll find in any city of its size.

Getting There and Getting Around: Fly to San Diego, the nearest big city, and drive to La Jolla. Drive, walk, or bicycle along La Jolla's beachside streets or use the city buses.

Where to Be a Good Sport

Although swimming and fishing are two of this country's favorite participation sports, they aren't the only ways to inject a little action into your beach day.

HANG GLIDING

Some good spots are Nags Head, North Carolina; Torrey Pines, Playa Del Rey, or Pismo Beach, California. For more information about where the best hang gliding is, contact the United States Hang Gliding Association, Inc., P.O. Box 66306, Los Angeles, CA 90066.

Nags Head (N.C. Travel and Tourism Division)

KITE FLYING

Catch the International Kite Flying Contest that's held in January in Sarasota's Lido Beach in Florida. Or do-it-yourself at these beaches recommended by the magazine *KiteLines* (7106 Campfield Rd., Baltimore, MD 21207): In California, Marina del Rey, Redondo Beach, Pacific Beach, Carmel; in Oregon, Cannon Beach and Lincoln City; in New York, Southampton and Jones Beach; in Massachusetts, Cape Cod, Martha's Vineyard, and Nantucket; in North Carolina, Kitty Hawk (Wright Brothers country!); in Flordia, Sanibel Island and Key West; in Virginia, Virginia Beach. Kite flying is big in Bermuda and in Canada's Vancouver and British Columbia.

SAILING

Sailing's not only an exhilarating, enchanting beach-based activity, it's one of the best ways to beach-hop and discover your own special retreats. You don't need to own a yacht or even be knowledgeable in this sport to enjoy it. You can charter a boat for a day, a week, or more; you can hire a full crew, or bare-boat it. There are bare-boat or windjammer cruises in protected waters along the coast of New England and all around the Caribbean Islands. They're informal, so be prepared to rough it. You can help out if you want, or relax completely — just sun yourself, take in the sights, swim or snorkel off the side. Expect big family-style meals on board and a few strategic stops along the way. You can even buy a learn-to-sail package for a vacation you'll never forget. One school with a good reputation is the Offshore Sailing School, with branches on Martha's Vineyard off Cape Cod, Hilton Head Island off South Carolina, Captiva Island off Florida, and Tortola in the British Virgin Islands. As you might suspect, these are all superb sailing waters. Other great sailing grounds are:

• *Marina Del Rey* (California). The largest man-made small boat marina in the world.
• *Newport Beach* (California). Hobnob with 10,000 boats including those owned by biggies of the world.
• *Sausalito* (California). Sail around the Bay or Sacramento River Delta's inland waterways.
• *Long Island Sound* (Connecticut and New York). Protected cruising water.
• *The Coast of Maine.* Variety — and fog, islands, rocky beaches.
• *Chesapeake Bay* (Maryland and Virginia). Large estuary with river mouths, coves, harbors.

• *The Caribbean.* Calm, protected waters and lots of inlets to explore make the islands a sailor's playground. Best of all are the Virgin Islands and the Grenadines.
• *Bahamas.* Very protected waters.
• *Newport* (Rhode Island). America's oldest resort, a center for yachting and host of two famous ocean races (the Newport to Bermuda race and the Annapolis to Newport race), and sometimes the America's Cup. Naragansett Bay is where to go for small boats and short cruises. Larger craft are a short sail from other yachting meccas.

Sunfishing

Resort hotel beaches in the U.S. and Caribbean have Sunfish for guests, and often will supply instruction as well. Regattas are held at many beaches, including the Sea Cliff Yacht Club Beach, New York; Weed Beach, Darien, Connecticut; Aruba's beaches; Wickford, Rhode Island, Town Beach; Miami Yacht Club Beach.

(Lee Male)

(Bahama News Bureau)

SNORKELING AND SCUBA DIVING
See *A Nature Lover's Guide.*

SURFING
There are hundreds of surf sites in the United States alone. The greatest are in Hawaii, surfing's home state. Take a drive along Kamehameha Highway on Oahu and you can't miss the surfers. Waikiki is the best beach; Haleiwa, Sunset, Goat Island, and the famous Pipeline are also recommended for spectators or experienced surfers.

California is another surfing state — the surf's up all along its coastline, and you can't go wrong at Santa Cruz, Jalama, Santa Barbara, Malibu, Hermosa Beach, Huntington Beach, San Onofre, and San Diego.

To this list, the American Surfing Association (in Newport Beach, California) adds: the Carolinas (especially San Sebastian); Long Island, New York; New Jersey; Padre Island, Texas; and Virginia. Exceptional surf conditions also exist in Argentina, Australia, Brazil, Ecuador, England, Fiji, France, Indonesia, Ireland, Israel, Kenya, Mexico, Morocco, New Zealand, Peru, Puerto Rico, South Africa, Tahiti, Trinidad and Tobago, and Uruguay.

CLUB MEDS
For sports with a French accent, and all the guesswork removed, there's Club Med, which has been putting together prepaid vacation packages for over thirty years. There are about 80 Club Med villages in 25 countries, including Africa, the Bahamas, Europe, Mexico, the Middle East, Polynesia and the Pacific, South American, and the West Indies. Their goal is to provide a special vacation for everyone — singles, couples, and families. Children are accepted from age 6 up; there's a special mini-village for kids at Fort Royal on Guadcloupc. Once you sign for the package and pay the fee, sports equipment and instruction are free, which encourages everyone to participate. Although not all sports are available at all clubs, expect to find: windsurfing, tennis, swimming, calisthenics, jogging, water-skiing, sailing, snorkeling, scuba diving, yoga, horseback riding, deep-sea fishing, archery, fencing, volley-ball, and *petanque* (bocce ball). (For more information, write to Club Med, P.O. Box 4460, Scottsdale, AZ 85258.)

FOR YOUR INFORMATION

Before you take off for the best beaches in the U.S., Canada, Mexico, and the Caribbean, you might want more detailed information than the space in this book permits. The best source of information for the most popular tourist areas — such as Florida, California, Mexico, and the Caribbean — is a travel agent. Agents travel themselves and often can share personal knowledge; they will also arrange for transportation and accommodations. Because travel agents aren't interested in infrequent short hops that are hard to set up or that don't require air transportation and the accompanying commissions, you'll also need guidebooks and tourist boards. The guidebooks listed here will provide you with a wealth of information that you can peruse at your leisure before seeing a travel agent. But watch out! These days you should be prepared for change — what you find may not match what you've read about. Carefully researched information — especially on prices — may be out of date by the time a book is printed.

General Travel Guides

Most of these travel guides are updated annually. They're all available in paper back and are considered bibles in the industry:

• Stephen Birnbaum's *Get 'em and Go Guides*, published by Houghton Mifflin Co.

• Fodor's *Modern Guides*, published by David McKay Co., Inc.

• Arthur Frommer's *$__-a-Day Guides* (the amount keeps going up), published by Simon & Schuster, Inc.

Tourist Boards

Tourist boards that represent individual states and geographic locations are particularly useful for up-to-date detailed information. The more specific your request, the better.

GETTING IN

If you're traveling to Canada, Mexico, or the Caribbean, you'll need some proof of U.S. citizenship: a birth certificate, voter registration card, or a passport (even an expired one will do). A driver's license will be accepted as proof only in Canada. Occasionally a tourist card is also required, but these can be issued upon arrival. Most officials will also ask to see a return ticket. As of this writing, you can visit Cuba only as part of an organized tour; passports are needed, plus a visa, which can be obtained by the tour operator.

United States

If these agencies can't supply what you need, they'll refer you to the proper local agency. Unless otherwise specified, the toll-free (800) numbers may be dialed anywhere in the U.S. except the state being called.

• Alabama Bureau of Publicity and Information, 532 South Perry St., Montgomery, AL 36130; 205-832-5510 or 800-633-5761.

• Alaska Division of Tourism, Pouch E, Juneau, AK 99811; 907-465-2010.

• Arizona Office of Tourism, 1700 West Washington, Suite 501, Phoenix, AZ 85007; 602-252-5662.

• Arkansas Department of Parks and Tourism, 1 Capitol Mall, Little Rock, AR 72201; 501-371-7777 or 800-643-8383.

• California Office of Visitor Services, P.O. Box 1499, Sacramento, CA 95805; 916-322-1396.

• Colorado Office of Tourism, Division of Commerce and Development, 1313 Sherman St., Room 500, Denver, CO 80203; 303-839-3045.

• Connecticut Department of Economic Development, Travel Director, 210 Washington St., Hartford, CT 06106; 203-566-3385 or 800-243-1685.

• Delaware State Travel Service, 630 State College Rd., P.O. Box 1401, Dover, DE 19901; 302-678-4254.

• Washington, D.C., Convention and Visitors Association, Suite 250, 1575 I St. N.W., Washington, D.C. 20005; 202-789-7000.

• Florida Division of Tourism, 405 Collins Building, Tallahassee, FL 32301; 904-487-1462 or 800-874-8660.

• Tour Georgia, Box 1776, Atlanta, GA 30301; 404-656-3590 or 800-241-8444.

• Hawaii Visitors Bureau, 2270 Kalakaua Ave., Suite 801, Honolulu, HI 96815; 808-823-1811.

• Idaho Division of Tourism and Industrial Development, Capitol Building, Boise, ID 83720; 208-384-2470.

• Illinois Office of Tourism, 222 South College St., Springfield, IL 62706; 217-782-7139.

• Indiana Tourism Development Division, 440 North Meridian St., Indianapolis, IN 46204; 317-232-8860.

• Iowa Development Commission, Tourist Development Division, 250 Jewett Building, Des Moines, IA 50309; 515-281-3100, -3679 or (in Iowa) 800-362-2843, exts. 3100, 3679.

• Kansas Department of Economic Development, 503 Kansas, 6th fl., Topeka, KS 66603; 913-296-3481.

• Kentucky Department of Tourism, Fort Boone Plaza, Frankfort, KY 40601; 502-564-4930.

• Louisiana Office of Tourism, Inquiry Department, P.O. Box 44291, Baton Rouge, LA 70804; 504-342-4900.

• Maine Publicity Bureau, State House, Augusta, ME 04333; 207-289-2423.

• Maryland Office of Tourist Development, 1748 Forest Dr., Annapolis, MD 21401; 301-269-3517 or 800-638-5252 or (in Maryland) 800-492-7126.

• Massachusetts Division of Tourism, Department of Commerce and Development, Leverett Saltonstall Building, 100 Cambridge St., Boston, MA 02202; 617-727-3201.

UNITED STATES con't.

• Michigan Travel Bureau, Department of Commerce, P.O. Box 30226, Lansing, MI 48909; 517-373-1195 or 800-248-5703 or (in Michigan) 800-292-2524.

• Minnesota Tourist Information Center, 480 Cedar St., St. Paul, MN 55101; 612-296-5029 or 800-328-1410 or (in Minnesota) 800-652-9747.

• Mississippi Division of Tourism, P.O. Box 849, Jackson, MS 39205; 601-354-6715 or 800-647-2290.

• Missouri Division of Tourism, P.O. Box 1055, Jefferson City, MO 65102; 314-751-4133 or 800-325-0733 or (in Missouri) 800-392-0711.

• Montana Department of Highways, Travel Promotion Unit, Helena, MT 59601; 406-449-2654 or 800-548-3390.

• Nebraska Division of Travel and Tourism, Department of Economic Development, P.O. Box 94666, Lincoln, NE 68509; 402-471-3111.

• Nevada Division of Tourism, Capitol Complex, 1050 East Williams, Carson City, NV 89710; 702-885-4322.

• New Hampshire Division of Economic Development, Office of Vacation Travel, P.O. Box 856, Concord, NH 03301; 603-271-2665.

• New Jersey Division of Travel and Tourism, Box 400, Trenton, NJ 08625; 609-292-2470.

• New Mexico Travel Division, Commerce and Industry Department, Bataan Memorial Building, Santa Fe, NM 87503; 505-827-5571 or 800-545-2040.

• New York State Division of Tourism, 99 Washington Ave., Albany, NY 12245; 518-474-4116, or (in New York State) 800-342-3810.

• North Carolina Travel and Tourism Division, P.O. Box 25249, Raleigh, NC 27611; 919-733-4171.

• North Dakota Travel Division, Capitol Grounds, Bismarck, ND 58505; 701-224-2525 or 800-437-2077 or (in North Dakota) 800-472-2100.

• Travel Ohio, P.O. Box 1001, Columbus, OH 43216; 614-466-8844 or 800-848-1300 or (in Ohio) 800-282-5393.

• Oklahoma Division of Tourism Promotion, 500 Will Rogers Building, Oklahoma City, OK 73105; 405-521-2464.

• Oregon Travel Information Office, 101A Transportation Building, Salem, OR 97310; 503-378-6309 or 800-547-4901.

• Pennsylvania Bureau of Travel Development, Department of Commerce, 206 South Office Building, Harrisburg, PA 17120; 717-787-5453 or 800-323-1717.

• Rhode Island Department of Economic Development, 1 Weybosset Hill, Providence, RI 02903; 401-277-2601.

• South Carolina Division of Tourism, Box 71, Columbia, SC 29202; 803-758-8735.

• South Dakota Division of Tourism, Joe Foss Building, Pierre, SD 57501; 605-773-3301.

• Tennessee Tourist Development, P.O. Box 23170, Nashville, TN 37203; 615-741-2158.

• Texas Department of Highways and Public Transportation, Travel and Information Division, Austin, TX 78701; 512-475-2028.

• Utah Travel Council, Council Hall, Capitol Hill, Salt Lake City, UT 84114; 801-533-5681.

• Vermont Travel Division, 61 Elm St., Montpelier, VT 05602; 802-828-3236.

• Virginia State Travel Service, 6 North Sixth St., Richmond, VA 23219; 804-786-4484.

• Washington State Department of Commerce and Economic Development, Travel Information, General Administration Building G-3, Olympia, WA 98504; 206-753-5630.

• West Virginia Travel Development Division, 1900 Washington St., Building 6, Room B553, State Capitol, Charleston, WV 25305; 304-348-2286.

• Wisconsin Department of Business Development, Division of Tourism, P.O. Box 7606, Madison, WI 53707; 608-266-2161 or 800-356-9508 or (in Wisconsin) 800-362-9566.

• Wyoming Travel Commission, Frank Norris, Jr., Travel Center, Cheyenne, WY 82002; 307-777-7777.

ELSEWHERE

• Caribbean Tourism Association, 20 E. 46th St., New York, NY 10017; 212-682-0435.

• Canadian Government Office of Tourism, 1251 Avenue of the Americas, New York, NY 10020; 212-757-4917.

• Mexican National Tourist Council, 405 Park Ave., New York, NY 10022; 212-755-7212.

BEFORE YOU GO...

Before you go tearing off to the sand, sun, and surf, take a tip from the Boy Scouts: Be prepared. Make sure you have all the paraphernalia you need to keep cool, comfy, warm, sheltered, shaded, chic, fed, and afloat. In other words, let's go shopping!

Suiting Up

What better way to begin a shopping spree than with the nucleus, the all-important core, the indispensable central character of everyone's beach wardrobe: le bathing suit? And what better spokesman for the subject than the internationally famous, suave, debonair swimsuit designer, Oleg Bikini? (Few people realize that Mr. Bikini is the true originator of the skimpy two-piece bathing suit that *bares* his name. Even fewer know that when the aforementioned garment went out of style, Mr. Bikini went underground and began designing suits under the pseudonym Eliot Freemont-One-Piece-Bathing-Suit.)

Mr. Bikini has kindly consented to dip into his collection and put together a pageant of his favorite bathing suits and bathing beauties — past and present — for this book.

Commentator: Mr. Bikini, we're ready to begin.

Mr. Bikini: Hoo-wee — ha! Lookit that one...practically naked. Oh my God! Did you see that? The back! The front! The side! Wait — there *is* no side. I know material is getting expensive, but this is ridiculous. I can't take it. I'd better — how you say — take this lying down.

Commentator: Mr. Bikini, please calm down. We're all waiting for the show.

Mr. Bikini: Oh. Yes, so sorry. I got carried away. Let's see.

Here we go...the 1800s. Can you imagine swimming in this little number? Heavy, cumbersome, but then in those days the key was modesty rather than style and comfort. People went to the sea to partake of the fresh air, perhaps to "bathe" (dunk), but hardly to swim.

Short trunks and overshirts were the rage for both sexes around 1915, especially the spiffy stripes worn by these two gay blades.

By the 1900s, more people knew how to swim. Suits became a bit more streamlined; the sailor look was appropriately popular.

The suit that "changed bathing to swimming" — as worn by the insanely popular circa 1920s Jantzen diving girl. Briefer than ever, and perhaps the first example of unisex clothing. Swimsuits continued to get briefer, more stylish, and practical. By the thirties halters, low backs, cutouts, stripes, and banners of color brightened up the beach scene.

When it became acceptable for men to bare their chests, the detachable "topper" was developed, a style that persisted into the forties.

(Jantzen)

REMOVING TAR AND OIL
You pick up your foot and there it is: a real-life remake of *The Blob.* With oil spills depositing the stuff destined for your car on your feet (and bathing suit bottom), there's no oil shortage at the beach. Many beaches and beach resorts supply bathers with paint thinner to remove the sticky stuff. But you might prefer to use your own, gentler remover: suntan or baby oil. It takes longer to remove the stuff, but is much better for your skin.

(Jantzen)

At long last...latex!...and lightweight, stretchy fabrics that made swimming easier, and figures better looking. Fabrics continued to become more lightweight and comfortable into the fifties and sixties, as experiments continued and technology boomed.

They became briefer, too. My beloved bikini burst on the scene and eventually was worn by almost everyone of every age, size, and sex. Of course, I may be a bit prejudiced, but others agree that the bikini is the best suit to wear if your waist and midriff are your strong points, and your legs your weak point. Those with out-of-proportion figures can buy the tops and bottoms separately for a perfect fit.

The baggies worn by surfers were a temporary abomination — and the less said about them the better!

Then along came the seventies, when the Olympic influence and the burgeoning fitness craze conspired to bring back the one-piece tank suit, or *maillot*...but with a twist: They were "skin suits" that fit like a suntan, clung like crazy, and felt like nothing during a swim. The real thing comes from Speedo, Arena, Head, and the Finals; fashion suits that have been racing-suit-inspired are sold everywhere. (They also have a built-in-bonus: They elongate the torso, especially if made in a solid, dark color; vertical side stripes nip in the waist even more.)

In other words, as in other types of design, form follows function. Today's suits are made of manmade fibers that move when you do, hold their shape, show off yours, and dry in a wink.

As to the future of the swimsuit, turn to *A Skinny-Dipper's Guide* and you'll see what gets my vote.

(Head Swimwear)

SUITING YOURSELF

Raised consciousness or not, men tend to have fewer "figure problems" than women. Most common is the over-sized gut, which you can always suck in at crucial moments. But just try sucking in your hips! The Shaping Up exercises that appear at the end of this section will help. If it's too late, keep these tips in mind when you shop for your new swimsuit.

- Early season pale skin, or skin that never seems to tan, looks best in pastel fabric with some shimmer and shine.
- Wavy stripes add curves to tiny figures.
- Shirring adds flattering curves to bosoms, waists, and bottoms.
- High-cut legs slim the thighs by adding the illusion of length.
- A busy design is distracting and makes a less-than-flat-as-a-board middle unnoticeable.
- Strapless styles are most practical on medium- or small-busted women. Choose a convertible halter with some underwiring if you're larger than average.
- Swimdresses with overskirts work wonders for thighs; some new ones have separate hold-you-in panties underneath.
- Bored with no-texture Lycra? Try the new textured suits introduced by Cole.

(Cole of California)

(Danskin)

(Healthtex)

KID STUFF

Hey kids... let mom and dad know you want to be cute and comfortable at the beach too.

The future diving champ is wearing a suit that's 94 percent cotton, 6 percent spandex.

111

Covering Up

Covering your head when you swim or sun serves several purposes: It keeps your brains from frying, keeps your hair from turning to old-mown hay, and keeps your hair from whipping your precious face to death. It's also a great way to express your personality (or someone else's), a means to exude that certain *je ne sais quoi,* and a way to attract an awful lot of attention.

JEEPERS PEEPERS

Sunglasses should do more than make you look cool, sexy, rich, or silly. They should protect your eyes and the delicate skin surrounding them from the harsh rays of the sun. Here's how to make sure they do, courtesy of eye-care experts and sunglass manufacturers like Foster Grant and Bausch and Lomb:

• Reflecting or mirrored lenses provide the best protection from the super-bright light at the beach.

• Gray-tinted lenses, which are the choice of the U.S. Air Force, offer maximum protection against ultraviolet and infrared rays. Brown and green lenses are nearly as good. Blue and purple, however fashionable, leave your eyes vulnerable to ultraviolet radiation; yellow, orange, and pink admit infrared rays.

• Polarized lenses reduce reflected glare from water and sand.

• Cheapie glasses have low-quality lenses, which can distort your vision, causing your brain and eye muscles to strain constantly. This can result in headache, neck pain, fatigue, and tension.

• Photochromic lenses that automatically darken in bright light and lighten in the shade don't offer enough protection at the beach, except on not so sunny days.

• Plastic lenses are lightweight, but scratch more easily than those made of glass.

• The shape of the frames you choose can flatter or detract from the shape of your face. (Foster Grant suggests you stick to the rule "opposites attract": a square face looks best in round or oval frames, a round face in square or rectangular frames.) For the most protection and comfort, make sure the frames are large enough to protect the entire eye area and that they don't rest on your cheeks.

• There are basically two things to remember about sunglass care:

  1. Clean sunglasses often by first rinsing them in clear water to remove sand and body salts that can scratch the lenses as you wipe them.
  2. Don't sit on them!

(Chuck DeLaney)

(Picture Collection Cooper-Hewitt Museum Library)

WHO'S THAT MAN BEHIND THOSE FOSTER GRANTS?
Maybe you remember the company's highly successful advertising campaign in 1966, in which the question "Isn't that _____ behind those Foster Grants?" was asked. (Woody Allen, Anthony Quinn, Jane Fonda, and Raquel Welch were among those who filled in the blank.) The man behind the company was Sam Foster, who began by making plastic haircombs, umbrella handles, and novelty items over 60 years ago. Ten years later he moved on to sunglasses, adopted injection molding of plastics to mass produce them, and the rest is history. Today, Foster Grant is the largest manufacturer of sunglasses in the world.

(Marianne Dickinson)

LIVING A SHELTERED LIFE

You can hang out by the beautiful sea longer if you protect yourself and your little ones from too much sun or wind.

Your basic beach umbrella may seem a little provincial in these days of sun and wind screens like those sold by Hammacher Schlemmer. The top one is polyester, costs about $60, and comes in bright yellow, orange, or blue, complete with carrying case — very 1980s.

The one on the bottom is a good old canvas wind screen in bright stripes; it rolls up for storage (and costs about $20).

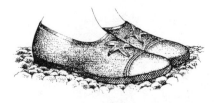

If you'll be visiting rocky or shell-laden shores, some sort of foot protection is a must. These famous Swim Sneaks (by Dorsay, 142 MacArthur Ave., Garfield, NJ 07026) have been foot-savers for years. Clear plastic "jellybean shoes" in bright colors serve the same purpose and are fashionable when worn in town.

A sweltering day on land can turn into a chilly day on the sea. Banish breezes with a Windbreaker-type jacket. This one, from O'Neill, is part of their *BreezeBreaker* line, which is made from thin neoprene (wetsuit material) in the body, and light, loose waterproof material elsewhere; snug wristbands keep water out. It's also great for windsurfing, water-skiing, and other active sports — and looks good enough for just plain hanging around.

The sun and wind aren't the only elements that will make you want to cover up.

There's wetness, for one. But rain won't dampen your spirits if you're prepared with water-repellent or waterproof togs. Simple, back-to-basics stuff like a poncho and parka are classics. Banish boredom along with wetness with the new rain-shower chic bright colors.

For dry but chilly days or hours, soft, cozy jogging/sweatsuits are ideal. (You might even be inspired to jog.) And the wrapped look is always stylish (see box).

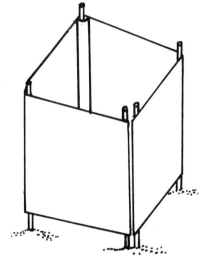

— 40″ — — 40″ — — 40″ —

Fold and stitch 3/4″ casing   **Stitch casings**   **1″ hem**

DO-IT-YOURSELF CABANA

Make your own ultimate shelter — a portable cabaña to open up and use as a wind and sun screen; to close up and use as a private dressing room.

Materials Needed: Four ¾-inch dowels, 6 feet long each; one heavy cotton or canvas panel, measuring 62 by 122 inches, and two measuring 1½ by 62 inches (for casing strips); matching thread.

1. Turn under ¼ inch and then ¾ inch to stitch hem along the long sides of the panel and short ends of the casing strips.

2. Form a casing at each short end of the panel the same way you stitched the hem.

3. Fold under and stitch the remaining (long) raw edges of the casing strips. Stitch as shown to the panel, forming three equal-sized sections.

4. Slip in the dowels and your cabaña is complete.

WRAP IT UP

A plain rectangular piece of cloth, or a few, could be the basis for the only beach cover-up you'll need. It can be versatile, too. Experiment and invent your own techniques. Add a safety pin or two for security; a flower or decorative jewelry pin for style and variety.

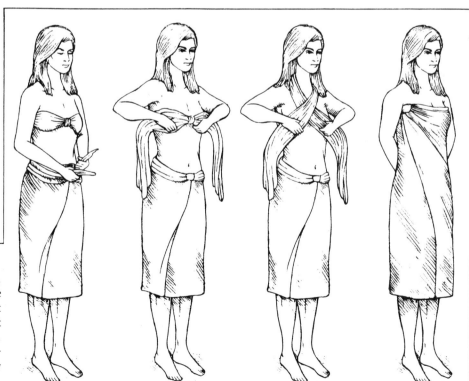

Wrap a skirt... a strapless top... a halter top... or a Dorothy Lamour sarong.

115

Eating Out

Nothing in the world stimulates the appetite like fresh air, especially salt air. Beach picnics can be as sumptuous or as simple as you like; just about everything tastes terrific when it's served alfresco. At the beach, having enough to drink is extremely important since the sun and activity take their toll in body fluids. But there are a few special considerations when planning and packing outdoor meals.

For ideas about gathering, catching, and preparing food right on the beach, see BEACH FEASTS, *Playing Around.*

FOOD

- Choose food that suits the climate. Hot weather calls for light foods such as fruits, vegetables, cold soups, and lean protein sources (like fish). Chilly weather is the time for hot soups, meats, and heavy foods (like rich cheeses).
- Take great care with foods that require refrigeration. Egg-based foods (mayonnaise, custards, deviled eggs, egg or tuna salad), raw or cooked meats, and seafood must be well chilled (below 45°F) to avoid the potentially high risk of food poisoning. (An hour out of refrigeration is the maximum safe period.)
- Put well-chilled foods in insulated coolers — and keep them chilly with chemical ice packs or ice cubes in a plastic bag.
- Select an insulated cooler for lightness (Styrofoam is light and cheap) and effectiveness. (Thermos and Scotch make coolers that keep foods cold for a long time.)
- Use durable, lightweight, leakproof containers.
- Put bruisable fruits and crushable items in rigid containers.
- To minimize the need for lots of utensils and for ease in serving, prepare "finger foods" and single portions.
- Cold dishes need extra seasoning.

(Coleman)

BEVERAGES

- Choose beverages well and bring plenty of them.
- Alcoholic beverages are very popular at beaches (who can resist a fresh banana daiquiri by the Caribbean?), but keep in mind that alcohol plus sunshine usually equals a very dizzy head.
- Sparkling water or seltzer with a slice of lime is terrific as a thirst-quencher and has no calories.
- Try iced mint, rose hip, or hibiscus tea instead of regular tea.
- Lemonade is a favorite refresher, especially if it is not too sweet. Dilute fruit juices with club soda.
- Choose chillable light wines over full-bodied reds for summer picnics.
- Having a beer-lover's beach party? Check into purchasing brew by the keg — there's plenty to go around, it's cheaper, and there are no bottles and cans to worry about.

S'MORES

What's a beach house without a barbecue? And what's a barbecue without s'mores? S'mores are delicious, have no nutritive value whatsoever (but lots of calories), and boy do you deserve them after slaving over a hot pit all afternoon. You'll need thin plain cookies — graham crackers are best — a Hershey bar, and marshmallows. Roast the marshmallows over the dying coals and place one on a cookie. Put a square of chocolate over it and top with another cookie, sandwich style. Bite. Chew. Smile. Ready for s'more?

BEYOND BOLOGNA

As you may have gathered, beach fare doesn't have to be the same old boring bologna sandwiches and tepid Kool-Aid. Pick up a copy of *The Picnic Gourmet* by Joan Hemingway and Connie Maricich (Vintage Books, 1978; paper). Check out the menu for their Cuban-Style Boating Picnic (just like Papa Hemingway used to eat):

Gin with fresh coconut juice
Spanish peasant soup
Marinated oysters
Morro crab with mayonnaise
Cuban potato salad
Cuban stuffed avocados
Guava fruit with cream cheese
Meringue torte
Wine, beer

— From *The Picnic Gourmet,* by Joan Hemingway and Connie Maricich. Copyright ©1975, 1977 by Joan Hemingway and Connie Maricich. Reprinted by permission of Random House, Inc.

HOW TO BLOW (UP) YOUR COOL(ER)

Definitely in the what-a-great-idea department is the *Nautilus,* the world's first inflatable ice chest. It comes in several sizes, from seven quarts (about $15 — holds seven beverage cans plus ice cubes) to forty-eight quarts (under $30). Use it also to protect cameras, binoculars, and other delicate gear from bumps, becoming wet, even from sinking when you're in a boat. When the beach party's over, deflate and fold it up for easy carrying.

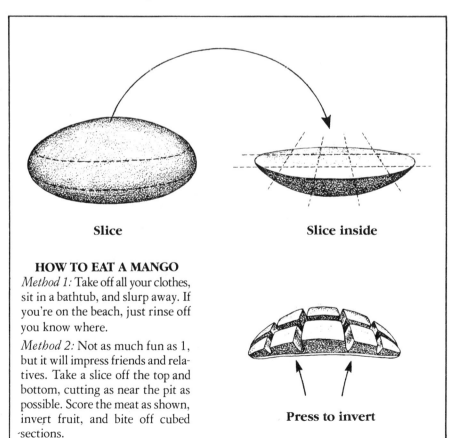

Slice

Slice inside

HOW TO EAT A MANGO

Method 1: Take off all your clothes, sit in a bathtub, and slurp away. If you're on the beach, just rinse off you know where.

Method 2: Not as much fun as 1, but it will impress friends and relatives. Take a slice off the top and bottom, cutting as near the pit as possible. Score the meat as shown, invert fruit, and bite off cubed sections.

Press to invert

SURE-FIRE THIRST QUENCHER

It may sound strange, but lemonade's tartness is what makes it so thirst-quenching. So why not vinegar? James Beard suggests this refreshing and cooling drink: Mix a spoonful of fruit vinegar (such as raspberry, strawberry, or black currant) with sparkling water; add ice if there's some around. Fruit vinegars are "new" on the market (our grandmothers used to make them) and also add a wake-up tang to summertime desserts such as cold poached fruit. Put a bottle in your picnic basket.

Getting Carried Away

Neat practical tricks for packing up all your cares and woes...and sunglasses, towels, combs, and reading matter.

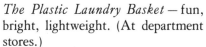

The Canvas Tote — a classic for boaters and beachers alike. L.L. Bean, Inc., Freeport, ME 04033, has them in two sizes with contrasting trim (for about $10).

Fishing Gear Bag — with compartments for everything, waterproof lining too. (At fishing and hunting supply stores.)

The Plastic Laundry Basket — fun, bright, lightweight. (At department stores.)

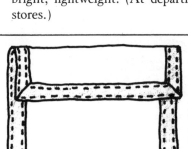

The Water Wallet — the place to stash your cash. Drop it in the brink; it floats and keeps your mad money dry. (At marine supply stores, and Sage Mart, 22 Ridge Rd., Bethel, CT 06801; $2.98.)

LeSportsac — according to some, le best of all. Lightweight, sturdy, damp-proof, good-looking, chic, versatile: The big ones fold down to practically nothing and slip into their own little zippered carrying cases that you can also use alone for small-time schlepping. Though they don't have the snob appeal of the original LeSportsac, the imitations have all the remaining attributes, except for the high price tag.

And then there's always the minimalist school — the old throw-whatever-you'll-be- needing -into-a- towel- or- blanket-and-roll-it-up-into-a-log technique. (Popular with the roughing-it crowd.)

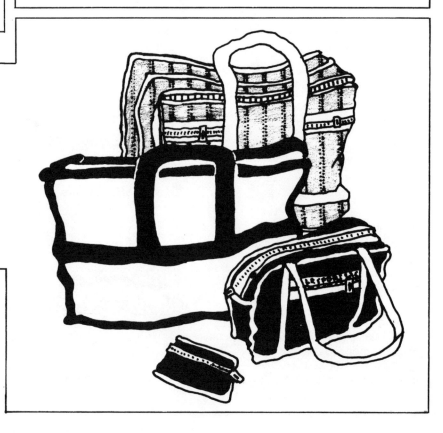

Settling Down

If you've reached the point when it's time to throw away your old army blanket/bedspread/tacky little towel for something with a bit more panache, now's your chance. Here's how to get comfy in style:

Woven straw mats are lightweight, roll up into neat little bundles, add a touch of the well-designed East, and smell like new-mown hay when new.

An investment in beauty for the luxury lover is a handwoven cotton rug. Make it yourself or buy it in a craft store or home furnishings shop like Conran's in New York (mail-order address: 10 Cedar St., New Rochelle, NY 10801).

Beach-Quilt-in-a-Bag (Heritage Quilts, N.Y.) is a quilted beach blanket that absorbs water and repels sand. It comes with its own tote, which has enough room for more beach gear.

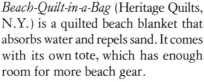

Pack 'n' Pad Tote from Sportsline serves several purposes — folded up, it's a cushion for hard surfaces and pebbly beaches or a tote to carry all your beach items; unfolded, it's a quilted mat for sunbathing comfort.

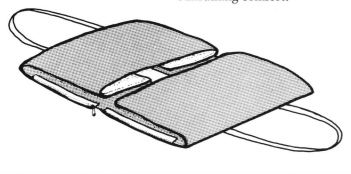

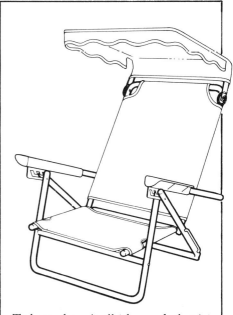

To keep above it all (the sand, that is) opt for a folding sand chair (this one by Duralite comes with its own canvas canopy or lounge (Duralite makes deluxe, redwood-slat models).

119

Going Wild

Being prepared holds special sway for those who succumb to the call of the wild and prefer their beaches as undeveloped as possible. It may be just you — and/or you and your companions — against the world.

Deluxe campgrounds or "wilderness outfitters" and trip packagers generally supply you with varying amounts of necessary gear — tents, sleeping bags, boats, and maybe more. But if you're supplying these items yourself, remember that the space and energy crunch doesn't necessarily disappear when you hit the great outdoors. You've got to transport everything with you. Efficiency and being unencumbered are the key rules for campers and wilderness trekkers.

GIMME SHELTER

Keep your home away from home as simple as you can stand it. You've a wide variety these days; depending upon your needs, priorities, and bank account, choose from:

The sleeping bag is for those who don't mind the bugs or the possibility of becoming drenched (from under $50).

A simple tarp, tube tent, or fly sheet also provides minimum protection (under $50).

A one-person shelter adds bye-bye-bugs netting, waterproof nylon; but it can definitely cramp your style (about $100).

The simple A-frame tent is low-cost and easy to stake down. Front and side eaves protect against weather and condensation build up and allow for screened walls (about $100).

FOR THE MAIL-ORDER CAMPER

Three of the best-known mail-order suppliers of outdoor and sports gear are listed below. Their catalogs will provide a treasure trove of up-to-date information that will help your selection.

• *L.L. Bean, Inc.,* Freeport, ME 04033.
• *Eastern Mountain Sports, Inc.,* Vose Farm Rd., Peterborough, NH 03458.
• *Eddie Bauer,* Third and Virginia, Seattle, WA 98134.

(The North Face)

Family-size tent sleeps four, has room enough to stand up, and extra "luxuries" such as lots of ventilation, handy inside pockets, and privacy curtain ($300 and up).

For those who prefer to rough it in more comfort, there are new "flyweight" on-the-ground tent-trailers, designed to be towed by compact cars. One, the *Apache Cub* (made by the Vesley Company, 2101 N. Lapeer Rd., Lapeer, MI 48446), is a combination boat, tent, and trailer.

One beach camping nuisance is staking down in the shifting sand. Space-age dome or arc tents are completely self-supporting and require no stakes or ropes for stability (except in wind). So they're ideal for seaside pitching; once erected, they can even be lifted and repositioned. (Prices start at about $100.)

[Moss Design]

NICETIES AND NECESSITIES

There are oodles of containers for holding, carrying, and dispensing water:

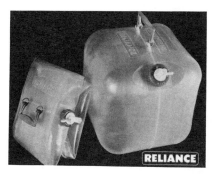

Some collapse when empty to save space.

For sissy tough guys, there are even portable sinks...

A camper's best friend may be a knife, and the undisputed champ is the Swiss Army Knife. These knives come with a lifetime guarantee and won't rust. Depending upon the model you choose, you can have several size cutting blades, screwdriver, corkscrew, can opener, scissors, toothpick, tweezers, saw blade, fish scaler, metric rule, and magnifier. It's the only knife you'll ever need.

Others are on wheels to save your strength and have spigots for easy use.

...and portable chemical toilets.

121

Beauty and the Beach

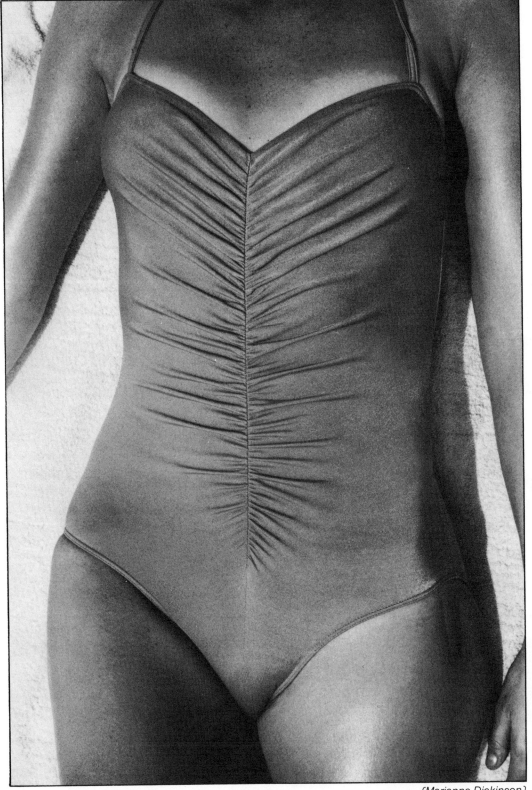

(Marianne Dickinson)

TAN, DON'T BURN

Imagine lounging lazily under the soothing golden light. You feel that familiar warm, almost erotic glow as the sun beats down on your clean, bare skin. You feel one with nature as your troubles melt away and you begin to drowse, perhaps dreaming of how beautiful and healthy you'll look with a deep rich tan, symbol of the good life and your most precious souvenir of a perfect vacation. Mmm . . .

WAKE UP, SUN WORSHIPER! Your days are numbered and your golden dreams may become a nightmare. Heat, wind, and water (whether salt, fresh, or chlorinated) all contribute to dry, damaged skin and hair. Dermatologists unanimously agree that the sun's ultraviolet rays are the single biggest cause of premature aging. The sun, in small doses, does do some good: It helps control acne, manufactures vitamin D, relaxes you, and improves your appearance overall. But these benefits are only temporary. Ironically, the very deep delicious tan color and taut feeling that make you look so good today will eventually damage the inner layer of your skin causing sags, bags, and wrinkles. The effects of too much of a good thing are temporary and immediate (sunburn and possibly sun poisoning) as well as permanent and delayed (wrinkles and possibly skin cancer).

You've probably been cautioned a hundred times before; and no self-respecting beach aficionado is going to stay inside or sit swathed in Victorian garb. In order to have your cake and eat it too, *protection*—not *abstention*—is the key.

Yes, Virginia, There Is a Safe Tan

The first step on the road to golden tandom is to know your skin and choose a suntan product accordingly. The new SPF (Sun Protection Factor) ratings make this easier: the higher the number, the more protection from the sun's burning rays. A 2 rating means you can stay in the sun twice as long without burning as you would with no protection, a 4 means four times, and so on. The highest rating is 15. In general, the lighter your skin, the higher SPF rating you require. Even if you have naturally dark skin, you should use *some* protection.

When sunbathing, take into account other factors—for example, the rays reflected off light-colored surfaces such as sand, water, and cement, which increase the sun's power. Water also allows ultraviolet rays to penetrate. Remember, the sun is at its strongest at midday, at higher altitudes, and close to the equator.

Tan gradually, slowly increasing the exposure time each day. (The length of time depends upon your skin type, the strength of the sun, and the SPF rating you use.) This allows your skin cells to produce *melanin,* the pigment that makes you look tan and is responsible for protecting you against the burning rays. This natural defense mechanism takes time to develop. A burn does not turn into a tan; that's a separate process. Follow the rule: Never spend more than two hours directly in the sun. (A slowly acquired tan lasts longer, too.)

A tan is a natural form of sunburn protection; but it's not perfect. As your tan deepens, you can lower your SPF rating, but don't go without any protection at all. On some sensitive areas—face, lips, nose, shoulders—you may want to stick with a higher rating.

For best results, take this tip from Dr. Stephen Kurtin, noted New York dermatologist: Apply a suntan product (preferably one containing PABA) the night before you plan to be in the sun to get the most out of it. Don't forget to reapply frequently, especially if you swim or perspire. Nothing lasts forever.

Avoid using products such as perfumes, deodorant soaps, medicated makeups, and creams; these can cause light sensitivity. Other causes of mysterious blotches and rashes after sunbathing are the Pill, tranquilizers, and antibiotics.

- To prevent the Hotlips Syndrome, apply good old petroleum jelly, or one of the specially formulated lip balms with sunscreen. APO Lip-Seal is one that has PABA in a wax base that resists lick-off, yet doesn't feel sticky. It's part of a line of outdoor cosmetics that includes APO Suntan Lotion and Sun Cream for sun worshipers, Wind-Guard for sailors, Frost-Guard for scuba divers, and Insect-Guard for picnickers. (From Reyco-Reynes Products, Inc., P.O. Box 1203, Sonoma, CA 95476.)

- Although the sun helps a bad complexion, the heat can aggravate it and so can greasy suntan lotions. Don't skip your face—look for greaseless preparations, such as Coppertone's For Faces Only.

- Sun care doesn't stop when you roll up your beach mat and head for home. Shower or bathe to remove oil, sweat, dirt, sand, salt, and chemicals. Apply a light moisturizing after-sun lotion, preferably while your skin is still slightly damp. Those containing aloe, a natural burn remedy, are particularly soothing.

- Try these remedies if you've really overdone it:
  - Bathe in lukewarm water and laundry starch or oatmeal.
  - Apply compresses of witch hazel, white vinegar, or tea diluted with cool water.
  - Soothe especially red areas by applying wet tea bags directly.

HAIR TODAY, STRAW TOMORROW?

To help prevent the elements from drying out your crowning glory, Jules Medina of Sunshine Studio hair salon in New York suggests you apply a protective coating. Your usual hair conditioner will do, as will plain baby oil or even your suntan lotion in a pinch. Leave it on while you're at the beach (pull back your hair, braid it, or go with the "wet look"); then wash as usual when you get home.

- Did you know that you may react differently to the sun during different times of your life? Studies have shown that:

You're most resistant to sunburn between these years:

3½-5
13-17
50-60

You're most vulnerable to sunburn between these years:

6-8
25-30 (women)
30-35 (men)

- The latest wrinkle in skin care is that too much sun at a very young age may be the most harmful kind of exposure. Norman Orentreich, M.D., clinical associate professor of dermatology at New York University School of Medicine, says that because more cells reproduce and do so faster, the chance that sun-damaged abnormal cells will replicate themselves is greater. (In fact, young experimental mice exposed to the same amount of sunlight as their elders produced more skin cancer.) So slather children frequently with a strong sunscreen. Keep the very young out of strong sun altogether to avoid subjecting their tiny systems to heat and sunstroke.

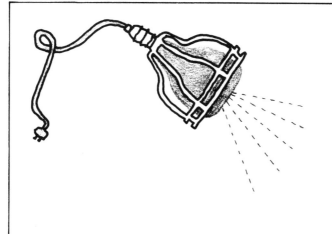

MAN-MADE TANS

It seems like such a good idea. You walk into a tanning salon and get a head start on or prolong your tan. Don't. The manmade ultraviolet rays are just as dangerous as the real thing, and the strength of the bulbs can vary widely so it's difficult to say how much is enough. Forget home suntan lamps and reflectors, too; dermatologists have nightmares about them.

Shaping Up

One of the most important preparatory steps you can take before zipping off to beachland is to see that your physical self is in tiptop working order. The snazziest swimsuit and the most perfect tan can't disguise that candy bar middle or those office-worker hips. Do you dread that crucial moment — The Unveiling — because it reveals a body you wished belonged to someone else?

Unfortunately, there's no substitute for staying in reasonably good shape all the time; going on a crash make-over program won't slim you down or tone you up enough to render you a perfect 10 if your present rating's a 3. So incorporate the following exercises into a regular fitness regime. These are killers, but they work. Repeat each at least 10 times (on each side, if applicable). If you're really tough, gradually work up to 100 repeats. Do these exercises coupled with a sensible diet if you need to lose weight and no one will dare call you a 97-pound weakling or a baby whale. (Consumer Guide's *Rating the Diets,* published by New American Library, 1979, separates the fat from the fads.)

Extra Tips: You can do these exercises at the beach, and take advantage of the wide open spaces and fresh air. Running and swimming are both excellent all-round slimmers and trimmers. You can enjoy them along with the other sports and activities found in *Taking the Plunge* and *Playing Around.*

(Marianne Dickinson)

1. KARATE PUSH-UPS (for arms, chest): With legs apart, do pushups by bending at waist, lowering your torso and scooting forward with straight body. Raise up and return to starting position.

2. MOUNTAIN CLIMBERS (all-over toning): In squatting position, "climb" in place by bending and straightening alternate legs.

3. SQUAT THRUSTS (all-over toner): Squat down and thrust both legs out in back. Bring legs back under you and return to standing position.

4. SIDE BENDERS (for waist, "love handles," front and back of thighs, sides): Bend from side to side, touching elbows to floor next to your hip.

5. FENCER'S LUNGE (for front and back of thighs, buttocks): Lunge forward to alternate sides, dipping down as far as possible.

6. SIDE LEG RAISES: Raise top leg the same number of times on each side. May be done as 4 variations, each stressing slightly different muscles of the inner and outer thigh, buttocks, and hip: (1) foot flexed, toes facing downward, body rolled forward slightly; (2) foot flexed, toes forward; (3) foot pointed; (4) top leg out at 45-degree angle, foot flexed.

7. FIRE HYDRANTS (for thighs, hips, buttocks): Lift bent leg out to side, hip level. Straighten, keeping leg high; then bend and return to starting position.

8. LEG RAISES (abdomen and thigh toner): Palms down and under buttocks, bend knees into chest while raising lower body up and over, bringing knees to nose and buttocks off the floor. Straighten and lower legs to floor slowly.

9. CRUNCHES (for abdomen, back, thighs, buttocks): Touch alternate knee to opposite elbow, never letting legs touch ground. Variation: Raise both knees simultaneously.

10. MORE CRUNCHES: Same as before, but extend arms in front, sit up as knee comes up, to balance on buttocks.

(Club Med)

Tips for Travelers

HOW TO SAVE MONEY

- Plan ahead.
- Choose your vacation destination carefully. You tend to spend more money when you're displeased with a resort.
- Go off season. You pay half price or less; it's less crowded then too, and service may be more personal.
- Don't drive. If you do, stay closer to home, travel light, and send for this free leaflet: "How to Save Gasoline and Money" (Public Affairs, Office of Public Inquiries, U.S. Department of Energy, Room GA-343, Washington, DC 20585).
- Don't travel alone; singles, unfortunately, get the price shaft.
- Eat like a native.
- Investigate package deals; they're a price advantage due to volume buying and booking.
- The *National Directory of Budget Motels* edited by Raymond Carlson (Pilot Books, 1980; paper) lists low-cost accommodations in 48 states.
- Consider camping out (in a tent, not a gas-guzzling RV).
- If you're exchanging money, find out the current exchange rate in advance and get foreign currency at banks, which give the best rates.

PUCKER UP FOR SAFETY
Going to the beach means being near the water. Take a tip from this conscientious couple: Be sure you're prepared for safety by practicing preventive mouth-to-mouth resuscitation, every chance you get. Remember, it could save a life (or at least a relationship).

HOW NOT TO FORGET ANYTHING

Use this check list, or make your own.
- ☐ Bag for beach-found treasures
- ☐ Bathing suit
- ☐ Blanket
- ☐ Camera and film
- ☐ Chair
- ☐ First-aid kit
- ☐ Drinks
- ☐ Food
- ☐ Hat
- ☐ Mat
- ☐ Pail and shovel
- ☐ Q-Tips
- ☐ Radio
- ☐ Reading material
- ☐ Sketchbook and pencil
- ☐ Tissues
- ☐ Suntan lotion
- ☐ Toys for kids of all ages
- ☐ Towel
- ☐ Sunglasses
- ☐ Umbrella
- ☐ Windbreaker

(And of course, *The Beach Book!*)

SPECIAL ITEMS
Bathing cap
Goggles
Nose clip
Sports equipment (fins, mask, snorkel, inflatable boat, binoculars)
Swim shoes

(Charles McShan)

TAKING THE PLUNGE...

Safe fun in the sun. The mind of a lifeguard. Swim like a fish. Ride a wave — lying down, or standing up. Water-ski with the pros. Visit the underwater world of Jacques Cousteau. Shiver your timbers. Somersaults and porpoise dives...ballet legs and doilies...swan dives and forward pikes...dribble in deep water. It's all here, so come on in, the water's fine.

(Bob Smith, Evening Outlook)

Safety First

Yes, the water is there for your enjoyment, but if you want to make sure that all your beach days have happy endings, you'd better play according to its rules. Water accidents are unpleasant to think about, but they do happen. Did you know that about 8000 people drown each year? (That's about one every hour.) And that *over half* of the victims didn't expect to be in the water? Even if you don't plan to take the plunge, peruse these pointers. Most rely on good old common sense, so remember to pack that, along with your bathing suit. For more information, pick up one of the several books on this subject that are published by the American National Red Cross.

TEN RULES FOR EVERYONE

1. Never go in the water when you're alone. There should be at least one other swimmer near at all times, preferably a qualified lifeguard.

2. Learn and teach your beach companions how to swim or tread water. At least learn "drown-proofing" or "survival floating," techniques that even nonswimmers can learn and that enable you to stay afloat for a long period of time while using very little energy. *(See Common Emergencies, next page.)*

3. *Look before you leap.* Check the depth before diving; enter unfamiliar water cautiously, feet first, looking for rocks, holes, and strong currents. Lifeguards can advise you of these conditions and of jellyfish and sandbars, too. Stay clear of jetties, pier pilings, and so on — and be aware of any currents that may cause you to drift.

4. Obey posted rules and regulations; they're put there for your benefit, not to ruin your fun.

5. Don't overestimate your ability, a common mistake of weekend swimmers and at the start of a vacation or swimming season.

6. Keep a constant eye on children; the very young should wear flotation jackets at all times.

7. There's no evidence that a heavy meal causes cramps, but you'll be mighty uncomfortable swimming strenuously if your stomach is distended with food. Light meals are fine before a swim.

8. Don't jump into the water if you're overheated. A plunge in the brine may seem just the ticket after a jog or volleyball game, but the sudden temperature change can cause cramps.

9. Nearly half of all drowning victims have significant levels of drugs in their systems, so avoid alcohol or other drugs when near the water.

10. No midnight dips unless the area is properly lighted and/or a buddy or lifeguard is around.

(Florida News Bureau)

Nonswimming beach tots should wear flotation devices, but not this one, which is only safe in water as deep as you see here -- in other words, on dry land. The best type is the one made by Elton Corporation (Rochester, NY). By the way, most experts frown upon teaching under-four-year-olds to swim because they lack the muscular control to lift their heads out of the water to inhale. They're also quite susceptible to infections that can be spread in pool water. They can, however, be taught to enjoy the water and thus be better prepared to learn how to swim when the time comes.

COMMON EMERGENCIES AND HOW TO HANDLE THEM

In all emergencies, keep cool so you can think clearly. Save your panic for later, when it's all over.

1. Never attempt a swimming rescue by yourself; even those trained in life-saving make solo rescue attempts only as a last resort. If you're well intentioned but inexperienced, the danger of a double drowning increases. Anyone — even nonswimmers — can save a life by extending a pole, branch, rope, board, towel, or article of clothing for the victim to grab. As you pull someone in to safety, stay low to the ground, so you don't get pulled in, too. If the person is too far away for that technique, toss anything that floats — a wooden board, life preserver, a kickboard, a life jacket — for support until help comes.

2. In case of a submerging, seconds count. Once the victim is out of the water, check his or her breathing and pulse and begin to perform cardiopulmonary resuscitation immediately, if necessary. (Learn how at the Red Cross or Y.)

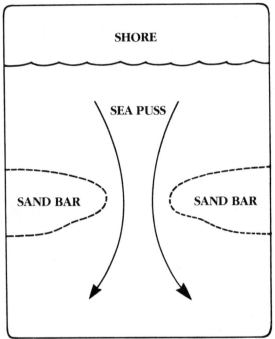

A rip current is formed when the water breaks through a sandbar.

3. A muscle cramp gets you into trouble usually because you panic and become exhausted, not because it restricts your movement. You can often prevent a full-scale cramp by heeding the warning twinge that precedes it; stretch the muscle and knead it with your thumb until it eases up.

4. If you should become caught in the neck of a *rip tide* (a long, narrow, seaward-moving streak of water; also known as sea puss or rip current), don't attempt to swim directly back to shore. Instead, swim parallel to the shore (and thus, perpendicular to and out of the rip) or let the rip carry you out past the breaking waves. Once you're free of the current you can swim back to shore.

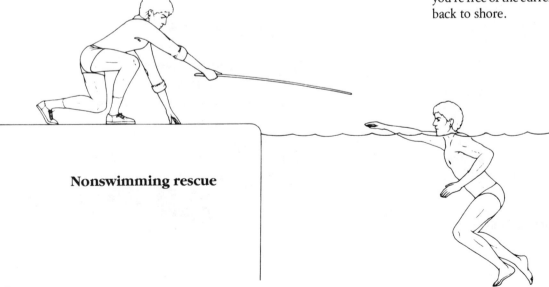

Nonswimming rescue

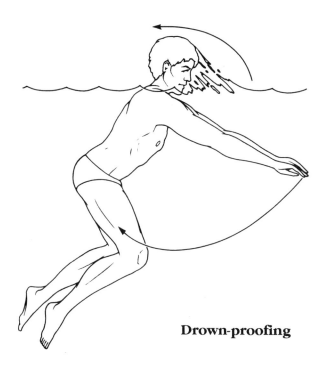

Drown-proofing

5. If you get caught in a river current, swim diagonally across. You'll end up farther downstream, but on dry land.

6. If you should become entangled in a pocket of weeds, extricate yourself by swimming slowly in the same direction as the stems flow.

7. If you're in a boating accident or some other mishap that leaves you far from shore or if you become tired or winded or experience a muscle cramp, do "survival floating."

To begin, take a deep breath, then lower your face into the water and relax your body as much as possible as you assume a vertical floating position. When you need more air, exhale through your nose and mouth as you press your arms downward or bring your legs together and raise your head. Inhale, then go limp again into the face down floating position. Continue until help comes or the cramp subsides.

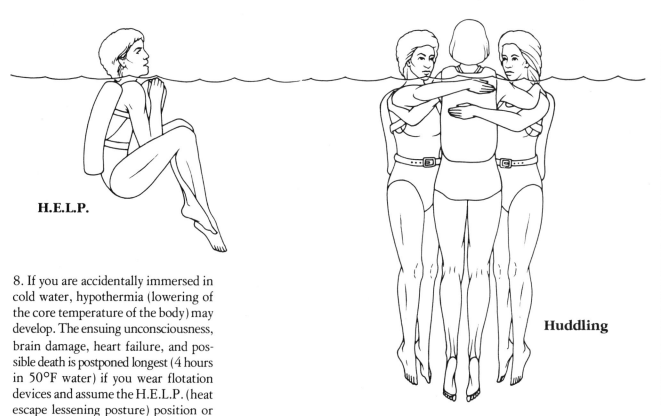

H.E.L.P.

Huddling

8. If you are accidentally immersed in cold water, hypothermia (lowering of the core temperature of the body) may develop. The ensuing unconsciousness, brain damage, heart failure, and possible death is postponed longest (4 hours in 50°F water) if you wear flotation devices and assume the H.E.L.P. (heat escape lessening posture) position or huddle together in a group.

THE LIFE-SAVING PATROL
by Gustave Kobbé

One of the chief charms to me about a life-saver is the fact of his usually being utterly unconscious that he is a hero. If you ask him why he is in the service, he will probably tell you that he has lived all his life along the shore, fishes in the summer, and finds life-saving the best means of making a living in winter. Heroism indeed! — you will say — when the chief attraction of his calling to him seems the regularity with which payday comes along.

But there are some occupations which are in themselves heroic: and you can't mention a calling which involves shoving a boat's nose into salt-water that hasn't a touch certainly of the picturesque and romantic and generally of the heroic about it... There is something heroic even about the boat itself. How small, how frail it seems compared with each successive breaker that curves and bursts into a cataract as it nears shore. Yet life-savers launch it fearlessly upon that vast contumescence of wind and sea. Now it rises seemingly upon a mountain, now it plunges into an abyss. The watchers ashore hold their breath. Will it ever reappear? Yes, there it rises upon the succeeding breaker, kept head on to the sea only by the desperate strength of the crew. Will it be pitch-poled, or thrown on its beam-ends? Will that breaker whose white crest curves almost over it burst and fill it? Somehow it seems to live — live and move with the strength of its heroic crew.

— from a nineteenth-century newspaper

THIS PLACE IS ROMANTIC

LIFE GUARD

BUT LITTLE THINGS DRIVE ME FRANTIC

C-20

© C. T. B CO.

81 Life Guards on Duty at the Beach, Atlantic City, N. J.

7A-H3503

(Al De Matteo)

In the Swim

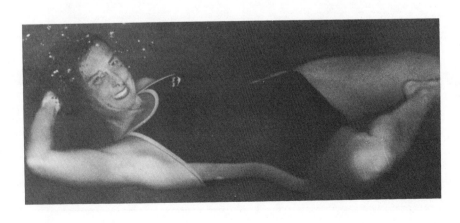

An Interview with Esther Mermaid, the 2000-Year-Old Swimmer

Interviewer: This is the first interview wherein you've revealed your true age. Why haven't you stepped forward before?

Esther Mermaid: Because I compete in the Masters Swim Program, which is divided into age groups, and there's no 2000-years-and-up category. But since I've just published a book on swimming, I figure I need all the publicity I can get.

Q: Is Esther Mermaid your real name?

A: Of course not; it's Jane Katz. The Mermaid bit was my agent's idea.

Q: You hold several national records. To what do you attribute your ability?

A: After swimming for 2000 years, you get pretty good.

Q: Are you really 2000 years old? Can you prove it?

A: Well, no...my birth certificate was lost in the Great Flood.

Q: You don't look a day over 18. What's your secret?

A: Swimming, dummy! Water keeps you young. Have you ever heard of Ponce de Leon and the Fountain of Youth? Poncey, we called him...now there was a nice guy, but he didn't realize that you can't just drink the stuff, you have to paddle around in it too.

Q: Isn't all that just a myth?

A: Listen, have you ever seen a whale visit Clairol for a touch-up? Do sharks sleep with their teeth in a glass on the night table? Do babies need face lifts? No, and they don't wear bifocals, either. That's because they've been floating around for nine months in —

Q: Water?

A: You got it, buddy. The longer you're out of the womb, the older and tireder you get, right?

Q: I never thought about it that way. Tell me, you must remember some great moments in swimming history.

A: Oh, yes. On Atlantis, where I was born, we invented swimming by imitating the animals and hair styles — the doggie paddle, the frog kick, the dolphin kick, the swan dive, the flip turn. The big mistake was the butterfly. We were all lying around drinking one night, and some joker says, "Hey here's a good one no one will be able to do. Let's call it the butterfly." Get it? Butterflies can't swim! Only the world took it seriously, and perfectly sane people have been trying to learn this ridiculous stroke ever since.

Q: Are there any other reasons to swim regularly?

A: Well, seeing as how this is a book on beaches, I'd better point out that it's a good idea for beach lovers to swim well since they'll be near all that water.

Q: Any other reasons?

A: It helps you lose or maintain your weight. For one thing, you can't eat while you're swimming. (Cheesecake is particularly difficult.) And you burn up about 500 calories in an hour of steady swimming. The major muscle groups are used in swimming the various strokes, so it's an excellent aerobic exercise that also whittles the waist, tones the hips, and it does wonderful things for your upper body, too.

Q: I'll say [admiringly]. How about giving us some advice on how to swim better.

A: Be glad to. Just turn the page.

HOW TO SWIM LIKE A FISH

So, you think you know how to swim. You probably do — according to a Nielsen survey, nearly half the population of this country swims regularly. But do you know how to swim *well*? Does more water end up around the pool than in it after you've been swimming? Do you look more like Englebert Eggbeater than Mark Spitz? Do eight-year-olds beat you to the other side of the pool? Can you *barely make it* to the other side of the pool? After you give the butterfly your best shot do observers compliment your sidestroke? Even if humans really can't swim exactly like fish, you *can* clean up your act.

The Art of Swimming Better

Think of swimming as a performing art, like dance. Aim for a smooth, graceful, rhythmic, fluid motion, with no wasted effort. Don't fight the water, let its buoyancy work for you, so you can devote your energy toward swimming *through* water rather than trying to stay *on top* of it. The less splashing, the better.

In general, your *body position* should be elongated and streamlined. The water should be about hairline level, except when your head emerges to exhale during some strokes.

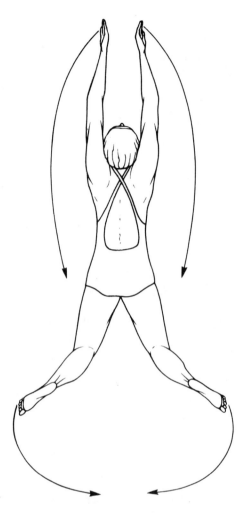

Breaststroke
Armstroke ends at about shoulder width
Inhale as head lifts naturally along with shoulders
New narrow whip kick

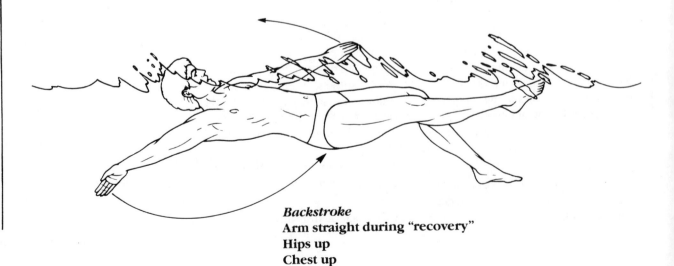

Backstroke
Arm straight during "recovery"
Hips up
Chest up

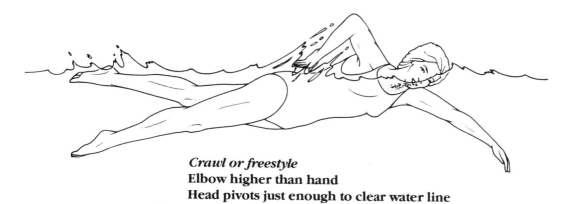

Crawl or freestyle
Elbow higher than hand
Head pivots just enough to clear water line

Your breathing should be rhythmic and constant. Inhale and exhale fully through your nose and mouth; exhaling through your nose is especially important in those strokes that require your head to be underwater to prevent water from entering your nose. In the crawl stroke, many people persist in practicing "Coney Island Breathing" — the head stays above water and whips from side to side during each armstroke. This is a very inefficient, tiring technique. Your head should pivot on your neck to the most comfortable side, at the point at which that arm is down and out of the way.

This next tip should shock most people: In most strokes, more power comes from the arms than from the legs. In the crawl stroke, the ratio is 80 percent arms and 20 percent legs; in the backstroke it's 75:25; the butterfly, 70:30; in breaststroke and sidestroke, 50:50. Arms are a more efficient source of power, too, especially in the long run, because leg muscles are larger and require more oxygen and energy.

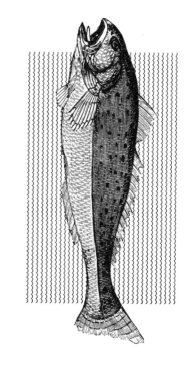

Your kicking should utilize the large muscles of the thigh and hip. In the flutter kick, used in the crawl and backstroke, just make the surface of the water "boil." Kicking water high into the air — Old Faithful style — is useless. Legs should be straight, but relaxed — not locked. Flex your ankles easily on the upbeat, and point your feet on the downbeat to make the most of the resultant whipping action.

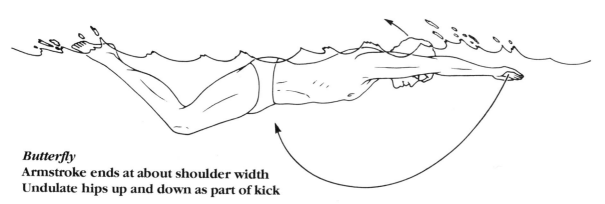

Butterfly
Armstroke ends at about shoulder width
Undulate hips up and down as part of kick

**Come on in
The water's fine.
I'll give you
Till I count to nine.
If you're not
In by then,
Guess I'll have to
Count to ten.**

— Old rhyme

OCEAN SWIMMING

The incessant barrage of waves rolling toward you means there's never a dull moment in ocean swimming. Jumping over, diving through, and riding with the sea swells makes for exhilarating sport; being slapped in the face or churned into mincemeat doesn't, but you can accentuate the positive and darn near eliminate the negative with a little practice, timing, and luck. Though the ocean may sometimes prove to be too rough or dangerous for even the strong swimmer (check with a lifeguard or other swimmers), challenging a moderately feisty surf is the most alluring element for many a beach goer. If you're a novice or a weak swimmer, you should, however, begin the baptism on a day (and at a beach) when the surf is relatively gentle.

How to Do It

The first step is to get you past the breakers. Wade out slowly, and as a wave comes toward you, turn sideways to offer it the least amount of body surface; bend your knees so you can give with the wave and absorb the shock. Next, jump when the wave hits you; raising your arms above your head and screaming "AAGGHH" usually helps.

Alternate walking and jumping until you get past the breakers — this usually happens just at the point at which the water is over your head, so start treading. Now face each wave and allow it to lift you up (a delirious sensation, and a natural progression from jumping). You can also rise up with the wave sideways, or facing toward the shore.

Though the waves usually break at about the same place, they may not. If it breaks early, you can dive through it. You can dive through even if it doesn't break, too.

Or you can cannonball through the wave if it breaks early and it's too forceful to dive through. In between waves, relax and tread or swim; you'll find the salinity makes you more buoyant than fresh water. But keep on the lookout for the next wave.

To get back to shore in one piece, repeat the wading/jumping process, gradually making your way to shallow water. Once you get to a certain point, run like crazy and hope the breakers don't catch you.

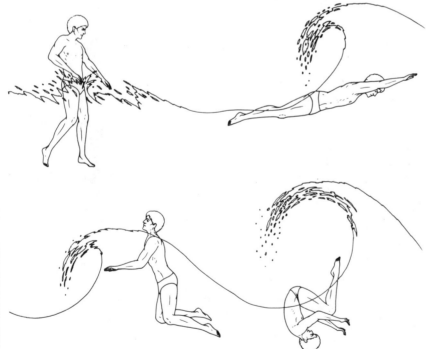

"Sink or swim, live or die, survive or perish."
— Daniel Webster

IT FLOATS

If you're serious about swimming, the number one participation sport in the U.S., get *Swimming for Total Fitness* by Jane Katz with Nancy Bruning (Doubleday/Dolphin, 1981) which teaches you how to swim, how to swim better, how to swim for fitness, and how to swim competitively.

Total Swimming, by Harvey S. Weiner (Simon and Schuster, 1980) delves into swimming and the inner self.

Stretching exercises are particularly pleasant when done on a beach. *Stretching* by Bob Anderson (Shelter Publications/ Random House, 1980) tells you why and how to incorporate stretching into any exercise program, with special sections on such beach sports as swimming, water polo, surfing. The author also publishes packets of stretching cards and stretching charts. (For more information, write: Stretching, Inc., Box 767, Palmer Lake, CO 80133.)

Swim Swim magazine is an entertaining source for fitness and Masters (adult competitive) swimmers alike. It features stories, how-to's, advice columns, pool listings, and workout groups, new products, articles on exercise and nutrition, exotic locations to swim, and portraits of swimming greats. Available by subscription, and published quarterly. *Swim Swim*, P.O. Box 5901, Santa Monica, CA 90405.

Surf's Up!

(David Seidman)

Swim out to meet the wave and immediately turn around to face the shore in ready position. As the wave swells and begins to *spill* (at its highest and steepest, just before it breaks), take a big breath in and begin to swim in the direction the wave is traveling. One good armstroke and one powerful kick should put your body parallel to the water's surface and moving along with the wave.

If your body's in the right position—and only experience and practice will let you know if this is so—drop your head and torso and bring your weight forward, arms extended overhead.

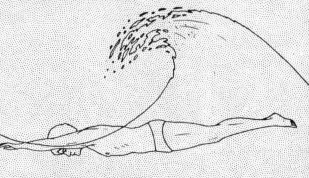

BODY SURFING

Body surfing has to be one of the purest sports around, with nothing between you and the powerful surge of the sea. It's full of thrills (and spills). Learning how to do it is usually simply a matter of monkey-see, monkey-do with a dash of trial and error mixed in. But as you experiment and practice, keep these pointers in mind.

The ideal conditions for body surfing are waves that are at least two feet high and that break softly at least thirty feet from a sandy, gently sloping shore. Avoid beaches with rocky or coral-rich bottoms, even if surfing in deep water. Don't even consider *sandbusters*—beaches where waves break perilously and thunderously close to shore.

How to Do It

Timing is of the essence in this sport: You must be in exactly the right place at the right time. Watch the surf for a few minutes to get an idea of the rhythm and timing of the breaking waves; check out where most of them break. Wade or swim out to about waist deep (unless the waves are breaking farther away from shore). Wait for a "good one"; when you spot it, go get it!

If you sense you're heading for a *wipeout* (an early and violent break in the wave that spells the end of your joy ride), drop one shoulder and roll out of the wave, or tuck yourself into a firm little ball to prevent injury during the inevitable tumble. Most waves simply slow down as they near the shore, and so will you. That's the time to get up on your feet, take a deep breath, compare notes with your fellow surfers, and go back for another round.

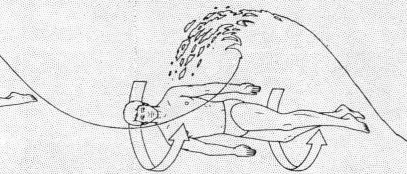

As you catch the wave and gain momentum, bring both arms down to your sides in a double armstroke for one final push. Then quickly raise your head and shoulders; your body will ride the wave to shore, just like a surfboard.

Once you've mastered the basic art of body surfing, experiment with variations such as corkscrewing, shown here. As you ride the wave, drop one shoulder and raise the opposite hip so your body revolves through the water.

ONE SURFER'S STORY

Interviewer: Why did you start surfing?

Tony Friedkin: I started body surfing in Malibu when I was six. I was board surfing at eleven. I'd sit on the pier at Malibu and just go "Ooh, ooh...that looks so unreal." And the whole life-style seemed so attractive to me: the beautiful people, the fantastic bodies, the chicks. It was such a magnificent energy and I was completely taken in by it.

Q: How has surfing changed over the years?

A: Well, surfing culture has evolved incredibly. I mean look at the phenomenon we're talking about. Jesus thought he was heavy walking on the water. Surfers dance on the water!

Q: How does one learn how to surf?

A: You pretty much have to learn on your own. There are people who will give you lessons, but most kids learn through an evolution from swimming to body surfing to watching board surfers and finally to trial and error with board surfing. Surfers associate with others of similar ability and they watch surfing films.

Q: What's the average career span of a surfer?

A: A surfer must have enormous physical ability—it's not just skill. We're talking about strength, stamina, and the ability to hold air in your lungs for long periods of time. Surfers start surfing at eleven years old. Their first peak is at about sixteen or seventeen after they've been surfing for around six years. Their style is fantastic. They're real hot, they're anxious, and their bodies are as flexible as rubber bands. Then they evolve for the next ten years or so until they're around twenty-five or twenty-six and that's when they develop a maturity that comes from experience and wave knowledge. That I think is the high point in a surfer's career. After about thirty, your style and knowledge are so well developed that your learning is relatively minimal.

By your late thirties getting up early in the morning, battling with the highways, and the crowd hassles are all factors that kind of deter you from keeping on surfing. Besides, you usually have other responsibilities in your life by now and it probably doesn't seem as appealing to live your life totally for surfing anymore.

Q: How does sex relate to surfing?

A: Well let's put it this way, there's probably only one thing that will stop a surfer from getting up early in the morning and going out to check the waves and that's being in bed with an incredible woman. Of all the forces that can pull a surfer away from the sea, a woman is probably the strongest. You're dealing with a sensual experience when you're surfing and you're dealing with a sensual experience when you have sex. On the other hand, after a great day of waves, you've got to come down, but you want to hold on to that wonderful sensation...

Tony Friedkin is a surfer and a photographer who lives in southern California, twelve blocks from the ocean. This interview originally appeared in longer form in the May/June 1978 issue of *WET* and is reprinted by permission. ©Wet Magazine 1978.

THE ABCS OF
SURF BOARDING

A. Paddle with your arms until the wave comes and lifts you.

B. Hold on to the edge of the board and pull yourself up to a kneeling position.

C. Stand up, knees bent, and use your arms to help you balance. Usually the left foot is in front, but stand whichever way is most comfortable. (If you fall, try real hard to fall off to the side or to the back so the board doesn't hit you.)

Master board surfing first lying in the prone position, then gradually progress to standing in Step C.

SURFING FACTS

• The highest ridable waves occur in Makaha Beach, Hawaii; waves are consistently thirty to thirty-five feet high.

• The first World Surfing Championship was held in Sidney, Australia, in 1964.

• The longest surfing ride in the world is found at Matachen Bay on the Pacific Coast of Mexico, where you can ride for up to 5700 feet. (This occurs only four to six times a year, though.)

• The first surfer to win two consecutive World Surfing Championships was Joyce Hoffman, in 1965 and 1966.

• "Wake surfing" makes it possible to surf on lakes and ponds. To do it, you need a heavy boat's wake to take the place of natural surf. You can also surf in Big Surf, the Arizona pool described in *A Landlocked Guide.*

For more surfing fun and info, try to get hold of *The Surfer's Almanac* by Gary Fairmont R. Filosa (Dutton, 1977).

a.

b.

(O'Neill)

Surfing is the oldest American sport: the Hawaiians were zipping along on their big *olo* boards and their little *omo* boards way before 1492. *Windsurfing* is the latest water sport to come along. It's a combination of surfing and sailing that's the next logical step to take once you've mastered your board. Instead of the wave providing the speed and power to what's essentially a surfboard with a mast on it (what? no roller skates?), the wind does — and how! For additional information, contact the Windsurfing Association, 1038 Princeton Dr., Marina Del Rey, CA 90291.

C.

SURF MUSIC

Unlike any other field of human endeavor, going to the beach comes complete with its own custom-tailored sound track. In 1961, thanks to a handful of California-based musicians, Surf Music was born, and for better or for worse it has been with us ever since.

Groups like the Beach Boys, the Frogmen, the Trashmen, Dick Dale and his Deltones, the Fantastic Baggies, the Marketts, and the Tradewinds recorded instrumental and lyrical odes to the summer, the surf, and the sun. Frequently employing the argot of the surfing crowd, instrumentals were called "Pipeline" and "Wipeout" and lyrics spoke of "baggies," "woodies," and "hanging ten."

Most famous of all were the three brothers and two friends who combined Four Freshmen harmonies with Chuck Berry rock-and-roll rhythms when they

cut the single, "Surfin'." At that moment the Beach Boys — the Wilson brothers (guitarist Carl, drummer Dennis, and resident genius Brian), Mike Love, and Al Jardin — launched their never-to-be-forgotten career as the foremost musical exponents of the California beach lifestyle.

Brian Wilson quickly became the poet laureate of surfers, penning tunes such as "Surfin'," "Surfer Girl," "Ride the Wild Surf," "Surfin' U.S.A.," "Noble Surfer," "Surf Jam," "The Surfer Moon," "The Rocking Surfer," "Surfer's Rule," ad nauseum. The Beach Boys had become one of the most popular bands in the world before anyone ever heard of four Englishmen from Liverpool. With their apt vocal harmonies and the aid of top-notch session musicians, the band's albums painted vivid aural pictures of life in southern California.

Pictures that, as is true with much good art, were far more interesting than their subject matter. They toured the country and the world singing hymns of sun, sand, and waves; and if they were not exactly profound, at least they sang like angels.

Twenty years later, their career is still going strong and the Beach Boys seem as permanent a fixture as the beach itself. Their early albums provide the perfect background music for a day by the ocean. Their later albums (*Pet Sounds, Smiley Smile, Wild Honey, Surf's Up*) in which the post-nervous breakdown Brian forsook some of the banalities of the beach without losing sight of his roots, can provide insights into the magic and mystery of the sea, its surf, and its borders.

The New Wave in Surf Music

If the beach party philosophy of life appeals to you and you are afraid that you missed all the fun because you were a mere tadpole in the sixties, don't despair. Beach music is making a big comeback in the eighties.

Jan and Dean are once again touring the country to SRO crowds and enthusiastic responses. New bands have captured the spirit of the surf and all the time more are jumping on (you'll pardon the expression) the sandwagon. For instance, the B-52s have created what they call "beach music from outer space," the Sincero's album is called *The Sounds of Sunbathing* and the Ramones celebrate "Rock Rock Rock-Away Beach."

So when you pack up the car to head for the dunes, don't forget your portable radio or tape recorder. Any music can be beach music as long as it conveys a feeling of fun, fun, fun 'til your daddy takes the Toyota Corolla away.

WHAT EVER HAPPENED TO...?

In 1962, Jan Berry and Dean Torrence had a national hit record with a piece of fluff called "Baby Talk." But it wasn't until 1963, when Jan teamed up with Brian Wilson of the Beach Boys to write and produce a single called "Surf City," that the singing duo of Jan and Dean had their first number-one record and joined the swelling ranks of those who represented the California surf sound.

In some ways Jan and Dean were even more typical of the West Coast lifestyle than Brian Wilson and company — they were the Beach Boys without pretensions. Totally obsessed (on record at least) with sun and surf, girls and cars, they reflected a philosophy of life as one long party. The fun ended for Jan when he was injured in a car wreck in 1966, effectively removing Jan and Dean from the music scene for the next ten years.

SURF TALK

Before heading out in search of the perfect wave, you'd better know a hamburger from a hot dog:

baggies: *loose-fitting bathing suits worn by surfers in the sixties.*

barge: *large, awkward board (not to be confused with a* Queen Mary, *a board that's too big for the surfer).*

to bomb: *to fall, spill, or be wiped out.*

boomer: *wave that crashes down violently.*

to dig: *to paddle hard.*

droppers: *large waves.*

glass-off: *a sudden smoothing of the surf.*

goofy-foot: *stance with the right foot forward.*

hamburger: *a crash on the rocks.*

hang five: *draping the toes of one foot over the edge of the board.*

hang ten: *ditto, with both feet.*

highway surfer: *one who rides around with a surfboard on his car, but never uses it.*

to hot dog: *do fancy stunts.*

kamikaze: *a deliberate wipeout.*

peeler: *a perfectly curling wave.*

roto-moto: *turning around on the board for the whole ride in.*

woodie: *wood-paneled cars driven by surfers in the sixties.*

TAKING THE PLUNGE...

Water-Skiing

Pyramid of Aqua-Maids
Florida Cypress Gardens

You don't need to spend your winters careening down a mountain slope in order to enjoy the exhilaration of skiing. Water-skiing is as easy as falling off a log. It can be learned in an afternoon and enjoyed for a lifetime.

Water-skiing has only one prerequisite: You must know how to swim, as you will be doing a lot of it, especially at the beginning. Even with this ability it is highly recommended that you wear a life preserver of some sort; even a good swimmer can get in trouble when he or she takes an unexpected dunking.

How to Do It

First choose your skis. Their size depends on your weight (no cheating):

    up to 120 lbs. — 5′ ski
    120-175 lbs. — 5′6″
    175-200 lbs. — 5′9″
    over 200 lbs. — 6′ or 6′3″

Then, begin training on land, with a partner holding the towline about seven feet from the bar. Put on your skis and grasp the bar firmly with both hands. Then lower into a squatting position, so you end up sitting back on your skis, with your knees between your elbows, arms straight out. Keeping your back and arms straight, have your partner pull you to your feet — arms still straight, knees flexed. DO NOT SHIFT YOUR WEIGHT FORWARD TO HELP YOU GET UP! When the boat pulls you, any motion to aid in getting up will, in fact, topple you over.

When you're ready to make a go of it, trot on down to water that's about neck deep and put your skis on. Wet feet will slide more easily into wet bindings, and if you fall in the middle of your run, you'll have to know how to put them on in the water anyway.

Grasp the towline and get into the squatting position you practiced on land. Make sure that your knees are between your elbows, the ski tips protruding from the water, the towline running between them.

Signal the spotter that you are ready and he will have the driver taxi the boat slowly until the towline is taut.

It's now or never — make sure you're sitting back on your skis and your arms are straight but relaxed as you yell "GERONIMO!" or some equally momentous phrase. The driver will smoothly accelerate; without trying to help, let the boat pull you up. It should only take a speed of ten or fifteen miles an hour. You've done it!

O.K. You haven't done it. If at first you don't succeed — LET GO OF THE TOWLINE! This may seem painfully obvious to you now, but many a perfectly intelligent beginner has swallowed half the lake before realizing that they were not going to get up again this way. (If you fall, you should try to go over sideways or backward to avoid hitting your skis.)

Once you're up, stay in the trough of the boat's wake — nothing too fancy at first. Just riding behind a fast boat should provide all the thrills you'll need for a while. But if you tend toward rapid ennui, you can lean left to veer left, and right to go right. If you want to try crossing the wake, swing wide and try to cross it at a 90-degree angle.

(Connelly Skis)

(Cypress Gardens, Florida)

THAT'S SHOW BIZ!

Like water-skiing enough to consider making a career out of it? According to interviews with show skiers in *The Water Skier* (published by the American Water Ski Association, P.O. Box 191, Winter Haven, FL 33880), here's what it takes and what it's like:

"It takes a love for the sport, almost a 'ski fever'; you just can't get tired of it. You have to be aggressive and outgoing."

"It takes determination to become a show skier, a lot of hard work and get-back-up-and-do-it-again, self-confidence, and the ability to perform. It's a good idea to go to a ski school, and ski clubs are the greatest."

"Most of the time I feel lucky if I just make it through the show."

"It's glamorous to be recognized, but it's hard work, and I'm just too plain tired a lot of the time."

"I love water-skiing, and it's nice to be paid to do what I like to do. How many people have the opportunity to work at something they enjoy so much? I look forward to every day, and there's no such thing as a Sunday night."

"This may sound corny, but sometimes I feel like I'm living in a dream."

"What makes me happiest about doing this is knowing that it's made my mother so proud."

153

Skin and Scuba Diving

Skin diving (or snorkeling) and scuba (scuba is an acronym for self-contained underwater breathing apparatus) diving give you a glimpse of what goes on in the colorful, mysterious, beautiful, silent world that exists underwater. All the caverns, reefs, canyons, mountains, lost ships, plants, and animals hidden beneath the sea are suddenly available to the diver. Inland lakes, rivers, springs, quarries, and caves reveal their own special secrets.

Both skin and scuba diving can mean hours of fascinating fun as long as you have respect for the water. Of the two, skin diving involves the least expensive equipment and preparation, and no decompression problems. All you need is a mask, snorkel, fins, a wetsuit in chilly waters, and the ability to swim.

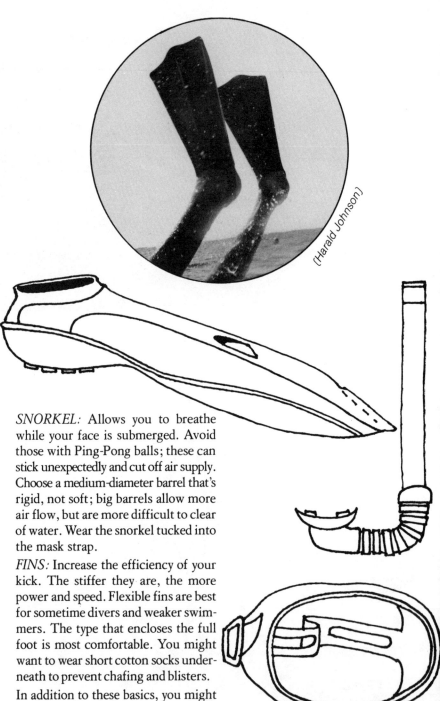

(Harald Johnson)

Equipment

Whether you buy or rent, here's what to look for and how to use it. All rubber goods should be rinsed with fresh water after use and stored away from direct sunlight.

MASK: This is your window to the underwater world. It should cover the eyes and nose, protect eyes and improve underwater vision. Everything underwater appears one-quarter larger and closer, but if your eyesight isn't perfect, you should check into masks that have prescription lenses. The rubber should be soft and comfortable. To test the fit, hold the mask to your face; inhale to create suction; let go with your hand. If it stays put, the fit's right. To keep the lens (which should be shatterproof glass not plastic, which scratches easily) fog-free, rinse it with water and coat it with saliva, or one of the special fog-resistant products available.

SNORKEL: Allows you to breathe while your face is submerged. Avoid those with Ping-Pong balls; these can stick unexpectedly and cut off air supply. Choose a medium-diameter barrel that's rigid, not soft; big barrels allow more air flow, but are more difficult to clear of water. Wear the snorkel tucked into the mask strap.

FINS: Increase the efficiency of your kick. The stiffer they are, the more power and speed. Flexible fins are best for sometime divers and weaker swimmers. The type that encloses the full foot is most comfortable. You might want to wear short cotton socks underneath to prevent chafing and blisters.

In addition to these basics, you might want a *wet suit* in cold water to prolong your dive time and cotton or work *gloves* to protect your hands from fish spines, coral, and so on.

For more information about recreational skin and scuba diving, refer to a manual such as *Sport Diving* by A.P. Balder (Collier, 1978) or contact the Underwater Society of America, 732 50th St., West Palm Beach, FL 33407.

How to Snorkel

You usually snorkel in relatively shallow water so the sights along the bottom remain visible as you swim along the surface. Occasionally you might want to go down for a closer look. Take a deep breath before you plunge and hold it as you submerge. To prevent water from trickling into your mouth, seal the mouthpiece with your tongue, or by biting down on it. When you re-surface, blow out forcefully through the tube and the water will spout out. Then resume breathing in a normal, relaxed rhythm.

DIVING TIPS

- Always dive with a buddy.
- Practice increasing your breath-holding capacity so your dives below the surface are prolonged.
- When in a new area, consult local clubs and dive shops for information about good spots and danger areas.
- Walk backward whenever you wear fins.
- Wear old clothes as protection from abrasive coral.
- Uninterrupted sandy beaches often offer little in the way of interesting sights, but rocky coastlines and coral reefs are usually teeming with aquatic life and interesting formations.
- If you go scuba diving, be sure you've received enough proper training and have practiced. Resorts may offer quickie courses, but it's advised that you train for several weeks in certified schools; the Y gives well-respected courses, too.
- Don't lose track of the time; it's easy to become overly absorbed in this mentally relaxing, yet physically demanding, sport.

You are about to take a journey into wonderland. It is probable that your state of mind will be one of astonishment — nay, of stupefaction. You will find it hard to remain indifferent to the spectacle unrolling itself before your eyes.

—Jules Verne

WHAT'S MY LINE?

Look! Out in the water! Is it a swimmer? Is it a fisherman? Is it a skin diver? It's a swimfisherman! And he, along with other adherents to this unusual activity, would say he's combining the best of several sports.

A swimfisherman, they say, is a Zen fisherman. He's in a "better attitude" to the fish, swimming in the water with them, presenting the lure more naturally. And he can release his catch if he wants, after the thrill is gone.

To be a swimfisherman, you need good swimming ability, fins, and either a regular spool of monofilament or a special handline spinning spool; a jig is the preferred lure. You may also want a mask and snorkel. As you swim out to where the fish are, hold the spool in your hand or tuck it in your bathing suit. Drop the lure, and swim parallel to the shore, your "bait" bobbing temptingly with every stroke. When a fish strikes, the spool will pop out of your hands or suit and spin as it floats on the water's surface. (In clear water, you may actually be able to watch them bite!) Pick the spool up and proceed as usual; when the fish is ready, angle the spool for the drag — there's nothing else to provide it: It's just you and the fish and the taut, trembling line.

(Harald Johnson)

Movable Beaches

What's a movable beach? Simple: It's any water-worthy vessel that gives you the freedom to get away from it all — or to get *to* it all. It's anything that floats (and, it is hoped, doesn't rely on engine power for mobility) that you can use to either discover hidden water-side havens inaccessible by land, or to use as a private mini-beach of your own that you can transport anywhere.

Sailing, Sailing

Why do people sail? Here's how one young salt feels about it:

Call me a modern Ishmael (or whatever else you like). But whenever I find myself growing grim about the mouth; whenever it is a damp, drizzly November in my soul; whenever I find myself involuntarily pausing before coffin warehouses and bringing up the rear of every funeral I meet; and when it requires strong moral principle to prevent me from deliberately stepping into the street and methodically knocking people's hats off — then I account it high time to get to sea as soon as I can. With a philosophical flourish my contemporaries seek out therapy. I will quietly take to the sea. My mediums are wind and water.

At the beach all the world's basic elements, less fire, are present. For the time being man has subdued only earth and fire. Water and wind still go unmastered. Air and water, wind and ocean; two opposing elements that often meet violently, and the only sign of peace between them is the sailboat — a creature that exists in both worlds. It's almost magical how this simple device can create a bond between the two powers and

somehow seems to be plugged into a very basic force of the planet.

Most any machine you can think of works against natural forces to achieve its goal. But moving along in a sailboat is the art of being in harmony with these forces. You're not overcoming forces, but manipulating and moving with them. All you need is your wits and a boat, and you can let your valium prescription expire.

What's even better is that you don't need a great vessel to work this magic. The beginner on a Sunfish is experiencing an adventure into another world as much as the bearded old salt in a world-girdling yacht. The essence is independence, and your reliance on cunning and courage. With this you'll find that when you look astern you'll see the world ashore in a much different perspective.

So if you can talk your way into a day's sail on a friend's — or a friend of a friend's — boat, do it. If you're determined to give it a try on your own, don't let anything stop you. Even if you have to settle for a cheap dinghy with a blanket for a sail and a how-to book from the library, get out there and fake it. (Or you can get in touch with one of the U.S. Coast Guard's civilian groups that offer free boating classes and will even check out your craft to make sure it's shipshape.) Take it from someone who's gone that route: you may come back wet, tired, and a bit banged up. But you'll probably be smiling too.

CAVEAT GREENHORN

Beware of the sailor!
His world is filled with tradition, machismo, and whatever else is trapped in his libido. Once out of sight of land his vessel truly becomes a floating kingdom. It's a freedom and responsibility that is rare in our society and affects the modern yachtsman in many ways. When you're invited along for a sail, remember these few rules for your safety and enjoyment. They may insure a second invitation.

• *Bring warm clothes.* Even in the tropic seas you'll occasionally be thankful for

a pair of warm socks and a sweater. Water-repellent togs such as slickers come in handy against sea spray and rain.

• *Go easy on cigarettes.* The boat's trapped gases and your match may yield explosive results.

• *Go easy on the libations.* Your stomach and the captain's patience will thank you.

• *Wear sneakers.* They will protect you as well as the boat's deck.

• *Time and tide wait for no man.* Get to the departing dock on time.

• *Once underway, forget schedules.* A vessel is always said to be "bound" for its destination. It has been long known that a sailboat can start out for a place, but there are no guarantees when it will arrive. That's sailing.

• *"There is one God in the universe, and only one captain of the Pequod."* Granted old Ahab was a bit extreme, but the idea still goes. You liberated women and rebellious young men had better be warned. Centuries of sea travel have taught captains that democracy is a clumsy way of dealing with problems. (Then again, a good mutiny is always fun!)

• *Go softly.* Whatever you bring should be carried in a soft, easily stowed, non-abrasive bag.

• *Don't be too helpful.* Do only what's asked. A helpful group of inept hands can really cause trouble.

• *Keep it clean.* The sailor's world is compact and orderly. Confusion is his enemy.

• *Water, water everywhere.* Fresh water is in limited supply on a boat, so go easy with it.

• *The head.* The marine toilet requires a degree in engineering and great endurance to operate. Ask for help before you befoul yourself and the boat.

• *Don't barf into the wind.* You only make this mistake once.

• *NEVER MESS WITH THE CAPTAIN'S STRAWBERRIES!* (Especially if he bears the slightest resemblance to Humphrey Bogart or answers to the name of Queeg.)

(Sally Cummings)

The Petersen Publishing Company publishes three separate regional boating magazines. *Rudder* covers the Atlantic Coast and the Gulf of Mexico, *Sea* takes care of the West Coast, and *Lakeland Boating* caters to the inland boater. For subscription information, write to the magazine of your choice at P.O. Box 1159, Los Angeles, CA 90028.

Soundings (Pratt St., Essex, CT 06426) is a monthly newspaper for recreational mariners and others interested in boats, the water, and the waterfront. Nine regional editions and several sections allow for flexibility and suitability of coverage.

To subscribe to *Cruising World,* the magazine devoted entirely to cruising under sail, write to Cruising World, 524 Thames St., Newport, RI 02840. A one-year subscription includes the *Guide to Chartering.*

According to the Sunfish Racing Association (P.O. Box 1345, Waterbury, CT 06720), novice "sunfishermen" should be able to swim and should wear a life jacket (a ski belt will not suffice). Lessons are also recommended to get you started. If you join the association (for a moderate one-time fee), you're entitled to mailings, a yearly regatta schedule, and a 2-year subscription to *Windward Log,* their newsletter.

ROW, ROW, ROW YOUR BOAT

(Phoenix Products)

So you have no rich friends with yachts. Your budget wouldn't supply the fuel for a motorboat's trip across your bathtub. Your car is so small you don't even want to discuss the possibility of transporting a boat. You don't even *have* a car!

Cheer up — you can still try out your sea legs...if you'll consider people-powered boats such as canoes, kayaks, rowboats, and rafts. You can rent them at most lakes, rivers, resorts; or buy them for close to a song and transport them easily. Better yet are the new foldables and inflatables, which are perfect for this new stringent decade. Europeans have been turned on to inflatables for years; they had to be, with their more crowded waters and smaller homes and cars. (The *Hindenburg* disaster, by the way, caused many an airship maker to turn to the boat business.) In this country, they're coming into their own; the grown-up version of blow-up pool toys are no laughing matter. Deflated, they squish into one or more small bags that allow you to fit the whole shebang into the trunk of a small car, check as baggage at the airport, store in a closet, tuck in a cor-

ner of a garage, or stow under the bed. Inflated (in minutes, with a pump), they're a nifty way to fish, float around, watch nature, and explore to your heart's content. No trailers or docking areas are needed, and you can usually carry (or backpack) them right to the water's edge.

Inflatables can be of the *single-layer* type (of PVC, usually) — these are the cheapest and lightest, and are fine for small-scale boating and protected waters.

They may also be of the *sandwich-type* construction, with an outer layer that's sun and abrasion resistant, a middle layer of strong reinforcing fabric or plastic web, and an inner layer of air-retaining material. These have withstood the test of wild river running, and have even been across the Pacific and Atlantic oceans.

Depending upon the style, you can propel inflatables with oars or paddles; some have optional sails or motors. There's nothing like the peaceful silence of paddling or rowing a small craft using (and developing) your own strength and power.

160

ROWING AND PADDLING TIPS

- Rowing a boat that's designed to be propelled by motors can be sluggish, hard work. If you're in one of these, counteract it by loading it slightly bow-heavy to lift the drag-producing part of the transom out of the water.

- Use your whole body when rowing — not just your arms.

- A long, strong, slow oar stroke is better than a fast short one.

- To maneuver a rowboat: pivot by pulling on one oar and pushing on the other; to slow down, hold both oars still in the water.

- The United States Canoe Association (c/o Jim Mack, 606 Ross St., Middletown, OH 45042) suggests you think of propelling yourself by sticking the paddle in the water and pulling the canoe up to the paddle — instead of pulling the paddle through the water. The canoe should move a few feet; the paddle only a few inches, through the water.

- Correct, efficient paddling means swinging the blade forward, twisting slightly at the waist, and reaching with your shoulder. Stab the blade into the water at a 30-degree angle, and pull no farther back than your hip.

- If you're paddling with a buddy, change sides to equalize the strain on your muscles.

- For safety's sake — always wear a life jacket, and stay with your craft if it capsizes.

HOPE FOR SEASICKNESS

The U.S. Coast Guard recommends taking promethazine (an antihistamine) and ephedrine (a decongestant) together to prevent seasickness. The medication is not for everyone (pregnant women and those with hypertension shouldn't take it, and some people may be allergic or become drowsy), and should be taken only under a doctor's supervision, but it is highly effective. Medications like these, including Dramamine, can be supplemented. Before and during a sea voyage, low salt intake and a high intake of vitamin B complex can work wonders in combating "the green look."

Nice to have, in case of rough water or a spill: paddle jacket and pants made out of quick-drying fabric; waterproof bags to keep lunch, matches, first-aid kits, and cameras dry. (Both from Phoenix Products, Inc.)

More Fun in the Water

So you're not in the mood to swim, surf, water-ski, skin dive, scuba dive, or sail. But you still want to fool around, do *something,* move a little, cool off, maybe even sneak in a bit of exercise. Step right up, jump right in, and turn back the clock. The water's a great place to throw away all your cares and indulge in some good old-fashioned play, just like when you were a kid. Whether you mess around in a pool, a bay, a lake, or a relatively surfless ocean, it's always more entertaining to have others join in; mirth, like misery, loves company. Just remember one thing — try to keep your squeals and giggles down to a dull roar so you don't disturb the wet blankets that are "too old" to join the fun.

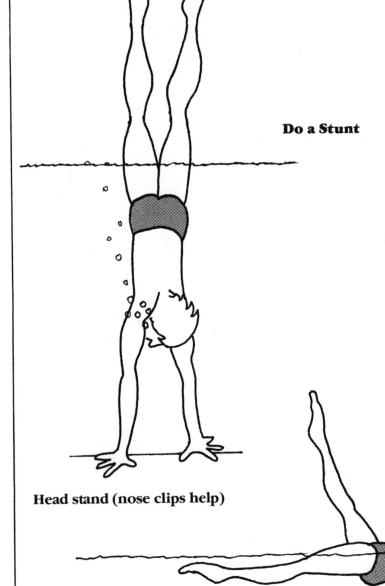

Do a Stunt

Head stand (nose clips help)

Ballet legs

Somersaults

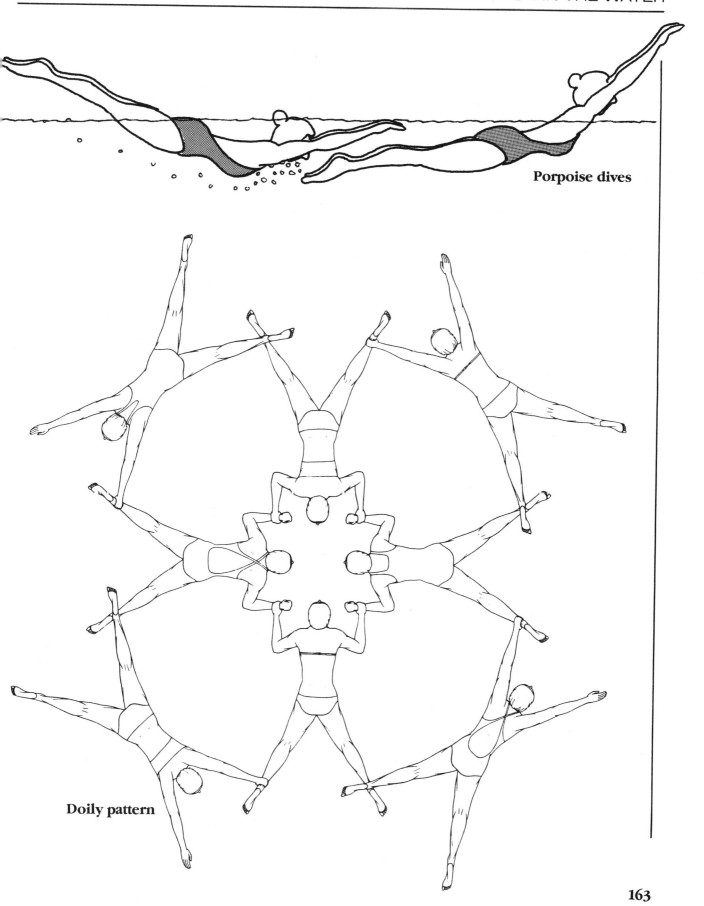

Porpoise dives

Doily pattern

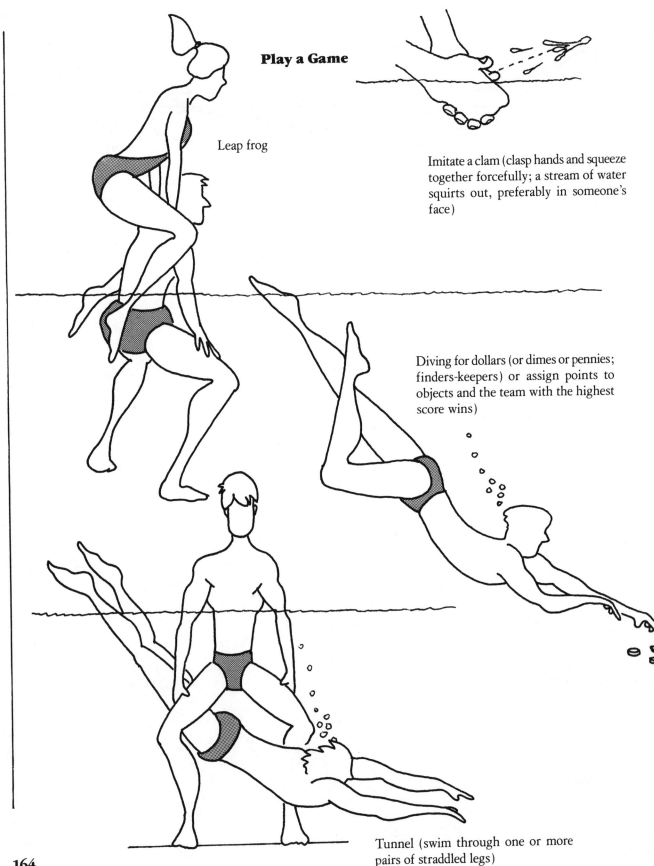

Play a Game

Leap frog

Imitate a clam (clasp hands and squeeze together forcefully; a stream of water squirts out, preferably in someone's face)

Diving for dollars (or dimes or pennies; finders-keepers) or assign points to objects and the team with the highest score wins)

Tunnel (swim through one or more pairs of straddled legs)

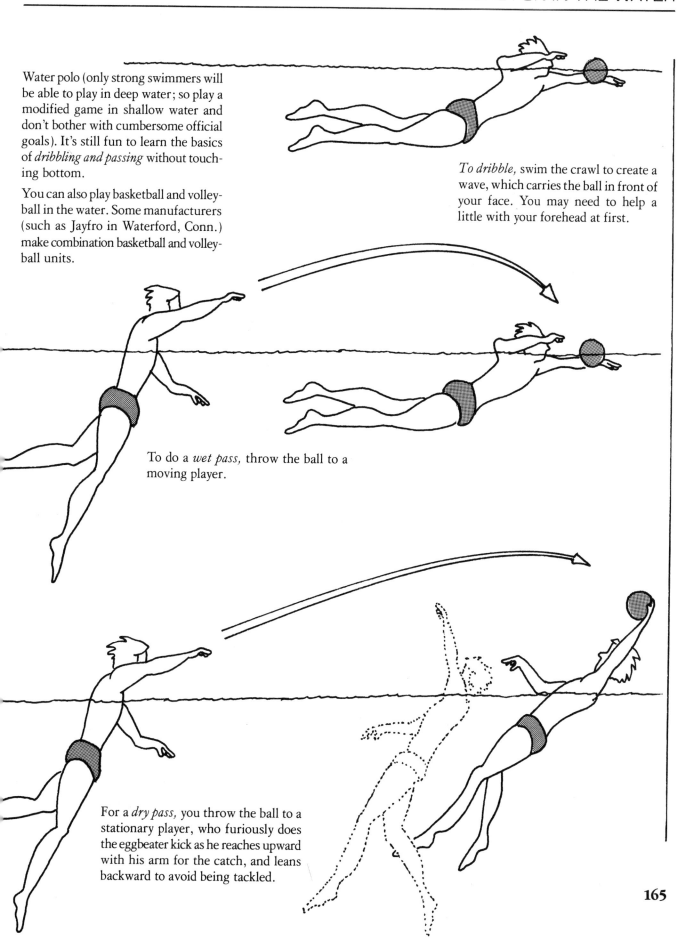

Water polo (only strong swimmers will be able to play in deep water; so play a modified game in shallow water and don't bother with cumbersome official goals). It's still fun to learn the basics of *dribbling and passing* without touching bottom.

You can also play basketball and volleyball in the water. Some manufacturers (such as Jayfro in Waterford, Conn.) make combination basketball and volleyball units.

To dribble, swim the crawl to create a wave, which carries the ball in front of your face. You may need to help a little with your forehead at first.

To do a *wet pass,* throw the ball to a moving player.

For a *dry pass,* you throw the ball to a stationary player, who furiously does the eggbeater kick as he reaches upward with his arm for the catch, and leans backward to avoid being tackled.

LEARN A TURN

Okay, you're swimming in a pool, and you get to the wall; what do you do? Grab the gutter, switch hands a few times, hang out, catch your breath, and then turn around and begin swimming again? Not anymore. Learn the open turn; impress your friends and relatives. Just promise you won't let on how easy it really is.

To begin, touch the wall with your leading arm (or grab the edge of the trough if there is one). Bend your elbow and tuck your legs and body into a ball, leaving your free arm behind you. As your feet touch the wall, turn your body so it faces the direction you want to go, and take a big bite of air. As you begin to push off from the wall (the more forcefully, the better), swing your contact arm to meet the free arm, drop your head into the water, and speed away.

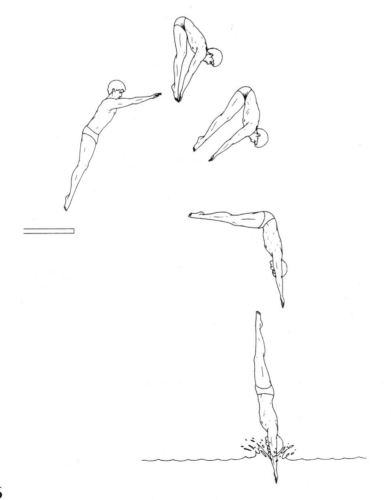

PERFECT A DIVE

All good divers — whether executing a simple standing dive or a forward one-and-a-half somersault with tuck — keep these pointers in mind:

- During the *stance* (sitting, kneeling, or standing) the toes are curled around the edge of the deck or board, body in balance, poised position.

- During the *take-off*, you should be energetic; push off aggressively.

- During the *flight*, your body should soar gracefully and smoothly through the air; keep your muscles taut and think streamlined.

- As you *enter* the water, make sure your chin is tucked down toward your chest (imagine you're holding an object there) to prevent bellywhops; hold your arms straight, covering your ears.

- As you *ascend* to the surface, form a smooth upward arc.

Safety Reminder: Never dive into water that's shallower than 3 feet; the higher your starting position, the deeper the water should be to protect you from hitting bottom.

DO AN EXERCISE

Hydro-calisthenics are the coolest way ever to get fit and have fun at the same time. The water's buoyancy and soothing effect make stretching easier and more relaxing; its resistance makes strength-building movements more effective.

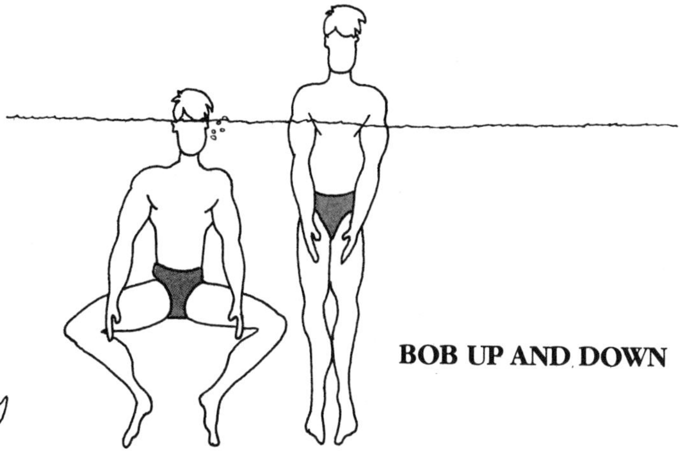

BOB UP AND DOWN

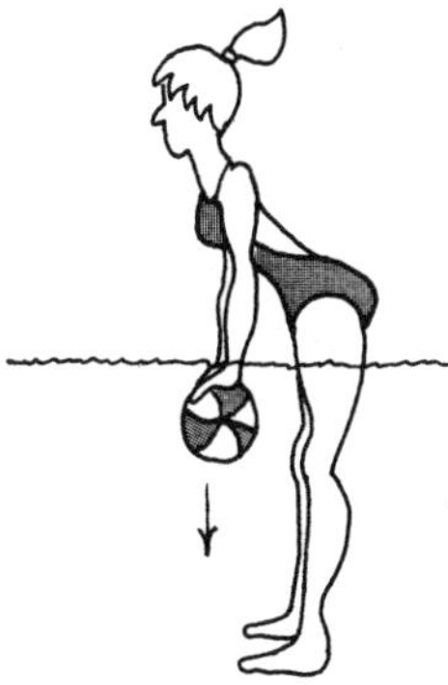

PUSH DOWN

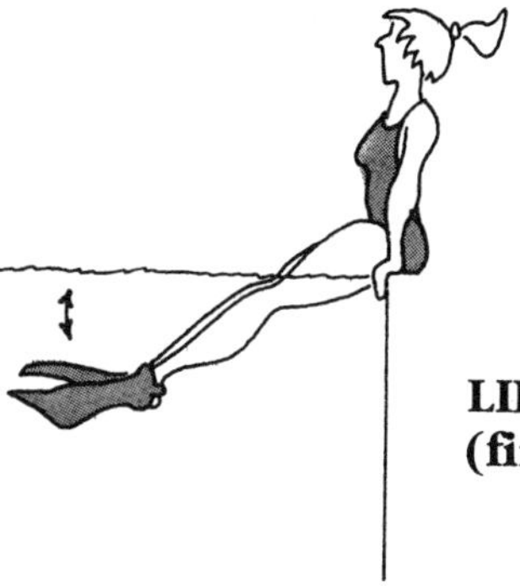

LIFT UP, THEN LOWER DOWN (fins add more resistance)

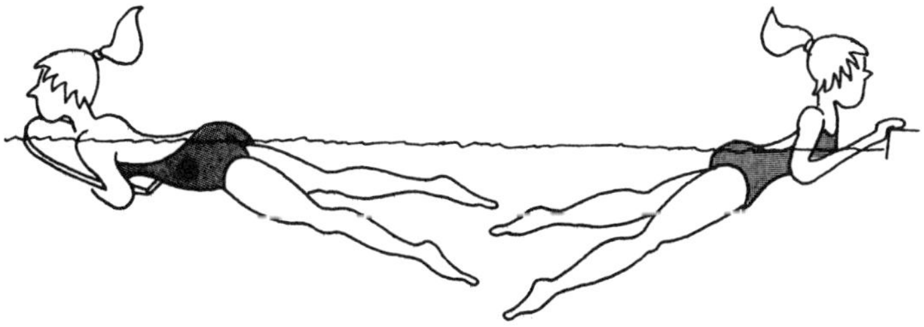

KICK (fins make this more effective)

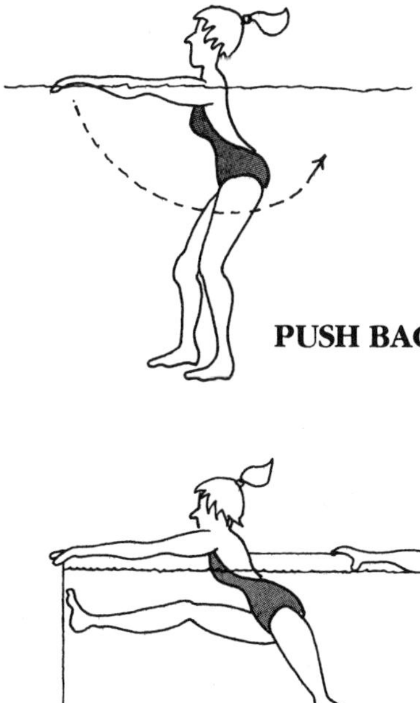

PUSH BACK, THEN FORWARD

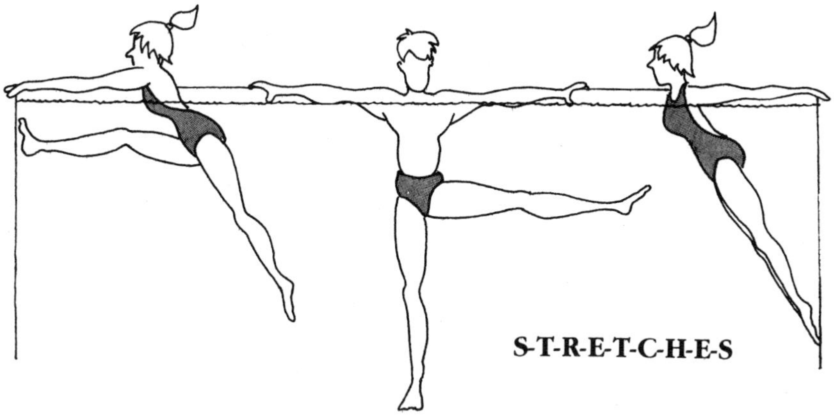

S-T-R-E-T-C-H-E-S

PLAYING ARO

All beach things great and small: whales and willets, continental drift and sand dunes, tidal waves and tide pools. Sea monsters, real and imagined. Magnificent mollusks. Weather wisdom. Shutterbugging. Eat up a storm. Fish for your supper. Making bugs bug off. Advice to the beach-lorn. Castles in the sand. Games galore. You don't have to get wet to get it going at the beach.

PLAYING AROUND...

AH, NATURE!

We pack off to the beach and relate to our surroundings the way we do to the supermarket: endless supplies of ordinary sand and water that's been laid out for our "consumption." Big deal. Once in a while the wind picks up enough so sand sticks to our oiled bodies; or a wave catches us off-guard and down we go; or we tread on a crab and he retaliates. For most of us, that's about the extent of our confronting the great outdoors. But way down deep, we may suspect that something more, something a little mysterious, is going on out there. But what is that something? Where is it? Hiding under an old Diet Pepsi can waiting to come out at night?

Wisely, the beach only reveals its wonders to those who deign to look — with patience and an interest in knowing. Nature may not be obvious at first to those of us who are surrounded by soot and concrete, the humdrum and the obvious, the neon and the fast action, the instantly gratifying. To see through its cover, you'll need a bit of basic knowledge, a little time, and a touch of imagination. (A pail, a notebook, binoculars, and a magnifying glass would help.)

All beaches have a tale to tell, be it the unspoiled beauty of a virgin beach or the ravaged honky-tonk of a former haven where beer cans seem to predominate. You can devote yourself to a single beach, a single type of beach, or all beaches. "Marinate" yourself for an hour, a week, a lifetime. Introduce yourself to the plants and animals that live there — from the gigantic whale to the minuscule creatures that sustain it.

Invest in a book about the area to which you'll be traveling. There are many excellent regional guides to beaches, such as Philip Kopper's *The Wild Edge: Life and Lore of the Great Atlantic Beaches* (Times Books, 1979), Peterson's *Field Guide to the Atlantic Seashore from the Bay of Fundy to Cape Hatteras* by Kenneth Gosner (Houghton Mifflin, 1979), and *The Tide Marsh Guide* by Mervin F. Roberts (Dutton, 1979; paper). Keep your eyes, ears, nose, and mind open to the miracles that surround you as you stroll along the fascinating place where land and water meet. You'll begin to notice a whole world you've been passing by for years.

Perhaps you'll find that a trip to the "real world" brings on a meditative mood: We're all a part of nature and dependent upon its other components for our very existence. You may find the realization that the never-ending cycle of birth, growth, death, and movement is curiously exciting and disturbing, yet comforting. There's a kind of beauty and immortality behind every cruel mortality, whether it's the life of a clam, an entire coastline, or your own. Or you may simply wiggle your toes in the soft sand, listen to the plaintive cry of a seagull, take a deep breath in, and sigh: "Ah, nature!"

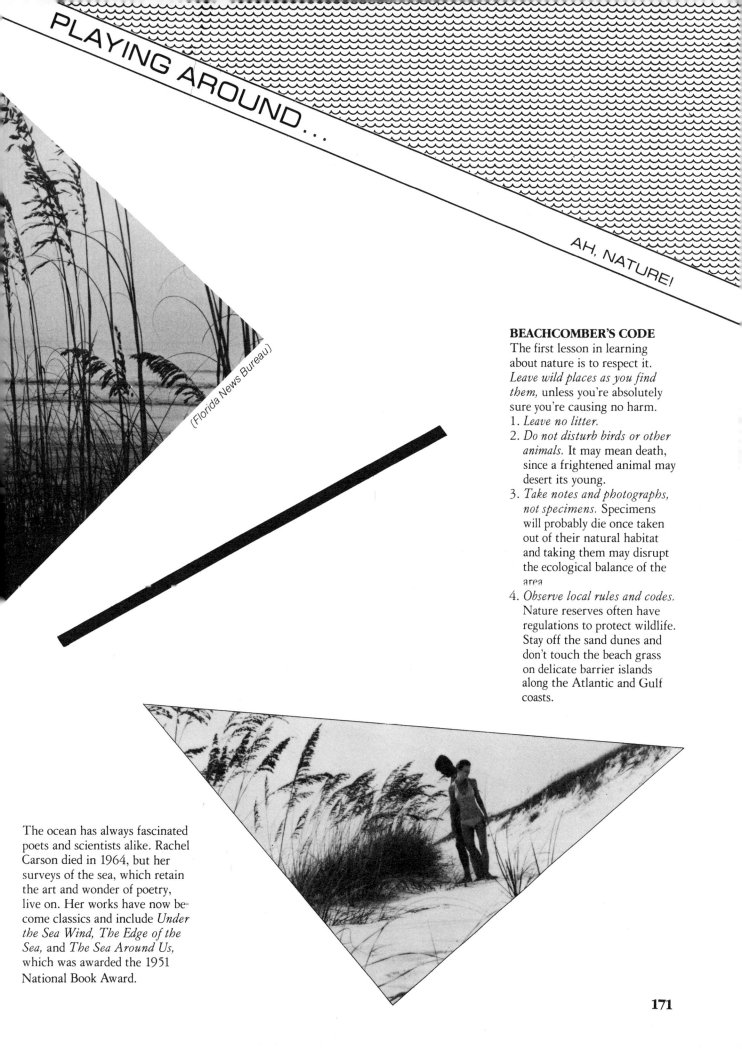

PLAYING AROUND...

AH, NATURE!

(Florida News Bureau)

BEACHCOMBER'S CODE

The first lesson in learning about nature is to respect it. *Leave wild places as you find them,* unless you're absolutely sure you're causing no harm.

1. *Leave no litter.*
2. *Do not disturb birds or other animals.* It may mean death, since a frightened animal may desert its young.
3. *Take notes and photographs, not specimens.* Specimens will probably die once taken out of their natural habitat and taking them may disrupt the ecological balance of the area.
4. *Observe local rules and codes.* Nature reserves often have regulations to protect wildlife. Stay off the sand dunes and don't touch the beach grass on delicate barrier islands along the Atlantic and Gulf coasts.

The ocean has always fascinated poets and scientists alike. Rachel Carson died in 1964, but her surveys of the sea, which retain the art and wonder of poetry, live on. Her works have now become classics and include *Under the Sea Wind, The Edge of the Sea,* and *The Sea Around Us,* which was awarded the 1951 National Book Award.

171

Types of Beaches

Most of the beaches that border the U.S., from Cape Cod south along Jersey and the Carolinas to Florida and around southern California, are gently sloping and have light-colored coarse sand. They contain most of our popular resorts so Americans tend to think they represent the world's beaches. They don't, but they *are* the beaches that have suffered the most ecological damage at the hands of resort promoters.

That this country is a land of contrasts is nowhere more dramatically demonstrated than along its coasts. Hundreds of miles of the Oregon-Washington coast are mountains and rocky prominences, interspaced with fine-grained gray-green beaches — wide and flat, and hard as a racetrack. Maine has a glacier-scoured, fjordlike indented shore. Delicate barrier islands, their sand battered by winds, storms, and tides, fringe the East and Gulf coasts; tranquil lagoons and semitropical vegetation lie behind some of them. The Gulf shore is characterized by coastal forests and marshes. Delta swamps surround the Mississippi; parts of the southern Pacific Coast are near desert. There is even a beach in California composed entirely of old tin cans, washed in from an ocean dump. The waves have arranged the cans into swirls and dunes, as they would any other beach material.

Looking elsewhere in the world, there is the beach at Nice on the French Riviera, which is largely composed of uncomfortable pebbles; much of the English coast is lined with small flat stones called shingle; many beaches of Labrador and Argentina are composed of large cobbles. On the windward side of Tahiti the beaches are volcanic black; on the other side, the lee, they are blindingly white, formed by the coral from the wide reefs. Not to forget the freshwater beaches: The vast and ever-moving dunes around Lake Michigan are world famous, and some of the beaches on Lake Ontario consist of perfectly smoothed and polished large oval stones in beautiful red and blue tones. The grassy bank of a freshwater pond in the woods is an old favorite among inland shorelines. Sitting on one of these shady banks in the summertime, you dangle your feet in the cool clear water; but in winter you may find yourself lacing up your skates from the very same bank for a spin around the smooth thick ice.

Whatever type of beach you choose to visit, take a look around. Even the casual observer can contemplate the miraculous diversity and the sensitivity with which beaches respond to the forces that act upon them.

The sand dune could be the most romantic landform on earth. These vagabond sand piles are all produced by wind and made up of the finest sands. The sandy cushion and the snug privacy created by the leeward side of each dune adds up to an attractive hideaway for an intimate picnic or rendezvous with a friend or sweetheart.

Sandy beaches are unstable, constantly changing structures: Plants have a hard time staying anchored, and the surface moves almost continually because of the waves and tidal energy that shifts the sand up, down, and along the beach. The profiles of a sandy beach can change immensely from season to season. In winter, storms erode the beach and deposit sand in offshore sandbars; the beach becomes steeper and narrower. Summertime waves shift the sand back to rebuild the beach naturally. Sandbars shrink and the profile returns to its wider, flatter state.

The scenic cliffs and rock outcrops that provide us with some of the most awe-inspiring views were mostly formed millions of years ago by geologic forces such as underground volcanoes, sedimentation and fractures, and offshore mountain-building and upward pressures. More recently, glaciers, weather, and the sea have gradually modified their appearance. These kinds of beaches aren't as fragile as sandy beaches, and they're usually located in highly exposed and dangerous areas. So they're generally sparsely used (and abused) by humans and are still in their relatively natural state.

(American Airlines)

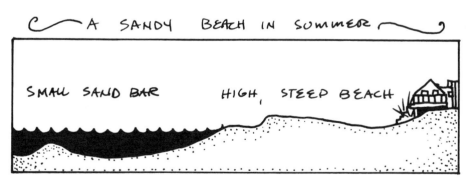

A SANDY BEACH IN SUMMER

SMALL SAND BAR   HIGH, STEEP BEACH

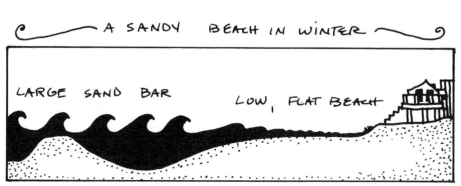

A SANDY BEACH IN WINTER

LARGE SAND BAR   LOW, FLAT BEACH

HERE COMES "THE SANDMAN"

Some beachcombers collect shells. Some collect driftwood. Some salvage the flotsam and jetsam that finds its way to shore, but who collects sand? A theater technician in New York City does! He has sand from more than 35 beaches, some from as far away as Australia, packed in pint Mason jars that enable him to look at his miniature beaches and run his fingers through the gritty stuff. A nice way to evoke memories of a beach's essential beauty...but if it catches on, our grandchildren might have nowhere to put their beach blankets!

AMAZING FACTS

⦿ Baby seals go for a week at a time without eating while their mothers forage for food. The papa seal fasts for up to two months while guarding his territory.

⦿ Mama whales feed their babies the equivalent of 200 glasses of milk with every squirt!

⦿ If all the gold that is contained in sea water could be extracted, there would be 13 billion pounds of it. That's more than 100 times the total amount mined on land, & more than $1,000,000 worth for every one on Earth!

⦿ The adult walrus has a built-in life vest. Two inflatable pouches, one on either side of his face, keep his head above water while he sleeps out to sea.

⦿ The water in the Persian Gulf sometimes reaches a temperature of 96.8° F near shore.

⦿ A 4-foot wave of 10-second duration contains the energy equivalent of 35,000 horsepower per mile of coastline.

⦿ Each pint of Dead Sea water contains 4 ounces of salt.

⦿ The humpback whale is the only animal with not one, but two hit records...
Songs of the Humpback Whale & Deep Voices (Capitol Records).

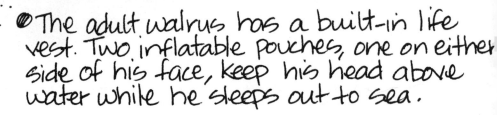

PART ONE

o o o

● The total coastline of the United States is 88,633 miles give or take a few feet. Alaska accounts for 33,904, Hawaii is contained by 1,052 miles of shoreline & Florida by 8,426.

● The octopus has 3 hearts.

● The salt contained in all the world's oceans would, if extracted, cover the Earth's continents to a depth of 500 feet.

● The longest drift-bottle on record was released on June 20, 1962, in Perth, Australia & recovered 5 years & 16,000 miles later in Miami, Florida.

● More golfers are struck by lightning than swimmers attacked by sharks.

● The most dangerous swimming area in the world is probably off the coast of Australia. Aside from a high incidence of shark attacks, it is also the home of the delightful <u>Chironex fleckeri</u>, the box jellyfish or "sea wasp". This creature has 25-foot tentacles that contain a venom deadly enough to kill a grown adult in 30 seconds. The truly amazing fact, however, is that there is protection from the sea wasp's sting. Its tentacles are completely unable to penetrate women's pantyhose, which has become required apparel for hapless Aussie lifeguards!

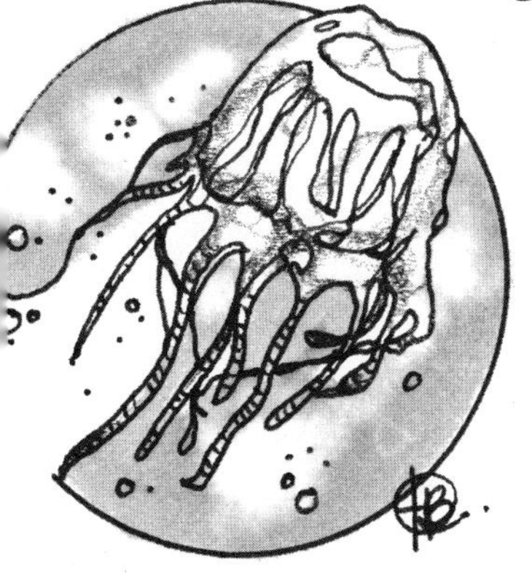

PERTH

MIAMI

175

PLAYING AROUND...

What a Wave Is

You're whooping it up body surfing when suddenly you realize you've miscalculated. Down you go, cement-mixer style, tumbling into the coarse sand and shell debris underneath. Maybe you'd like to know what is going on, even though it won't help your skinned knees one bit.

Waves are primarily created by wind, not tide as so many people think. As wind travels across water, what becomes the top of a wave (the crest) is pushed along while the lower part (trough) is held back by friction and so it moves slower than the wind-blown top. As the ripples build up, the wind catches them and increases their size and power. It's the wave, not the water itself, that moves forward because waves are actually a form of energy being transmitted through water. If this is hard for you to imagine, think of sound or light waves traveling through air — the air doesn't move, the waves do. To demonstrate this, try one or both of these little experiments. The next time you open a bottle of wine, float the cork in a pan of water, then make little waves by blowing across the water surface. The cork will bob up and down but it won't move forward. A variation is if two persons hold a long rope between them and one moves his end up and down rhythmically, waves will move down the rope yet the rope itself doesn't move from one person to the other.

Waves are formed or increased by the wakes of boats, by hurricanes, and by storms. Seismic waves from earthquakes, volcanic eruptions, and underwater landslides create those devastating waves called tsunamis, often called tidal waves.

There's a direct relationship between the shape of the shoreline and the kind of wave that hits it. A gently sloping shore slows down the waves and makes them curl over into white-capped breakers that topple into soft foam. On steeply sloped shorelines, the waves crest higher and crash with tremendous force. A very large and very curled wave phenomenon known to surfers as a "pipeline" is formed when a certain rare combination of wind and shoreline shape occurs. Waves that hit the shoreline in a frequency of no more than six or seven per minute will build up the beach but when waves break more often, the depositing action is interrupted. Storms produce not only larger but also more frequent waves which damage beaches. When waves strike at an angle to the beach, they tend to erode the shoreline; this is known as longshore drift. Understanding the formation and effects of waves is essential for many human endeavors from surfing to boat designing to beach preservation to off-shore drilling. But for now, watch out for the next one!

The Seashore World by David F. Costello (Thomas Y. Crowell, 1980) is a perfect companion for anyone who spends time at the seashore. It explains the forces of the sea, land formations, and animal and plant life.

Waves and Beaches by Willard Bascom (Anchor/Doubleday, 1980) is a classic that's been recently updated and revised. It will enhance your appreciation of our coastlines by describing aspects of beaches that you've never thought of, such as why beaches and waves behave the way they do.

176

AH, NATURE!

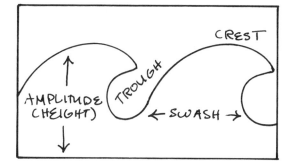

Anatomy of a wave. The mathematics is simple: A wave breaks when its height exceeds one seventh of its length (the distance between waves).

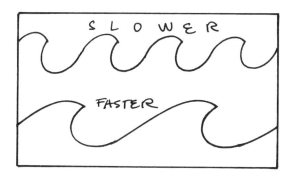

The farther apart the waves are, the faster the wave can travel; the closer waves are to each other, the slower they travel.

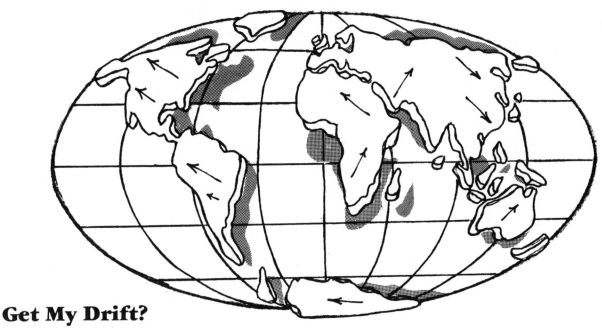

Get My Drift?

If you can wait around long enough (about 50 million years), the beaches you know and love will not only be unrecognizable, they will disappear completely. The Atlantic Coast will have earthquakes and volcanoes; California may have even more seaside fun to offer when it breaks off from the continent and becomes a Pacific island; island aficionados will flock to their favorite dot in the ocean, and find nothing but the deep blue sea — or perhaps a whole continent instead.

According to the theory of continental drift (or *plate tectonics*), all the continents are adrift on gigantic "plates" that have been wandering over the earth's surface for millions of years. During this process, which resembles a gigantic, slow-motion, intricate game of bumper cars, some land masses move away from each other and gradually crash into others, thus enlarging some oceans and creating new ones, and eradicating some coastlines and giving rise to others. Atlantis may be a myth, but scientists say the lost continents of Laurentia, Amorica, Avalon, Arcadia, Sonomia, Stikinia, and Wrangelia are what North America is made of.

On a Smaller Scale

The next time you marvel at the artistry of wind and water acting upon sand, give a thought to the other changes being wrought by the same action. This is especially evident in the necklace of low-lying sandy barrier islands strung along the Atlantic Coast from Maine to Florida and around the Gulf of Mexico to Texas. These islands are on the march — their beaches in a constant process of being worn away by currents and storms and the sand being redeposited somewhere else.

Hilton Head Island, off the coast of South Carolina, is a perfect example. Over the centuries, its coastline has changed from the dotted line to the solid one; it's predicted that 1000 years from now, the whole island will be gone. Another example is Cape Hatteras. When its famous lighthouse was built a century ago, it stood 1500 feet

away from the shore. Today, it's 200 feet away, and losing ground every year.

Interestingly enough, studies made by Duke University and East Carolina University have found that the devices (e.g. "groins") used to prevent beach erosion and subsequent loss of property actually hasten the overall process. Their advice is to let nature take its course and to avoid building on the seaward side of such islands, unless you like the security of living in a sand castle. In fact, there's a good case to be made against building *any* permanent structures on these living sculptures of nature.

What does this all mean? Philosophers may have their own deep meaning. For the average beach goer it means: Let's go to the beach today...tomorrow may be too late.

(Geological Survey of Canada, Ottawa)

HILTON HEAD ISLAND

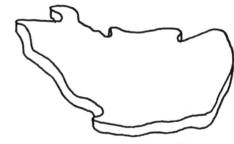

ANCIENT

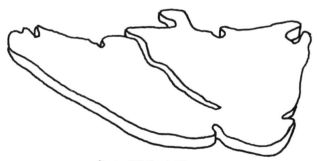

PRESENT

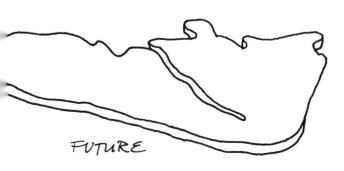

FUTURE

What Sand Is

Most North American beaches are sandy ones. What is sand and where does it come from?

Sand is primarily composed of rocks that have been worn down for millions of years by wind, rain, heat, and cold and by rubbing against other rocks. From rivers and streams these tiny sharp grains found their way to the ocean where wind and waves continued to shift and pound for a few more million years.

Most sand consists mainly of quartz and feldspar plus varying quantities of other minerals. The presence of mica makes a darkly glistening beach; semi-precious minerals such as garnet, tourmaline, topaz, sapphire, and amethyst add sparkling color. Beaches surrounding volcanic islands (such as Hawaii) are often all black or gray-green, the sand being derived from basaltic lava. Beaches of coral atolls will often be spectacularly white (or pink, as in Bermuda) with a hard, fine-grained sand made from the disintegrated coral skeletons. Ground-up shells also contribute to the composition of beaches. Even worn-down glass from bottles becomes beach material. So, the next time you brush the sand from your body, take a closer look and try identifying the sources of those tiny grains.

(Harald Johnson)

179

Seabirds

There are about 200 species of sea-birds, which are widely distributed from the tropics to the poles. You may see them inshore (within sight of land), offshore (between the shoreline and the continental shelf), and far out in the open ocean.

Penguins look like birds wearing tuxedos: light underbellies and dark on top. Their thick coats of short, waterproof feathers keep them warm in the cold waters in which they live. Penguins can't fly, but they're terrific swimmers.

Gulls (often called "seagulls") are the most common birds found near sea-shores. There are several common types of gulls, and they are also seen quite far inland. Although they're good swimmers, they don't dive the way other seabirds do. Seagulls will eat just about anything; when they catch shell-fish, they drop them from high in the air to crack their shells open to get at the meat.

The *albatross* is the largest seabird, and may have a wing span of 12 feet or more. It glides in the air easily, and may circle the globe several times a year. The only time you'll see this bird on land is when it mates and raises its young.

Willets, like most shore birds, are waders with no webbed toes and very little need to swim. They run after the small creatures left behind as each wave recedes.

180

Sandpipers are waders too, and long pointed beaks help them to reach the worms and crabs that burrow in the sand. As more and more shoreline is claimed by civilization, wading birds lose their territories.

Pelicans glide along just above the ocean, watching for fish. When they spot one, they let out a cry, fold up their wings, plunge headfirst and scoop up their prey into their big elastic throat pouches. The water drains out, leaving the fish.

FOR BIRDWATCHERS
Binoculars are a boon to identifying species of birds; so are guidebooks. Some of the best: Peterson's *A Field Guide to the Birds* (4th ed., rev., Houghton Mifflin, 1980; paper) and *A Field Guide to Western Birds* (Houghton Mifflin, 1972; paper), *Watching Birds* by Roger F. Pasquier (Houghton Mifflin, 1980; paper), *The Shorebirds of North America* by Garner D. Stout (Viking Press, 1967). The National Audubon Society, 950 Third Ave., New York, NY 10022, is another valuable source of information.

☆ ☆ ☆ ☆ ☆ ☆

Oceans magazine is a feast for the eyes — it includes beautiful color photographs of the sea, the creatures that live in it, and undersea ships, along with ecology-minded articles. For subscription information, write to Oceanic Society, 315 Fort Mason, San Francisco, CA 94123.

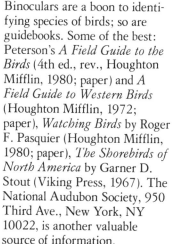

Terns fly low along the shoreline looking for fish. They are slender, streamlined with forked tails and are designed to fly and dive easily. Terns are related to gulls.

AMAZING FACTS

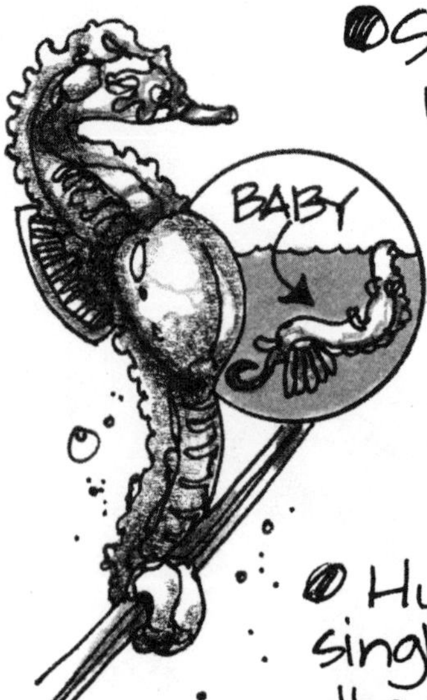

● Seahorses are the only fish that swim in an upright position. The extremely liberated male of the species carries the females' eggs in his pouch & gives birth to the baby seahorses.

BABY

● In 1868 a Hawaiian named Holua surfed a 50-foot tidal wave to keep from being crushed & lived to tell the tale!

● Huge swinging flamingo singles parties take place near the East African salt lakes. The males do the dancing & the females take their pick.

● In southern California a species of fish known as <u>Leuresthes tenuis</u>, or grunion, are washed up on the beach during a spring high tide. The females dig burrows in the sand & lay their eggs. The males fertilize the eggs & all flop back into the sea with the receding tide. The grunion eggs hatch on the beach & then they too are eventually washed back seaward.

● The horseshoe crab exists today in virtually the same form as it did 300 million years ago!

● The starfish can regenerate lost or damaged parts of its body. It can even remake an entire starfish from a piece of one leg!

...ooo PART TWO

"The legend of the unicorn owes much to an arctic aquatic mammal, the narwhal, whose modified incisor tooth spirals into an 8-foot tusk that was thought to have magical medicinal qualities in the middle ages.

The whale can swim up to 30 miles per hour, the dolphin 24 miles per hour, whereas the fastest human on record swam a whopping 5.19 miles per hour. Even penguins swim 22 miles per hour... not bad for a bird!

POLYP

● Coral reefs are actually limestone structures left behind by "polyps", tiny creatures who make them from calcium in sea water.

Most fish have a sixth sense... an organ called the "lateral line" that runs along their bodies detects vibrations & water displacement. This tips them off to approaching food & predators, often before their sense of smell or sight does.

KELP

● Kelp, a form of marine algae, grows faster than any other plant on Earth... 30 centimeters in one day!

The sea otter eats while floating on its back & it's one of the few animals who uses tools... in this case, a rock balanced on its tummy to crack open shellfish!

183

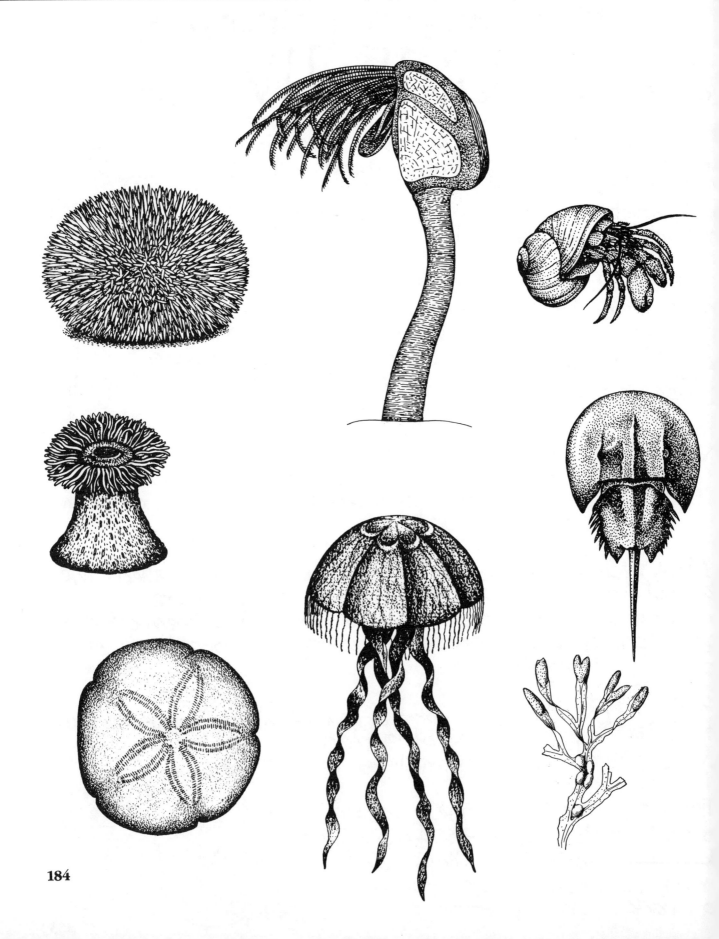

More Wild Creatures

As you stroll along the beach or peer under its waters, you may discover any number of sea creatures. (Even if you can't see them, they're there.) Here are some of the most common (not pictured elsewhere in this book) shown counterclockwise starting at the center top.

Barnacles. Tiny animals that anchor themselves to rocks and secrete a white shell around themselves. They extend tiny legs to search for food; you can hear their shells opening and closing if you listen carefully to a barnacle-covered rock. Contrary to popular rumor, barnacles aren't mollusks. They're crustaceans, and related to lobsters and crabs.

Sea urchins. Watch out for the spines on these globe-shaped echinoderms. Turn one over and you'll see the mouth parts and teeth, called "Aristotle's lantern."

Sea anemone. Called "the flower of the sea" because of its petallike tentacles, which withdraw inward when it's not covered by water. The poison this animal releases is deadly to its prey, but harmless to humans.

Sand dollar. An echinoderm (spiny-skinned animal) that lives in the sand; you'll seldom see whole, live ones, but fragments of their fragile skeletons are common.

Jellyfish. Swim by a kind of jet propulsion, alternately opening and closing bell-shaped parts of their bodies to provide thrust. The Portuguese man-of-war is one of the most beautiful — and fearsome, as the sting of their up-to-60-foot-long tentacles is very painful.

Seaweed. Really a type of algae. The *Fucus* (rockweed) shown here has air bladders that allow it to float and move with the currents, and make a loud popping noise when squeezed. Along with another rockweed, *Ascophyllum, Fucus* is used in clambakes.

Horseshoe crabs. Often found washed up on the beach either dead or alive. They're not harmful. Their tails aren't weapons, they are simply levers used to turn over if they get flipped on their backs.

Hermit crabs. Usually found in abandoned whelk and winkle shells, which they use for homes. When the crab outgrows the shell, it simply moves on to a larger one. If only apartment hunting was so easy!

Teeny tiny creatures. The ocean is filled with tiny organisms, that reveal their fascinating intricacy under a hand lens or microscope. A dipping net and a collection bottle are all you need to scoop these up and take them home or examine them right where you've found them. You'll discover plankton and algae as well as baby clams, crabs, shrimp, starfish, fish, and so on.

Whales, dolphins, porpoises. All of these magnificent, barely understood creatures are *cetaceans* (derived from the Latin *cetus,* "whale"). The whale is the largest animal on earth and is able to grow so large (100 feet, 100 tons for the blue whale) because the water supports its weight. Whales are warm-blooded mammals; their ancestors lived on land, but 65 million years ago returned to life in the sea.

People often confuse dolphins and porpoises. Both are small, toothed whales, but porpoises have rounded snouts and are the smaller of the two. Dolphins have pointed beaks and are the fastest and most playful and endearing of all. Whales are highly intelligent and communicate with each other; some have been taught to "talk" to humans. Their joyful, peaceful lives have led some to speculate that they're more intelligent than humans. Unfortunately, their particular type of smarts doesn't help them evade the wily bipeds who endanger the existence of many species through greed and carelessness.

Tales of dolphins coming to the aid of humans abound. One of the most amazing is the time a woman was the victim of a boat accident; one dolphin buoyed her up while two others circled her to protect her from sharks. After drifting for 200 miles, she happened upon a buoy; only after she climbed on it and was safe did the dolphins leave. Another incident involves four dolphins swimming around a fog-bound boat, causing it to change course just in time to avoid running into rocks. The dolphins continued to nudge the boat until it entered calm waters.

For more information about cetaceans, contact the *American Cetacean Society,* P.O. Box 4416, San Pedro, CA 90731, or *Save the Whales*/Greenpeace Foundation, 240 Fort Mason, San Francisco, CA 94123.

TIDE POOLING

Many of the smaller creatures on these pages will be revealed to you during low tide. When water retreats from a sandy beach, it can leave behind crabs, clams, jellyfish, seaweed, shells. On rocky shores, tiny pools of seawater remain in crevices and depressions as well, leaving many more tidal zone animals trapped in a kind of natural aquarium. Exploring these tide pools is especially popular along the west coast beaches, where there are thousands of them.

Myths, Monsters, and Mysteries of the Deep

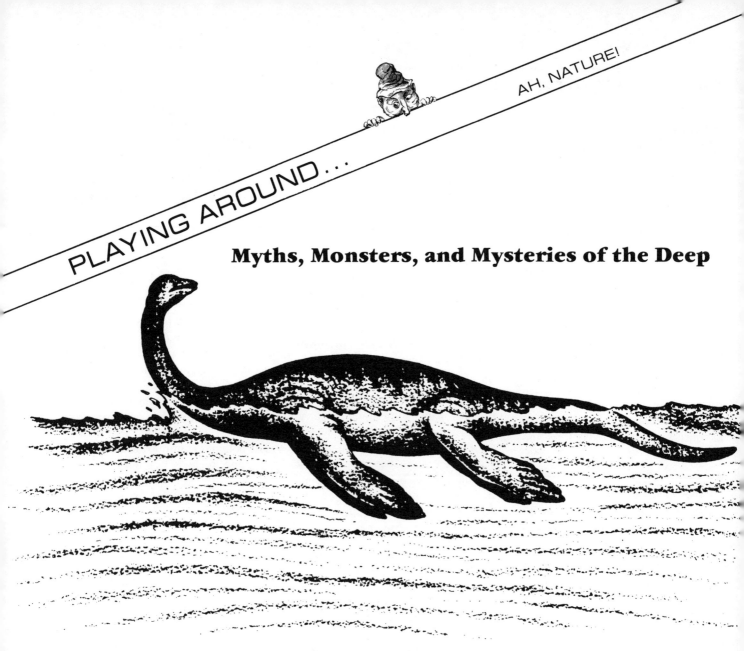

A sailor, alone on watch, surrounded by the shining stars in a black sky and a phosphorescent, gleaming sea has no way of knowing where sea ends and sky begins. A gust comes along, tossing up waves into mysterious glistening shapes of creatures that both tantalize and terrify.

Are tales of sea monsters and mermaids all just the wild imaginings of bored, superstitious sailors? Does the awesomeness of the sea naturally compel one to believe that fantastic creatures live in its depths? The waters that cover 70 percent of this earth are its least-explored realm, and that leaves a large reservoir for projections of human fears. But exactly what creatures have been "seen" rising from the deep?

Nessie, the famed Loch Ness Monster, was first reported in the sixth century and has been since spotted hundreds of times on the surface of that very deep and very murky Scottish lake. Similar in most respects to Nessie are Ogopogo, reportedly living in a lake in British Columbia, and its neighbors, Manipogo and Iogpogo, all of which have been sighted from shore and from boats since pre-Columbian times. Reports of a "great sea serpent" similar to Nessie have been made for many hundreds of years. The possible prehistoric progenitor for all these sea and lake "monsters" is still a hotly debated point; there are four main theories, two of which include dinosaurs, which are supposed to be long extinct.

And now it's theorized that mermaids,

those alluring fish-maidens, were manatees (sea cows) — but it's mighty hard to believe that those ungainly mammals were mermaids no matter how sex-starved those sailors were!

Scientists have had to admit some "monsters" do exist. It has been proved that the giant squid, or kraken, as it was known, existed. Huge man-eating sharks certainly seem like monsters. The dreaded sea snake, though relatively small (4 feet) is a reptile that inhabits tropical waters; its extremely poisonous bite kills humans. Orca, the killer whale, attacks dolphins and other small whales, but leaves humans alone. The lion's mane, or pink jellyfish (*Cyanea capillata*), of New England waters has hundreds of tentacles up to 200 feet long that can be fatal to

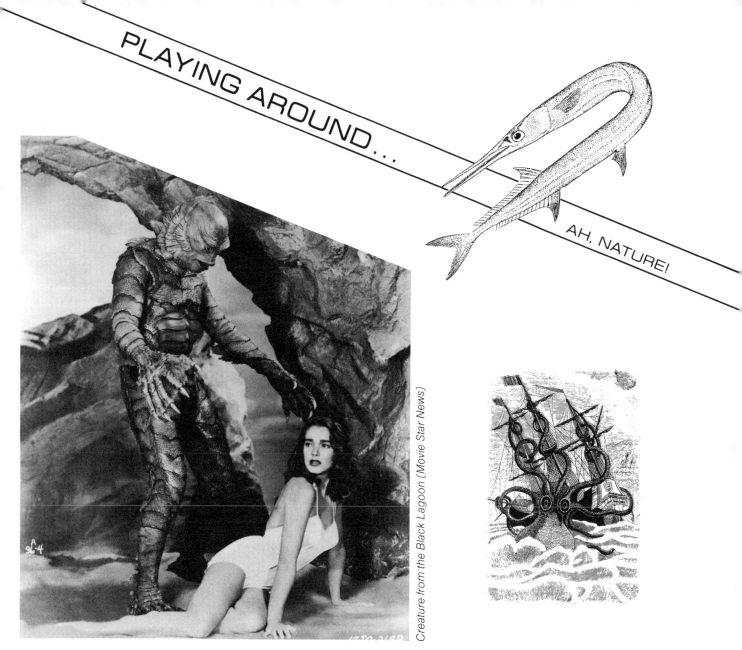

Creature from the Black Lagoon (Movie Star News)

swimmers. Even harmless creatures we know to exist can be too bizarre to readily comprehend. If a flying fish beached itself on the deck you stood on, its appearance would seem rather surreal. When early explorers came home and related what they had seen, the artists' renderings would be highly fanciful or grotesque representations of these new phenomena.

We are always creating new monsters and myths to replace the old. In books, songs, and film, we immortalize creatures who rise from the depths to wreak havoc — the great white whale Moby Dick, prehistoric creatures like Rodan and the Creature from the Black Lagoon, the great white man-eater of *Jaws*, and so on.

Water itself has powers we can barely comprehend. In science and psychological symbolism, water is regarded as the source of life — the "primordial soup." We carry the heritage of the sea in our bodies: We're about 70 percent water. Water as the womb environment probably accounts for the human fondness for bathing and underlies the psychological and spiritual benefits of newer explorations such as Rebirthing in hot tubs, and the work of Dr. John Lilly with isolation tanks.

Many cultures have myths depicting the beginning of the world or of life as arising out of the sea. One such creation myth is about the Great Turtle who rose from the ocean and on whose back the land is resting. And is there a more exquisite representation than *The Birth of Venus* by Botticelli, in which

the beautiful goddess is arising from the waves in a shell?

The ocean is a powerful symbol of the unconscious, the unknown in ourselves, deep, dark, and full of exciting, changeable, and sometimes frightening things. Water is hypnotic. Watch a waterfall and feel its pull...watch waves and become entranced. The sound of gently lapping waves is lulling; their surging power is awe-inspiring. Walking at the water's edge has inspired many a poet, artist, musician, thinker, scientist, statesman, sailor. In your exploration of the ocean's edge, you are very likely to explore your inner self as well.

MORE MONSTERS
For additional information, see *Beaches, Their Lives, Legends, and Lore* by Sean and Robert Manley (Chilton Book Co., 1968) and *In the Wake of the Sea-Serpents* by Bernard Heuvelmans (Hill & Wang, 1968)—this one's a classic.

There is, one knows not what sweet mystery about this sea, whose gently awful stirrings seem to speak of some hidden soul beneath.

— Herman Melville

Collecting Shells

Almost everyone has returned from a trip to the beach with at least a few shells tucked away as mementos, or for their beauty alone. Empty shells are easy to pick up on most beaches; you may even run across shell banks. They may not all be in tiptop condition, and you may have to search awhile to find a particular shell that isn't pale and worn, but that's part of the challenge and fun. Often fragments are so lovely in themselves that you won't feel the need to search further. (Serious collectors of rare specimens even rummage through the entrails of bottom-feeding fish.)

Most shells commonly found are from *mollusks*, animals whose shells provide both skeletal support and a home. While some shells can be found near freshwater, most are waiting for you along the seashore, and these fall into two major types. The *bivalve* shell has two parts joined at some point by a hinge and a few interlocking teeth. This type includes cockles, mussels, clams, oysters, and scallops, who usually bury themselves beneath the sand and so are likely to turn up on sandy shores. The snail-type or *gastropod* shelled creatures such as snails, whelks, winkles, conches, limpets, and abalones live on both rocky and sandy shores, but are most common along rocky coasts or coral reefs.

All you need to begin collecting shells is a good eye, a good back, and a good pail and shovel. When you get home, clean shells with a soft brush and plain water. If they're very worn, you might varnish or wax them to bring up the color. Display them on a shelf, tabletop, or in a clear glass canister, perhaps along with other beach treasures such as rock or coral. (If you're the crafty type, refer to one of the many books on shellcraft for project ideas.)

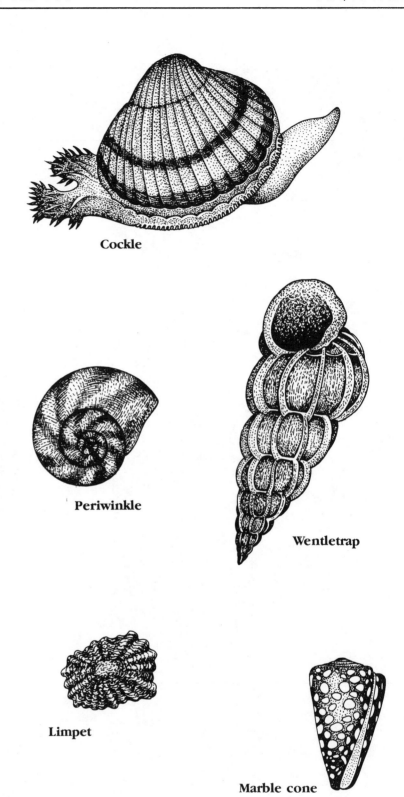

Cockle

Periwinkle

Wentletrap

Limpet

Marble cone

190

Cowrie

"Pelican's foot"

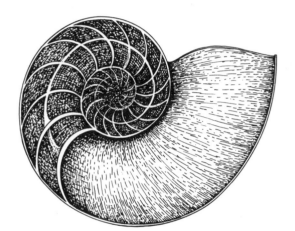

Nautilus (cross-section)

"The ocean? Sounds more like Mahler to me." (Actually, it's the sound of your own blood coursing through your body.)

The Beaches Are Moving: The Drowning of America's Shoreline by Wallace Kaufman and Orrin Pilkey (Anchor/Doubleday, 1979) provides an excellent portrait of the state of beach affairs — how shorelines work, how they maintain themselves, how misplaced good intentions not only fail to save the beaches, they sacrifice lives, and what can be done about all of this.

Weather-Wise

How many of your beach days have been ruined by a sudden unexpected downpour, or even an annoying light drizzle or overcast skies? Then, by the time you get home, the rain's stopped and the sun's out? Of course a cloudy sky doesn't preclude a trip to the beach, and eerie fog or even a rain shower have some charm. It's just nice to know what's up (and what will be down) so you can plan ahead and equip yourself with games, rain gear, and such. Before the gathering clouds spur you to pack it up and pack it in, learn how to read the clouds: an inexact science to be sure, but a fun one. (And if you're not too successful, remember the old saying: "If you don't like the weather...wait a minute.")

Other Weather Signs

Winds from the northeast or southwest generally bring fair weather. Those from the east often bring rain. *Barometer* readings indicate rising and falling air pressure. Generally a rising barometer means an improvement in the weather scene; but a rapid rise can bring strong winds. A falling barometer brings bad weather; a rapidly falling one means severe storms.

(NOAA)

If you're in the water when lightning strikes, get out — it conducts electricity. If you're in a small boat, head for home. Try to find shelter — a steel-frame building is best, but a car is safe too. If there is no shelter, head for the lowest spot.

WORDS OF WISDOM

Many old adages, such as these, have some basis in meteorological fact.

- *Red sky at night,*
  Sailors delight.
  Red sky in the morning,
  Sailors take warning.

- *Sound traveling far and wide*
  A stormy day will betide.

- *Evening red and morning gray*
  Sets the traveler on his way.
  Evening gray and morning red
  Brings down rain upon his head.

- *If a cloud looks as if it had been*
       scratched by a hen,
  Get ready to reef your topsails then.

- *Before the storm the crab*
       his briny home
  Sidelong forsakes, and strives for
       land to roam.

- *When trout refuse to bait a fly,*
  There ever is a storm a-nigh.

- *Seagull, seagull, sit on the sand*
  It's never good weather while
       you're on the land.

Stratocumulus usually appear in the evening and then disappear; no major change in the weather.

Altostratus can thicken and accompany a fall in barometer; expect a warm front and probably rain.

Stratus can precede some slow-moving warm fronts with low winds; can mean some drizzle, but not rain.

The Climate Advisor is a handy reference to year-round climate and weather in the United States, Canada, Mexico, and the Caribbean (over 340 different locations). For information, write to Climate Guide Publications, Box 323A, Station C, Flushing, NY 11367.

Cirrus often appear in combination with other clouds; no major change; possible warm front.

Cumulonimbus can accompany local thunderstorms. After the cold front passes, look for cooler weather, brisk winds, and sunny or partly sunny skies.

Cumulus are "fair-weather clouds" that often flatten out by late afternoon and vanish completely by evening; no major weather change, unless they build into cumulonimbus.

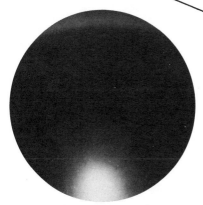

Cirrostratus may mean rain if followed by a falling barometer.

Nimbostratus can mean a slow-moving, stable warm front is arriving.

Altocumulus may lead to a warm front and rain or snow.

193

Beach Photography

If you think photography is using an Instamatic to snap Uncle Phil standing under a palm tree, and are ecstatic if it just "comes out," please turn the page. If you're one of the growing group of shutterbugs who want their photos to do something more, read on.

Three Steps to Better Photography

1. First of all, get a 35 mm SLR (single lens reflex) camera if you don't have one already. A manually operated 35 mm offers the most creative potential, in the form of interchangeable lenses and control of focusing and exposure. "Automatic" cameras take the mystery out of f-stops and shutter speeds, but the fun and challenge gets "thrown out with the bath water." And the batteries can go dead, leaving you in the lurch.

2. Learn how to "bracket." Take three different exposures of the same subject to make sure you've gotten the best one. Take one using the reading indicated on a light meter or on the printed guide that comes with the film. Then, take one over and one under that reading.

3. It's best to buy the body and lenses separately so you can get exactly what you need. The standard lens that camera "kits" (body plus lens) come with is a 50 or 55 mm, which is fine if you want ordinary pictures. A *wide-angle lens* (28 or 24 mm) gives more elbow room by encompassing more of the view. They come in handy for landscapes (and interiors). A *telephoto lens* (90 or 105 mm), on the other hand, magnifies objects and brings distant objects closer. They come in handy for portraits, some sports, and wildlife and nature photography.

CAMERA CARE

• Heat and humidity affect the film, especially color film; too much of both can affect your camera, too.

• To protect them both, store them away from direct sunlight, in a bag or at least covered by clothing.

• Sand can damage delicate mechanisms, too — and the lens may become scratched. So, keep your camera in the case and use a lens cap when you're not snapping away. Some photographers advise keeping it encased in a plastic bag with just the lens sticking out when you're beach bound.

S
M
I
L
E
!

RULES FOR THE
NATURE PHOTOGRAPHER

1. *Be patient.* Good photos cannot be rushed. You may have to stalk your subject, wait for the best action, or, for plants, wait for the wind to die down.

2. *Be quiet.* You don't want to scare your subject away.

3. *Be alert.* You may have only a second's opportunity. Be sure the lens cap is off, the shutter cocked, the exposure preset, and the focus adjusted (to average distance).

4. *Be knowledgeable.* It helps to know habits of creatures, where they are most likely to be found; then you can anticipate the best time to shoot. (For instance, whales expel air that might spray all over your camera and you if you're too close.)

5. *Be equipped.* Have a variety of lenses. A macrolens is an addition all nature photographers should consider. (A tripod and cable release are its companions.)

Invest in a good photography course or pick up a book on the subject. Of particular interest to beach photographers is *Outdoor Photography* by Erwin A. Bauer (Dutton, 1980; paper). It explains how to choose and use equipment, stalk wildlife, photograph animals, landscapes, and under water.

For those who are particularly interested in nature photography, there's *The Complete Manual of Nature Photography* by Guglielmo Izzi and Francesco Mezzatesta (Lippincott, 1980), who are two conservationists.

FLASH!
If you're going to use a pocket camera, at least let it be a Minolta Weathermatic. It's watertight so you can take it swimming, sailing, surfing, even snorkeling because it will still operate up to 15 feet under water. P.S. It floats. P.P.S. It ain't cheap (over $100).

195

BEACH FEASTS

No doubt about it: moving their jaws up and down is many beach-lovers' favorite sport. Bring-along foods are one thing (see *Before You Go*), but creating a food feast on the beach, using ingredients you've gathered or caught yourself (right at the dinner table, so to speak), is not only more satisfying, fun, and sociable, it's also by far more delicious because you'll end up with the freshest food there is. With a little talent, practice, knowledge, and luck, you may soon find that the only foods you need bring are lemons and butter.

Food to Forage

To begin with, you can forage for foods. The beach environment is full of edibles there for the picking, but species vary from East to West coasts, and from northern to tropical latitudes. Advance study is advisable so you'll know what your foraging prospects will be. Classics in the field are Euell Gibbons's foraging guides, *Stalking the Blue-Eyed Scallop* and the *Beachcombers' Handbook* (David McKay, 1964, 1967). You must also be sure that the shellfish you gather aren't from waters contaminated by red tides, sewage, or factory wastes. Some regions may restrict the amount you can pick; in some areas you may need a license.

On both coasts, *oysters* and many varieties of *clams* can be found near beaches and tidal creeks at low tide. *Crabs* are caught on any coastline, the best are found in the Chesapeake Bay and Pacific northwest. *Mussels* are common in salt and fresh water. Find *sea urchins* in tidal pools; pry *abalone* off Pacific coastal rocks, grab *grunions* (a small, beach spawning fish) on California beaches. Collect *scallops, periwinkles,* and *cockles* at low tide. Catching *lobster* (Northeastern or spiny Gulf) requires traps but its freshwater relative, the *crayfish,* is more accessible.

The beach environs yield delicious vegetables and fruits too. In Northern latitudes, pick *beach peas, sea rocket, beach plums, rose hips,* and various *berries.* In the tropics, find *coconuts, mangoes, bananas,* and *plantain* growing near beaches. *Kelp, dulse, rockweed,* and *sea lettuce* are all tasty, useful sea vegetables.

How elaborately you prepare the foods you've foraged is up to you. You can make bread from cattail pollen flour, and then spread it with rose hips jam or beach plum jelly. Concoct strand wheat cereal, candied scotch lovage leafstalks, and sea purslane pickles. Or you can keep it simple by tossing together a sea beach orach salad.

Is this any way to go shopping? You bet it is!

PLANTAIN

SEA ROCKET

EAT YOUR (SEA) VEGETABLES!

If you thought vegetables were yukky when you were a kid, wait till you try seaweed. Supposedly algae and kelp are the foods of the future, so you'd better begin getting used to them. The Chinese have been eating the stuff for centuries; so have the Japanese. Sea plants are an efficient food source — high in calcium, phosphorous, iron, vitamins A, B, C, niacin, protein, and trace elements, yet low in fat.

Before surprising the family with your own version of Seaweed Soufflé, refer to the tried-and-true recipes in *The Sea Vegetable Book* by Judith Cooper Madlener (Clarkson Potter, 1977; paper). According to the author, the Hijiki Sauté, which includes dried hijiki, carrots, and onions, has made many a convert.

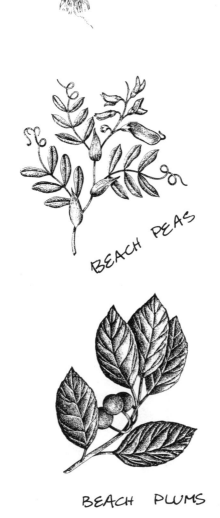

BEACH PEAS

BEACH PLUMS

PASS THE FINGERBOWL, PLEASE

If you find sampling and savoring local dishes one of the pleasures of traveling, meet Calvin Trillin, the seriously funny peripatetic food writer. Especially recommended for those enamored of *fruits de la mer* are "Off the Beach" and "Confessions of a Crab Eater" in his latest *Alice, Let's Eat: Further Adventures of a Happy Eater* (Vintage, 1979; paper). To wit:

If a research team systematically interviewed serious shellfish eaters about their most memorable shellfish experience, I suspect that the unifying theme of the testimony would be messiness. Ask anyone who has truly loved shellfish about the best he has ever had, and the answer tends to be a story ending with the table being hosed down after the meal, or mountains of shells being shoveled into trash bins. It is apparent to serious shellfish eaters that in the great evolutionary scheme of things crustaceans developed shells to protect them from knives and forks.

197

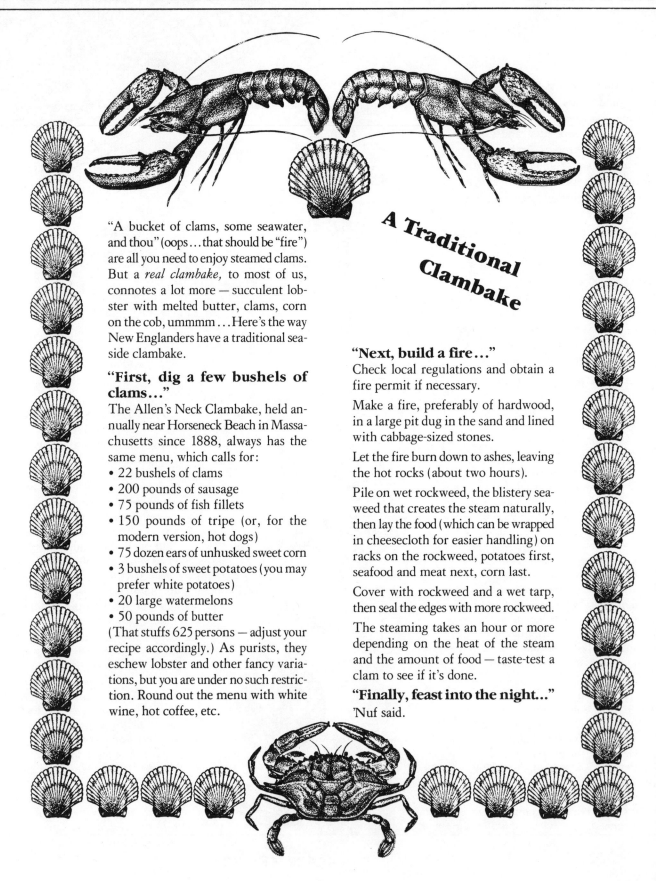

A Traditional Clambake

"A bucket of clams, some seawater, and thou" (oops...that should be "fire") are all you need to enjoy steamed clams. But a *real clambake,* to most of us, connotes a lot more — succulent lobster with melted butter, clams, corn on the cob, ummmm...Here's the way New Englanders have a traditional seaside clambake.

"First, dig a few bushels of clams..."

The Allen's Neck Clambake, held annually near Horseneck Beach in Massachusetts since 1888, always has the same menu, which calls for:

• 22 bushels of clams
• 200 pounds of sausage
• 75 pounds of fish fillets
• 150 pounds of tripe (or, for the modern version, hot dogs)
• 75 dozen ears of unhusked sweet corn
• 3 bushels of sweet potatoes (you may prefer white potatoes)
• 20 large watermelons
• 50 pounds of butter

(That stuffs 625 persons — adjust your recipe accordingly.) As purists, they eschew lobster and other fancy variations, but you are under no such restriction. Round out the menu with white wine, hot coffee, etc.

"Next, build a fire..."

Check local regulations and obtain a fire permit if necessary.

Make a fire, preferably of hardwood, in a large pit dug in the sand and lined with cabbage-sized stones.

Let the fire burn down to ashes, leaving the hot rocks (about two hours).

Pile on wet rockweed, the blistery seaweed that creates the steam naturally, then lay the food (which can be wrapped in cheesecloth for easier handling) on racks on the rockweed, potatoes first, seafood and meat next, corn last.

Cover with rockweed and a wet tarp, then seal the edges with more rockweed.

The steaming takes an hour or more depending on the heat of the steam and the amount of food — taste-test a clam to see if it's done.

"Finally, feast into the night..."

'Nuf said.

CLAMMING

At low tide, when the expanse of wet beach is the greatest, the soft wet sand at the water's edge is irresistible. You can squirm your feet around and be calf deep in cool soft sand in minutes. This is probably how the first humans on beaches found clams. Now clammers use shovels or rakes with curved tongs to capture this most popular mollusk, making the process a bit more like work. But the principle is the same; dig where bubbles appear in the wet sand at low tide. If you're lucky, this will uncover a bed of clams.

On the Jersey shore and much of the East Coast the prevalent clam is the quahog, the easiest to dig up. The flesh of the four-to five-inch-wide clam is tough, and they're usually ground up for canned chowder. Long Island beaches are good for cherrystones, which are the smallest quahogs, and a favorite for eating raw. The beaches of Cape Cod produce littlenecks, a great steamer or fryer.

On the northwest Pacific coast, clammers favor a more elusive variety, the long narrow razor clam. The razor clam is, as mollusks go, a speed demon.

The West Coast clammers' challenge, however, is the geoduck, pronounced "gooey duck." This huge clam can hide at depths of 3 feet and has a siphon (neck) as long as 3 feet. One "gooey duck" goes a long way.

COOKING FISH ON THE BEACH

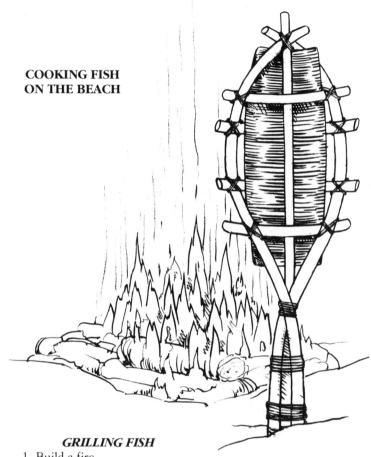

GRILLING FISH

1. Build a fire.
2. Small fish can be grilled rotisserie-style by inserting a greenwood stick in the mouth through the length of the fish and turning on a spit or by hand, over the coals. Fish will be cooked in 10 to 20 minutes, depending on size. (Scaling and gutting is optional.)
3. Larger fish — after being scaled and gutted, split and flattened — can be inserted between two long upright poles and braced with crosswise splits. Baste with butter or bacon fat. Hold poles at a slant to the fire to regulate the speed of cooking. Suggested for trout, small lakefish, salmon, halibut, bluefish.

A NATIVE FISHBAKE

1. Build a fire with stones added and let it burn down till only stones are left.
2. Scale the fish, split it open along the underbelly, and gut it.
3. Wrap the whole fish in large-leaf seaweed or banana leaves.
4. Pile seaweed on the hot stones, place the fish on the seaweed, and cover with more seaweed.
5. Baking time should approximate oven-baking time for the same size fish. Test for tenderness with a fork or toothpick. Suggested for pompano, mahi mahi, salmon, red snapper.

PLAYING AROUND...

Fishing, or: Guess Who's Coming to Dinner

According to the latest unofficial poll, people go fishing for three reasons: 1) It's relaxing. 2) It's exciting. 3) It's a great excuse to hang out near the water and do absolutely nothing. Almost incidental is what seems (to non-fishing, lip-licking bystanders at least) to be the raison d'ètre of all that silence and patience: the actual catch.

And yet...accidents *will* happen. Every once in a while there's a real tug on the line, and once the wild and unwilling creature that's taken the bait has been landed, it's time to make it a delectable part of your beach feast. But first, the catch.

Tips for Surf Fishing

1. Know where the fish are. (See *A Sports Lover's Guide.*)
2. Know the habits and preferences of the fish you plan to invite for dinner. For instance, striped bass are quite difficult to catch; kingfish are easy and like to nibble seaworms, clams, squid, and shrimp.
3. Learn to "read" the water. This can provide valuable clues as to the whereabouts of fish.
4. Buy the proper equipment and learn how to use it. (Sorry, in most cases string and a safety pin won't quite do, although a simple line wrapped around a tin can, a hook, sinker, and bit of bait is often all that's needed to persuade the inhabitants of rocky groins and inlets to bite.)
5. Be prepared to follow the fish. A school of fish don't stay put — they move constantly along the shore.
6. Ask questions of other fishermen, and from bait and tackle dealers near the area in which you intend to fish.
7. Be patient. One fellow in southern New Jersey fished for ten years, without success. He finally connected one morning; the prize? A 42-pound striped bass. The reaction? "It was worth it."

(Puerto Rico Tourism)

200

THE LURE OF FISHING

"It's not the actual catch that's so exciting. When you first feel a fish on the line, you feel a lot of energy — from the fish, and from yourself. And there's something really thrilling and, well, moving about that."

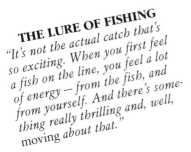

FISH STORIES

Sport Fishing USA is a good-looking encyclopedia on the fun, facts, frustrations, mysteries, and rewards of fishing. It is illustrated in color; has articles on fish, fishermen, fishing environments, and fishery science; and will provide you with almost as much fun as the sport itself. This 464-page hardcover book is available from Superintendent of Documents, U.S. Government Printing Office, Washington, D.C. 20402. (Specify item #2Z9; stock number 023-010-00235-2.)

The Whole Fishing Catalogue by the Editors of Consumer Guide (Simon and Schuster, 1978; paper) gives you fishing strategy, techniques, how to match tackle, license data, prime angling sites, and evaluations of fishing tackle and accessories.

201

WHAT'S COOKING?

Steamed clams, broiled lobster, she-crab soup, shrimp jambalaya, mussels in white wine sauce, broiled red snapper. Here's a selected list of the best of the seafood cookbooks. One bite and you're back on the beach.

American Cooking (Time-Life, 1968, 1970, 1971). This series, entitled Foods of the World, is published in regional volumes, with recipes for everything from soup to nuts.

James Beard's New Fish Cookery (Little, Brown, 1976). Includes recipes for all common saltwater fish, freshwater fish, shellfish, and frogs, snails, turtles, etc.

The Beach Plum Inn Cookbook by Theresa A. Morse and Fred Feiner (Doubleday, 1977). Recipes from the famed inn on Martha's Vineyard.

Lobster Pots & Sea Rocket Sandwiches: A Guide to the Edibles of the Seashore by Catherine Derevitsky (Down East, 1979; paper). Lists edibles from bayberry to sea urchins with recipes and nutritional info, charming illustrations by author.

Maryland Seafood Cookbooks I & II. (Available from Seafood Marketing Authority, Department of Economic and Community Development, Annapolis, Maryland).

The Mussel Cookbook by Sarah Hurlburt (Harvard University Press, 1979; paper). International recipes and historical and biological background of this delicious abundant mollusk.

The Pleasures of Seafood by Rima and Richard Collin (Holt, Rinehart & Winston, 1977). Lots of different regional recipes, especially from the New Orleans area.

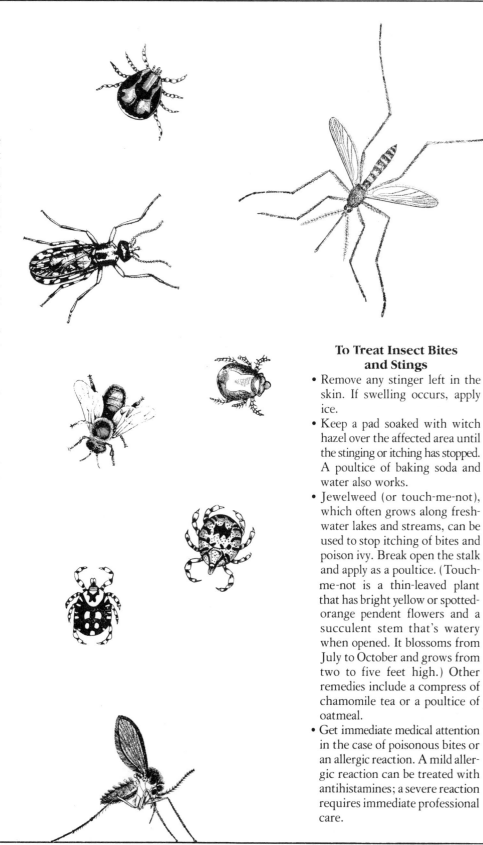

WHEN
YOU'RE THE ENTREE...

Chow time isn't the only time you've got to worry about insect pests. But it *is* the most annoying time, and these uninvited guests are attracted to foods other than human flesh. Follow these tips and you'll help keep hungry insect hordes from spoiling your outing.

Tips on Avoiding Pests

- Avoid swampy areas, still brackish water, and rotting organic matter — all of which attract insect pests.
- Flying insects are more likely to pester if the air is still, so choose a breezy location.
- Cover or containerize all foods.
- Remember that perfumes often attract insects, especially bees.
- Dry off after swimming — biting flies seem to like wet skin.

Repelling Pests

- Use a repellent substance on exposed skin (Cutter makes an excellent one for wilderness hikers). Oil of citronella also works.
- Burn "punks" (find cattails in marshes), citronella candles, or the commercial repellent rings.
- Protect your pet with a tick and flea collar, but be aware that moisture can cause some to become dangerously more potent, so remove the collar if there's a chance your pet will get wet.

About Insecticides

- Commercial fog insecticides are designed for backyard use and, as such, are fairly effective. They are nonselective poisons that kill all flying insects — not a very ecologically sound idea — but even they may not be able to make a dent in the greater outdoors. It's recommended that you try avoid-and-repel tactics rather than overkill.

To Treat Insect Bites and Stings

- Remove any stinger left in the skin. If swelling occurs, apply ice.
- Keep a pad soaked with witch hazel over the affected area until the stinging or itching has stopped. A poultice of baking soda and water also works.
- Jewelweed (or touch-me-not), which often grows along freshwater lakes and streams, can be used to stop itching of bites and poison ivy. Break open the stalk and apply as a poultice. (Touch-me-not is a thin-leaved plant that has bright yellow or spotted-orange pendent flowers and a succulent stem that's watery when opened. It blossoms from July to October and grows from two to five feet high.) Other remedies include a compress of chamomile tea or a poultice of oatmeal.
- Get immediate medical attention in the case of poisonous bites or an allergic reaction. A mild allergic reaction can be treated with antihistamines; a severe reaction requires immediate professional care.

And now, boys and girls, we come to the real nitty-gritty, the raison d'être that both sexes flock to brave the sand and surf: the never-ending quest for the perfect man, the perfect woman, the perfectly lit cigarette. For these and other centuries-old problems, we turn to our own beloved advice columnist, Dear Gabby.

Dear Gabby: How can I meet women at the beach?

It's not that different from anywhere else. Being good-looking helps. But not too good-looking, or you'll scare them away. The beach does have an informal atmosphere, though; and there's a lot of activity you can use as an excuse to start a conversation. But the best thing about meeting women at the beach is: everybody's running around half naked (sometimes more than half), so you know right off exactly what you're going to get.

If you take the aggressive road, stay away from your blanket as much as possible. *Circulate.* This is a big outdoor party. Walk, run, collect shells and compare them with the beach belle of your choice. Say hello to everyone as you make the rounds; after you've said hi to the chosen mermaid a few times, how can she refuse your invitation to join you for a quick dip, a short jog, a friendly game of backgammon?

Make sure you bring a blanket that's big enough for two. And puh-leese — no smelly old army blankets.

PLAY A MUSICAL INSTRUMENT

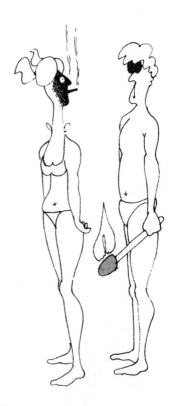

HELP LIGHT HER CIGARET:

Bring a well-stocked "bar" to the beach. A cooler stocked with interesting stuff, such as Tom Collins fixings, mineral water and limes, and imported beer, is irresistible when all the competition has to offer is lukewarm soda served in inelegant paper cups (or worse yet, straight from the can).

If you'd rather have *them* come to *you,* bringing the above-mentioned props won't hurt either. Wear some interesting article of clothing that doesn't make you look too silly — something you've picked up at another beach perhaps. Play a classical music station on your radio; read *Moby Dick;* pretend you're reading a book in a foreign language. Get a tattoo — real or fake — and flaunt it.

Read up on beach lore and the flora and fauna that's native to your beach. It depends upon the listener, of course, but most people will respond better to "Did you know that jellyfish swim by a kind of jet propulsion?" than to "Drown here often?"

(If you still need more help, write to Symphony Press, P.O. Box 515, Tenafly, NJ 07670, for *Summer Love.* It's by Eric Weber, the author of *How to Pick Up Girls* and *How to Pick Up Women.*)

204

Dear Gabby: How can I meet men at the beach?

This is the 1980s my dears, so everything I've said for the men goes for you too. Even the tattoo — I know one young lovely who has a darling little heart on her tummy. Of course, she affectionately calls it "Zippo" because, like the lighter, it never fails.

One more thing. Go easy on the make-up — or leave it off entirely. Unless he's into clowns, Mr. Right will hardly find technicolor cheeks a turn-on.

For additional advice, get *How to Meet Men Now That You're Liberated* by Audrey Gellis (Popular Library, 1978; paper).

COMPLIMENT THE WEATHER.

REVEAL YOUR BEST FEATURES

KEEP A FANCY BEACH BLANKET

BRING YOUR PET.

205

Dear Gabby: What do I do if someone kicks sand in my face?

Dear Gabby: How can I light a cigarette at the beach?

USE A BIGGER FLAME

STAND BEHIND A WIND BLOCK

Dear Gabby: How can I get the sand out of my bathing suit without feeling like an idiot or getting arrested?

There's really only one cure for removing sand from where you don't want it — a dip in the briny. Simply wade out to neck-deep water (waist-deep is enough for men), and conduct your business there. You may have to remove the offending garment and actually rinse it out, or you might get away with a light dusting in situ. Once you're through housecleaning, wade back toward shore — and run like a bat out of hell to avoid the breakers redepositing the nasty stuff.

Or, you can avoid the situation completely by (1) avoiding the bathing suit (go to a nude beach); (2) avoiding the sand (stay above it all by holding court from a beach chair or hanging out at the bar, snack tables, or boardwalk).

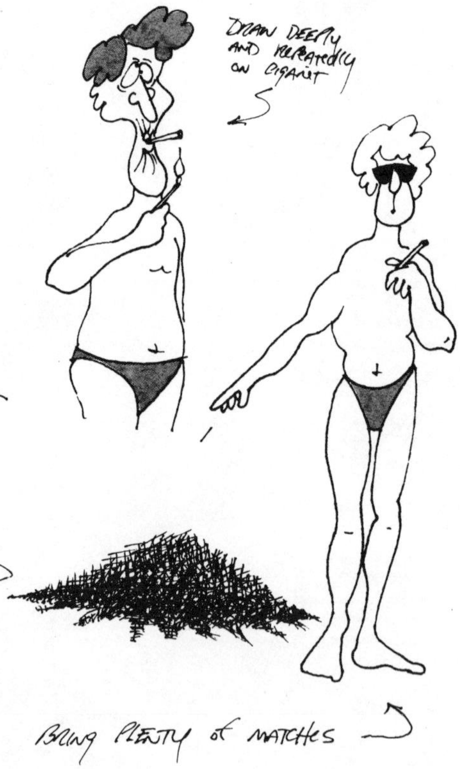

DRAW DEEPLY AND REPEATEDLY ON CIGARET

" GET BELOW THE WIND "

BRING PLENTY OF MATCHES

No Date Tonight?
Call Noctiluca Delight!
The beach at night is a whole new experience, and especially romantic if you can share it with a friend. What first-run movie can compare with the light of a full moon spilling over the sea, bouncing off the crests of water cascading musically over the beach? What disco can compare to the canopy of stars that leap out overhead after the moon has set? (As your eyes adjust, you may discern an entirely new cast of sea characters, creatures that remain burrowed in the sand during the day — not for the squeamish.)

More enchanting still is bioluminescence. This phosphorescent phenomenon occurs often in warm beaches with temperate waters. As you walk along the water's edge, you may find you're kicking up sprays of stardust — actually a tiny protozoan called noctiluca. Occasionally a breaker of bioluminescence will roll up on the beach, spewing cool flames of softly glowing living fire. Should the noctiluca population prove too weak — or the ambient light too strong — for the magic to appear, don't give up. Invite that special someone you've been dying to meet all day (or all summer) to a private light show. Get down close to the sand, cover you heads with the blanket you have resourcefully brought along, and begin digging. Even if the noctiluca doesn't come to the party, you might create a few sparks of your own.

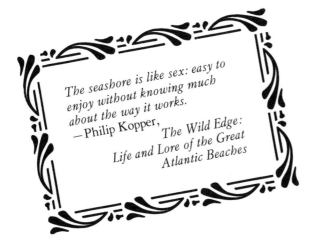

The seashore is like sex: easy to enjoy without knowing much about the way it works.
—Philip Kopper, The Wild Edge: Life and Lore of the Great Atlantic Beaches

AQUATIC ETIQUETTE
Swimming in the same ocean does not give a man the right to force his conversation or attentions on other — usually feminine — swimmers or sunbathers. Exhibitions of water-splashing, porpoising, wrestling and sand-throwing, often engaged in by very young men to attract feminine attention, usually make them offensive in the very eyes of those they seek to attract, and certainly make them loathsome to the run-of-the-beach bather in search of a little peace.

— from
Amy Vanderbilt's Etiquette

209

Sand Castles and Sand Sculptures

Sculptors and architects have always been purveyors of permanency. They seek immortality in their constructions of wood, stone, and steel. There is, however, a form of expression available on any beach to the sculptor or architect who does not eschew the ephemeral. Sand sculptures and sand castles provide hours of creative activity, and if they are washed away by the rising tide, at least they are more substantive than "castles in the air" and as permanent as some houses built on the ever-shifting sands of the barrier islands.

As Nietzsche said, becoming is more important than being (or words to that effect). Expressing yourself in a perfectly natural medium is an end in itself; the tide merely cleans your canvas, enabling you to start anew on the morrow. But enough philosophy. Let's get down to some of the basic techniques of sand modeling.

It is important to begin at low tide for the maximum amount of working and display time. Make sure you have plenty of suntan lotion, a shirt and a hat (hours of artistry in the sun can harm even the most suntanned body); bring a rake and some modeling tools, some buckets and shovels.

Pick the proper size plot for the project and rake it clean of all extraneous materials (shells, bottlecaps, stones, etc.). You can keep some of these objects for decorative purposes. Pour buckets of water over the entire working area to moisten the sand through and through. While working, add water as needed to keep the sand moist and pliable; rock salt would also work.

There are many techniques for modeling wet sand. Build up characters on flat sand or carve them out of angled mounds. Just as in the sculpting of clay, you can add or subtract sand to create the hills and valleys of your design.

Create sand castle towers easily with a pail by filling the pail with wet sand, inverting it, and tapping the bottom. Use ice cream sticks and spoons to carve windows and dig moats.

You can even paint sand sculptures with water-based spray paint or by sprinkling the finished work with dry, powdered tempera. Use shells and bottlecaps to create eyes, ears, and buttons. The sky (or in this case, the sand) is the limit in picking subjects to model on the sands of your beach. Models of television personalities, flora, fauna, and elaborate medieval castles have all been constructed in fun and competition.

For believers in the joy of doing, as opposed to the joy of having, sculpting in sand, like virtue, is its own reward.

210

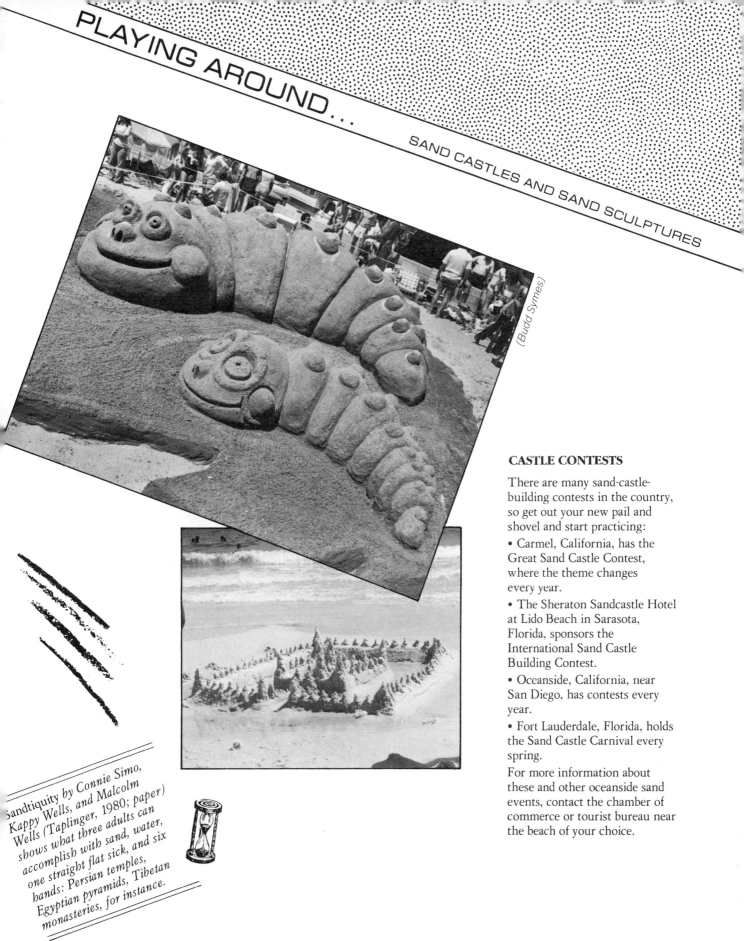

(Budd Symes)

CASTLE CONTESTS

There are many sand-castle-building contests in the country, so get out your new pail and shovel and start practicing:

• Carmel, California, has the Great Sand Castle Contest, where the theme changes every year.

• The Sheraton Sandcastle Hotel at Lido Beach in Sarasota, Florida, sponsors the International Sand Castle Building Contest.

• Oceanside, California, near San Diego, has contests every year.

• Fort Lauderdale, Florida, holds the Sand Castle Carnival every spring.

For more information about these and other oceanside sand events, contact the chamber of commerce or tourist bureau near the beach of your choice.

Sandtiquity by Connie Simo, Kappy Wells, and Malcolm Wells (Taplinger, 1980; paper) shows what three adults can accomplish with sand, water, one straight flat sick, and six hands: Persian temples, Egyptian pyramids, Tibetan monasteries, for instance.

GONE WITH THE WIND

The wide open spaces of the beach are a perfect place to let your spirit soar — whether you elect to let your body leave terra firma or not. But where to begin the transformation into a UFO?

Go Fly a Kite

Warm up to the idea of flying by flying a kite — a sport, an art, a hobby that was invented over 3000 years ago. In Asia, where the first kite was probably launched, kite flying is still taken quite seriously: fighter kites cut down their opponents, and festivals draw 50,000 spectators to watch such spectacles as a 45-by-35-foot kite flown by 40 to 50 men.

All *you* need is a simple little number (already assembled or in kit form) with a tail to steady it and keep wobbling to a minimum. These are still available for under $10; but the sky's the limit if you consider custom-made jobs, parafoils, multicolor rip-stop nylon, mylar giants, box kites, fighter kites, or flexifoils. Beaches are a favorite site because of their steady winds, open sky, and sparsely populated grounds. There is, however, such a thing as too much wind: 4 to 18 miles per hour is the best range. If the trees whip and toss, you're better off saving your venture for a calmer day.

You may need a friend at first to help you launch your paper bird, ersatz plane, or flying tiger, especially if there's only a slight breeze. Have your helper hold it about 100 feet away from you. As it is released, hold the line taut and the kite will climb. Give it as much slack as it needs to gain altitude. You can try "pumping" the line to help it lift in sluggish wind. Soon it will rise above the fickle ground wind to the steadier and stronger upper breezes. Remember to keep an eye on your kite as it flies in case it decides to take a nose dive or loop the loop.

When you're ready to call it a day, reel it in slowly, while your friend walks under it to catch it if it's fragile. (The sand is soft enough to cushion the landing of most kites.)

(Kitelines)

PARASAILING — THE FUN AND SAFE WAY TO FLY

Hang Gliding

The ultimate kite. You launch yourself through the air by running or jumping off a high level so the air current carries you and your vehicle — for how long depends upon the currents and your ability. Hang gliding is not for the dilettante — it's just air between you and never-never land. For more information on how to be high as a kite (literally and figuratively), write to the United States Hang Gliding Association, Inc., P.O. Box 66306, Los Angeles, CA 90066. They offer an information kit for beginners or interested parties that contains sources for dealers, schools, and so on. They also publish a monthly magazine, *Hang Gliding.*

HOW TO WATER-SKI AND FLY YOUR KITE TOO

Kiting, one of life's simple pleasures, is a natural at the beach. The swooshing of kites overhead is becoming more and more common at beaches.

For more information, write to Kite Lines, 7106 Campfield Rd., Baltimore, MD 21207. They'll tell you about the club and kite shop nearest you and send you their "Brief Guide to Safe and Sure Kiting" for a self-addressed, stamped envelope. For a fee, they'll also send you their quarterly magazine. On their list of recommended books are: *Kites* by Wyatt Brummitt (Western Golden Guide Series, 1971; paper); the *Penguin Book of Kites* (Penguin, 1976; paper) by David Pelham; and a beautiful coffee-table volume, *The Art of the Japanese Kite* by sculptor Tal Streeter (Weatherhill, 1974). Happy flying!

PLAYING AROUND...

MORE GAMES TO PLAY

Remember the beach party after the prom? Somebody yelled, "Let's form a pyramid!," people dropped to their knees, and the construction began. More often than not the person left to be the pinnacle was "Moose," the 250-pound second-string center, and when the bodies were untangled you knew how the Egyptian slaves felt.

A human pyramid, like the stone variety, requires the biggest building blocks on the bottom. This insures that the larger people will support the most weight and the lighter people will be stepping on their backs.

A soft part of the beach may be inviting as a surface, to cushion falls, but it will also increase the likelihood of the same, as the loose sand will not provide much stability for the foundation folk. A hard-packed surface will reduce the chances of collapse and will actually be less abrasive on the bottom line's hands and knees. To further reduce abrasion, a number of blankets may be laid on the sand at the start.

After finding an appropriate site, you're ready to begin the folly. The next step is figuring out how many people to put on the bottom. There's probably some mathematical formula (divide the number of people by the youngest person's age and multiply by number of bottles of beer that have been consumed, then subtract the date and add six), but since anyone in his right mind who wants to try this couldn't possibly be in his right mind, use this handy table:

The Human Pyramid

6 people total = 3 on the bottom
10 people total = 4 on the bottom
15 people total = 5 on the bottom
21 people total = 6 on the bottom

With more than 21 people, you will have a pyramid so high that the top bananas will get nosebleeds — so it's not recommended. Good luck.

Frisbee

There's always a couple of lunatics tossing a UFO (undesirable flying object) around. From those of us who for some strange reason don't appreciate sand in unexpected places and plastic burns: Stick to uncrowded stretches of beach, please.

(Budd Symes)

Kadima

A newish paddle ball game that originated in Israel and is perfect for beach play. Simply start 15 feet apart and maintain a volley for as long as possible. The better you get, the farther away you stand and the faster you hit the ball. Also called Beach Ball, Paddle Ball, and Radima — available at department and sporting goods stores.

Volleyball

An old favorite, and a serious one at certain beaches, where you must be an accomplished player to join in. It's strenuous, sweat-provoking, and satisfying — but resist the temptation to plunge into ice-cold surf to cool off afterward because your baking muscles may cramp up.

215

(Budd Symes)

Putting One Foot in Front of the Other

EIGHT ORGANIZED MILES

A beach walk can be a pleasant serendipitous stroll or a carefully planned activity. One book that gives you step-by-step game plans is *The Complete Book of Walking* by Charles T. Kuntzelman and the Editors of Consumer Guide (Simon and Schuster, 1979). For instance, for Key Biscayne, Florida, trekkies, they suggest beginning at the lighthouse on Cape Florida in the state park. Walk for one mile along the beach, staying in the park. Keep walking along the beach and you'll pass Key Biscayne, the hotel strip, the Miami Zoo, Crandon Park, and finally a beach that's surrounded by mangroves. To get back to point A, follow the beach round to Rickenbacker Crossway, cross to the bus stop at Crandon Marina, and retrace your steps.

When your beach blanket becomes too much of a security blanket and begins to feel more like a terry cloth Alcatraz, it's time for an easy amble along the shore. Inhale, exhale, explore, make a friend, even if it's only a seagull. The water is a cooling, soothing, softening salt bath for your tootsies; the gritty sand a natural pumice for those rough spots you could very well live without. It's one of the best exercises for your whole body: The sand massages your soles and makes your arches work overtime. You can walk for miles on the right beach without realizing it. Should you fail to resist the temptation to join everyone else and break into a run from sheer exuberance, try not to overdo it. Alternate walking and running sprints. This is especially necessary if you're a weekend athlete; but even old running hands will find that running barefoot on hard-packed sand is harder on the anatomy than a track and cushioned running shoes. Some beach runners recommend the usual heel-first landing. Others say beach condi-

tions dictate setting the foot down ball-first to avoid shin splints, but this technique may be harder on your calf muscles. Running on dry, soft sand is an even more strenuous workout, but it solves the problem of running on the angled surface that's characteristic of the water's edge.

Dr. Kenneth Cooper, popularizer of aerobic exercise, estimates that running on a sandy beach is about 20 percent more difficult than running on a solid surface. So if you manage a sand mile in 9:30, it's the equivalent of a regular mile in 8:30. Watch out for *hyperthermia,* or overheating. That can occur if you're not used to exercising in hot humid weather and your body generates more heat than it can handle. Danger signs are throbbing temples and a feeling of cold in your chest, sides, and back. Of course, these symptoms could also mean you're in love. In either case, cool off by taking a tepid shower or immersing yourself in tepid water. (Cold water could cause muscle cramps.)

216

BOARDWALK SPLINTERS

So you gave your feet some freedom and the boardwalk gave you
some splinters...Now what?

First, keep in mind that it isn't
always necessary to do anything
about a splinter. Your body has
its own defenses and will work a
deeply imbedded splinter up to
the surface in its own time. If
one end of the splinter is
sticking out, firmly grasp it with
a tweezer or your fingernails and
pull it out. Dab on alcohol or a
3-percent solution of hydrogen
peroxide. If a deeply imbedded
splinter is causing pain, try
soaking the affected area in
warm water or hydrogen peroxide for fifteen minutes then
squeeze gently. (Digging it out
with a needle or pin is not
recommended, but if you must
do it, sterilize the needle and the
skin area first.)

The best treatment, however, is
prevention. Unless your feet are
tougher than leather, wear
sandals or shoes when strolling
or running on boardwalks.

(Picture Collection Cooper-Hewitt Museum Library)

FREE SWIMMING BATHS, FOOT OF FIFTH STREET, EAST RIVER.—[FROM A SKETCH BY STANLEY FOX.]

FREELANCE FORTUNE HUNTING

Stalking the solid-gold Spanish
doubloon may be more your cup
of tea than Euell Gibbons's blue-
eyed scallop; if so, you need a
metal detector. Metal detectors
such as this one from Relco in
Houston, Texas, operate somewhat like magnets. They emit
lines of electromagnetic force
and so detect objects that conduct electricity and/or magnetic
lines of force. The job can be
complicated by mineralized soil
found near the sea, movement,
and temperature changes. Some
models are designed to take
these factors into account;
unfortunately, it may take a
while for them to pay for themselves: they cost up to $200.
(There are many books on the
market, though, that help guide
you in your hunt.)

(Chuck DeLaney)

I am right in the swim

THE POSTCARD PROBLEM

The toughest part of many a vacation has always been thinking up something clever and witty to put on the backs of the postcards you send home. (Which always arrive three days after you've returned, of course.)

- Think up one appropriate message and write it on everyone's card. (In Hawaii: "Dear so-and-so, This is a great place to get Lei'd.")
- Filch a greeting from *Postcard Poems* edited by Paul B. Janeczko (Dutton, 1979). If the brief poems by, among others, William Carlos Williams, Richard Brautigan, Ezra Pound, and Carl Sandburg are good enough for 13-year-olds, they're perfect for vacationers.
- Buy and write before you go. Send for the list of 1200 cards from 400 different cities made available by Foreign Cards, Ltd., P.O. Box 123, Guilford, CT 06436.
- Don't send any; save them for yourself as souvenirs. If all else fails, you can always fall back on "Having a wonderful time. Wish you were here." They'll understand.

WHAT TO DO
ON A RAINY DAY

You say it's the fifth straight day of rain and you and your fellow travelers are going buggy? When the weather turns rotten you needn't stay inside and mope all day:

- Read — make sure you've brought something along that you've been dying to tackle. (The trashiest, least socially redeeming novel usually fits the bill nicely; but of course you might opt for a biography, historic novel, or Calculus I.)
- Take up drawing; if that's hopeless, color in the drawings in this book.
- Do the crossword puzzle on page 219, even if you hate crosswords.
- Explore the surrounding area for local activities; check with the local chamber of commerce for museums, tours, exhibits, and so on.
- Toss on a rain slicker and brave the elements; get to know the beach in its different moods.
- Pick up a copy of *Games (and More!) for Backpackers* by June Fleming (Victoria House, 1979; paper). It's divided into three sections: make-it-at-home projects, in-the-field pleasures, and a catalog of store-bought packable pleasures. Written by someone who's been in the same boat, it's useful for anyone who's house- or tent-bound — but comes in especially handy if you've got kids on board.

On the Beach

by Stephanie Spadaccini

Across

1 Western hills
7 _____ City, New Jersey
12 Hawaiian island
16 Wine, in Paris
19 "Ain't That_____"
   (Fats Domino hit)
20 *Laugh-In's* Judy
21 Love, on Majorca
22 Direction from
   Southampton to
   East Hampton
23 Surf Citizens, U.S.A.
25 Sand castle resident?
27 "_____ a real nowhere
   man..."
28 _____ Lanka
29 Satisfy
31 Actor Alain_____
32 Aries
34 *Casablanca* piano player
36 Japanese general
39 Chemical suffixes
41 Leonardo da_____
43 San Francisco Bay city
48 Say cheese!
49 Terminating
51 Floating gangster type?
53 Stripper Lily St.-_____
54 Common abbreviation (pl.)
55 Roam, with "about"
57 Training colleges (abbr.)
58 Ms. Shearer

60 Small, in Saint-Tropez
62 Indonesian island group
63 Norwegian king
66 Foundation
69 Spanish queen
70 Brooch
71 Surfer's "fuel"
76 Vermont lake
73 Laughing sound
74 Army rank (abbr.)
75 Gets by, with "out"
76 Bush's title (slang)
77 Cry of discovery
78 Meadow
79 Take it easy
80 You at Myrtle Beach
81 Employ
82 *Happy Days'* Moran, et al.
84 Dog's lead
86 Friend, in Acapulco
91 Winter white,
   on Madison Avenue
92 Wonder
95 Buzzard's_____
97 *The Haunted Pool* author
100 Sailor
102 Improper
104 _____ *County* (1957 film)
105 Barbecue rods
106 Give the cold shoulder
107 Prophet
108 Swimmer's condition
111 Summertime tea addition
112 Adam and_____ a raft
114 Italian island resort
118 Summer mo.
120 Beach chair part
122 Charlie the Tuna?
125 Olympic swimmer of the 30s
129 Cardinals' monogram
130 Roles for Roddy McDowall
    and Kim Hunter
131 Map feature
132 Kind of whale
133 Ma Bell's co.
134 Beside, with "to"
135 *The Wreck of the Mary*_____
136 Hurries

Down

1 English resort city
2 Movie theater job
3 Vegas hotel
4 Mr. Hunter
5 Scottish uncles
6 Roebuck's partner
7 Alas, by Galway Bay
8 Taxi
9 Cupid
10 Author Seton
11 Seagull's home
12 _____ Street Beach,
   in Chicago
13 Friend, in Cannes
14 Havlicek's nickname
15 Goad
16 Where blonde actress
   vacations?
17 In a stupid manner
18 Landlocked state (abbr.)
24 Hoover's agy.
26 Oyster's relative
30 Feminine endings
33 Roman 1101
35 Food additive (abbr.)
37 "...walk_____the western
   wave..." (Shelley)
38 All-wet comedienne?
40 Sunday talk, for short
41 Neckline shape
42 *Picnic* playwright
44 _____, o, u
45 Prefix meaning "not"
46 Mr.'s mate

47 Employee of 24 Down (abbr.)
48 Waterway (abbr.)
50 Stopping point at a
   private beach
52 Summer coolers for city
   dwellers
56 Beached blonde celeb?
59 Warm weather workers
60 Folks
61 Western resort
62 _____ pandowdy
64 Roman greetings
65 Mae West, for one
66 Flock
67 Zoological suffix
68 Actress-turned-
   beachcomber?
83 Negative answers
85 Vital statistic
86 "I want_____, just like.."
87 Fellows
88 Believer (suffix)
89 Needlefish
90 Singleton
92 Friendly

93 Sleeping accommodations
   for a Seabee?
94 Printer's measures
95 City transportation
96 Frankie's companion at
   the beach
98 Actress Charlotte
99 Morning moisture
101 Bee (prefix)
103 Over, in Baden-Baden
107 Shoot at
109 Van Gogh had one
110 Puts to bed, with "in"
113 In the wink_____eye
115 Latin abbreviation
116 Sand hill
117 Greek peak
119 Grasp
121 Seas, on the French Riviera
122 The Concorde (abbr.)
123 Gender
124 Presidential monogram
126 Thrice (music)
127 Summer, in Cannes
128 Brighton Beach beverage

Beach Movie Trivia Quiz

Beach Party, released in 1960 by American International, touched off a whole cycle of youth-oriented musical comedies that were set at the beach. Singer Frankie Avalon and former Mouseketeer Annette Funicello were the perennial cute couple of the American International films of this genre; the films were so popular that Frankie and Annette became America's sweethearts. But Annette (as Dee Dee) and Frankie (as Frankie) weren't the only members of the casts:

A. The Match Game: Match the stars with the movie or movies they appeared in.

The Cast

_____ 1. Don Rickles
_____ 2. Deborah Walley
_____ 3. The Hondells
_____ 4. Paul Lynde
_____ 5. Buster Keaton
_____ 6. Buster Keaton as "Bwana"
_____ 7. A gorilla
_____ 8. Little Stevie Wonder
_____ 9. Morey Amsterdam
_____10. Dorothy Malone
_____11. Luciana Paluzzi
_____12. Buddy Hackett
_____13. Mickey Rooney
_____14. Martha Hyer

The Movies
a. *Beach Blanket Bingo*
b. *Beach Party*
c. *Bikini Beach*
d. *How to Stuff a Wild Bikini*
e. *Muscle Beach Party*

(Note: You get 5 extra points if you can remember the plots of each movie; 10 extra points if you can invent plots that are sillier than the originals.)

(The Museum of Modern Art/Film Stills Archive)

B. Three "Other" Beach Movies: Monkey-see, monkey-do.

1. *Wild on the Beach*
   a. The year of its release. _____
   b. The three singers or singing groups.
   _____
   _____
   c. The two principal actors. _____
   _____

2. *Gidget Goes Hawaiian*
   a. The year of its release. _____
   b. Who played Jeff? _____
   c. Who played Gidget? _____
   d. What does the word *gidget* mean?

3. *Surf Party*
   a. The year of its release. _____
   b. Who played Len? _____
   c. Who played Junior? _____
   d. The two singing groups. _____
   _____

C. Elvis and the Beach: Not strictly beach movies, but "the Pelvis" did make three that were set on the beach. What's the title and date of the movie in which:

1. Elvis is thrown into jail, but all ends happily with a wedding.
2. Elvis and "family" set up housekeeping on a beach, spend a day in court, but all ends happily when Elvis and an orphan fall in love.
3. Elvis loses his job as a sailor, becomes a nightclub singer and part-time lifeguard, conquers his fear of heights, and all ends happily when he decides to return to a career as a trapeze artist.

D. Surfer Movies: There are several, but the best and most well known is the one wherein three surfers embark on a three-month international adventure in search of the "perfect wave." Their odyssey takes them from Malibu to Ghana, with stops at Nigeria, Australia, New Zealand, Tahiti, and Hawaii. What's the name of this movie, and who was it's star? _____
_____

E. Horror Flicks: As if beach movies weren't silly enough.

1. An oceanographic professor in sea monster's clothing murders his way through this one.
   a. The director/star. _____
   b. The name of the movie. _____
   c. The music credit. _____
   d. The title song. _____

2. Radioactive waste material comes into contact with a human skull, turning it into a horrible monster in need of human blood.
   a. The name of the movie. _____
   b. The "secret" substance that saves the day. _____

(Movie Star News)

B	U	T	T	E	S		O	C	E	A	N		O	A	H	U		V	I	N
A	S	H	A	M	E		C	A	R	N	E		A	M	O	R		E	N	E
T	H	E	B	E	A	C	H	B	O	Y	S		K	I	N	G	C	R	A	B
H	E	S		S	R	I		S	A	T	E		D	E	L	O	N
	R	A	M		S	A	M				T	O	J	O		A	N	E	S
V	I	N	C	I		S	A	N	M	A	T	E	O		S	M	I	L	E
E	N	D	I	N	G		G	E	O	R	G	E	R	A	F	T		C	Y	R
E	G	S		G	A	D		I	N	S	T	S		N	O	R	M	A
		P	E	T	I	T					A	R	U		O	L	A	V
B	A	S	E		E	N	A				P	I	N		W	A	V	E
E	C	H	O		H	A	H				P	V	T		E	K	E	S
V	E	E	P		O	H	O				L	E	A		R	E	S	T
Y	A	L	L		U	S	E				E	R	I	N	S
	L	E	A	S	H		A	M	I	G	O		S	N	O		A	W	E
B	A	Y		G	E	O	R	G	E	S	A	N	D		S	E	A	M	A	N
U	N	D	U	E		R	A	I	N	T	R	E	E		S	P	I	T	S
S	N	U	B		S	E	E	R			W	E	T		I	C	E
E	V	E	O	N		L	I	D	O		A	U	G		A	R	M
S	T	A	R	F	I	S	H		B	U	S	T	E	R	C	R	A	B	B	E
S	T	L		A	P	E	S		I	N	S	E	T		K	I	L	L	E	R
T	E	L		N	E	X	T		D	E	A	R	E		S	P	E	E	D	S

Answers to Movie Trivia

A: 1. a, c, e
2. a
3. a
4. a
5. a
6. d
7. c
8. c, a, e
9. b, e
10. b
11. e
12. e
13. d
14. c

B: 1. a. 1965; b. The Astronauts, Sonny and Cher, Sandy Nelson; c. Frankie Randall, Sherry Jackson
2. a. 1964; b. James Darren; c. Deborah Walley; d. girl+midget (as you recall, Gidget was very petite)
3. a. 1964; b. Bobby Vinton; c. Jackie DeShannon; d. The Astronauts, the Routers

C: 1. *Blue Hawaii;* 1961
2. *Follow That Dream;* 1962
3. *Fun in Acapulco;* 1963

D: *The Endless Summer,* with Bruce Brown

E: 1. a. Jon Hall; b. *The Beach Girls and the Monster;* c. Frank Sinatra, Jr.; d. "Monster in the Surf"
2. a. *The Horror of Party Beach;* b. sodium

221

A Trip Down Memory Lane

Taking a Sun Bath in Front of Long Beach Bath House, Long Beach, Cal.

(Picture Collection Cooper-Hewitt Museum Library)

ASLEEP
BY THE SEA

Sea, sun, sand, surf, and finally...
sleep.

There comes a time when even the
most ardent beach nut has to call it
quits and get some rest after a busy day
of cavorting and carousing. Where you
lay your weary, sand-encrusted but
oh-so-happy head ranges from the
sublime to the ridiculous. (In these
pages, which is which depends upon
your point of view.) Here's a brief look
at the past, some options for the present, and a guess at future modes of
seaside living.

28:—The Finest Bathing Beach in the World, Cedar Point-on-Lake Erie.

(Picture Collection Cooper-Hewitt Museum Library)

The Bath House, Ocean Park, Ca.

222

UNDER A CANOPY OF STARS

Camping out is a classic case of less is more: the less you tote around, the more you feel you are camping. Gas-guzzling RVs are on the wane; many purists really rough it by not even bothering with tents. (Let the local climate and your tolerance for the unpleasantries and surprises of nature be your guide.)

Whether you subscribe to the spartan philosophy or personally believe instead that less is a bore, make sure your equipment is in good working order. A week or two before an extended trip away from home, take a short weekend excursion to give every item a test run. If anything's amiss, it will be no big disaster and can be remedied in time. And make sure you know how to deal with insect pests. Unless your camp is the size of the Taj Mahal, you'll have "nowhere to run, nowhere to hide."

A Home of Your Own

Dreams of your own hideaway by the sea can become reality — despite spiraling costs and shrinking real estate. For instance, you can still buy reasonably priced acreage in these inland and coastal watery bargain lands:

*The Finger Lakes region in New York *Northwest Florida, 15 miles inland from the Gulf* Jackson County, North Carolina *The Cumberland Plateau in central Tennessee *Indian Lake area in Logan County, Ohio* The Highland Lakes region of central Texas* Klamath Falls in Oregon*

Warm weather and casual living mean you can do without the usual amenities; vacation houses can skimp on size, insulation, heating...and what a perfect opportunity to use solar heating. Magazines such as *Woman's Day* and *Family Circle* regularly offer plans for building inexpensive cabins and such. Mobile homes are popping up like mushrooms.

But perhaps one of the most appropriate beach houses of all will be "grown" underwater, from materials contained right in the sea. Architect Wolf Hilbertz has found that electrolysis extracts minerals from seawater, causing them to be deposited on cathodes made of metal mesh. The resulting off-white coating is as strong as concrete and can grow an inch thick in six weeks. There are dozens of applications and spin-offs to this revolutionary new process, including hoisting water-grown structures onto prepared foundations right on the beach. The dome-shaped cabañas and prefab building components he's designed would cost as little as one-thousandth as much as conventionally built structures. You can visit Hilbertz's experimental reef off the island of St. Croix in the U.S. Virgin Islands (bring scuba gear). Perhaps his plans to grow his own private island nearby will have materialized by the time you read this. In the meantime, give your soul to the sandman and dream about how it feels to live in the ultimate beach house...a stone's throw from the sea and made of the same substance as seashells.

Good night, beach lover, wherever you are. See you at the cabaña.

[Marianne Dickinson]

ABOUT THE AUTHOR

Nancy Bruning spends as much time at the beach as possible. When she's not relaxing surfside, she writes books and articles about health, fitness, beauty, and leisure. Previously published works include *The Cold Weather Catalog* (with Robert Levine) and *Swimming for Total Fitness* (with Jane Katz).